MW00930405

The _Real_ Story of Creation

Defined Word Approach Reveals
Ancient Biblical Secrets

Willie J. Alexander

Truth crushed to earth shall rise again.
—William Cullen Bryant

You can't handle the truth.
—Jack Nicholson, _A Few Good Men_

WESTBOW
P R E S S
A DIVISION OF THOMAS NELSON

Copyright © 2012 Willie J. Alexander

All rights reserved. No part of this book may be used or reproduced by any means, graphic, electronic, or mechanical, including photocopying, recording, taping or by any information storage retrieval system without the written permission of the publisher except in the case of brief quotations embodied in critical articles and reviews.

ISBN: 978-1-4497-7313-7 (e)
ISBN: 978-1-4497-7314-4 (sc)
ISBN: 978-1-4497-7315-1 (hc)

Library of Congress Control Number: 2012920184

WestBow Press books may be ordered through booksellers or by contacting:

WestBow Press
A Division of Thomas Nelson
1663 Liberty Drive
Bloomington, IN 47403
www.westbowpress.com
1-(866) 928-1240

Because of the dynamic nature of the Internet, any web addresses or links contained in this book may have changed since publication and may no longer be valid. The views expressed in this work are solely those of the author and do not necessarily reflect the views of the publisher, and the publisher hereby disclaims any responsibility for them.

Front Cover Credit: NASA, ESA, and the Hubble Heritage Team STScI/AURA)-ESA/Hubble Collaboration. Acknowledgement: B. Whitmore (Space Telescope Science Institute) and James Long (ESA/Hubble).

This book's biblical verses come **only** from the "King James Version Holy Bible."

The author invites your feedback. Please contact Willie Alexander on Facebook at www.facebook.com/enteringthepromisedland and email at willie@enteringthepromisedland.com. The reader is also invited to visit our webpage at www.enteringthepromisedland.com.

Printed in the United States of America

WestBow Press rev. date: 12/12/2012

With boundless appreciation to those whose unconditional love is written into every page. To my parents, Nellie and Johnny Mack Alexander Sr., my wife Carolyn's parents, Minnie and Fleming Whitney Jr. and those very special surrogates who always embraced us, Essie B. and R. C. Brown and Carolyn's aunt, Velma Becks, yours was the beacon that showed the way. This work is dedicated to you.

Acknowledgments

A special thanks to my colleague, friend, and sometimes gadfly, Marsha C. Tucker. Her determination to keep me focused while writing this book was invaluable.

Contents

Forward

Pivotal moments — we all have them — when an associate or a neighbor becomes a friend because honesty has transcended politeness. And from that very moment, every contact with that person is forever burnished with care and respect, over time taking on an inestimable value.

In the dank cold of a January afternoon more than a decade ago, Willie Alexander first approached me about assisting with his writing. I listened. He talked. In my private moments, I wondered if some hard hits he had received as a defensive back in the National Football League had — well, you get the idea. Yet, I knew that Willie could not be dismissed as a former jock. The more he talked, the more it became apparent that he was a bottled-up man, one whose thoughts and ideas were racing around in his mind, trying to find a way out.

As the weeks and months passed, Willie shared his personal struggle. He straddled two worlds — the Black world to which he was born and had been a collegiate All-American athlete, and the business world populated principally by successful White males and a handful of minorities. That Willie was accepted in both places made him increasingly impatient with the comparatively slow pace of social progress in the world he had always known. At a meeting of the community's corporate leadership, his feelings spilled over with impromptu remarks to the assembled body. By all accounts, it was a memorable moment.

Sometimes, there is nothing more painful than the truth. While we may quake and have our knees knocking, it can also make us stronger, open to us a new way to look at the same situation, enhance our understanding and appreciation.

Fearful and unable to sort out his feelings, Willie sought out friends for answers and eventually went to the Holy Bible. First, to find solace.

Later, to validate the worth of his heritage. He used me as a sounding board. We debated my world versus his world, what we both experienced as kids in the segregated South. There were a couple of months when we did not speak. When he did reach out again, he had written the early chapters of his first book. He had entitled it "Entering The Promised Land." The primary audience would be people of color. His research would prove unalterably that the key biblical figures were Black. And with their heritage, he would challenge his people to shake off the mental and emotional shackles that have been their legacy, and to strive and work to elevate themselves. All of the above was accomplished through his study and publication of "Entering The Promised Land."

Greater things were on the horizon. In his research to prove his points, Willie discovered a new methodology for biblical study. He named and trademarked it the Defined Word Approach. I was skeptical, but very intrigued. He took each key word in a biblical verse and applied the Classical Hebrew meanings and cross-references to other Scripture to it, then applied what he found to the verse. The more he used his approach, the more he realized that through the ages the drivers of people have been the same: sex, procreation, acceptance, to name but a few.

"The Real Story of Creation" puts the Defined Word Approach to work. For the first time in Modern history, there is a way to read and understand the Bible, making it in its purest form a guide to life that is unaffected by the passage of time, contemporary theory or organized religion. Read this way, biblical language becomes elementary and far more relatable. You can touch it and it will touch you.

It has been my privilege to assist my good friend with this project. A decade ago, this would have seemed inconceivable. God does work in mysterious ways!

Marsha C. Tucker
December 5, 2012
Houston, Texas

Preface

Let me establish up front that I was brought up in a home where church, faith, and family were ingrained values. In the Deep South, Sunday was the most important day of the week. From morning to evening, everything we did revolved around the church. I believed then, and I do today. But my beliefs are deeper and broader than I ever could have imagined from the teachings I received. Then, the only issue I had with those teachings was whose wrath I feared more—the Almighty's or my mother's!

Many years later—long after I retired from professional football and had built my own business—I began to question. I still went to church regularly, but I often left feeling unfulfilled. Weren't the sermons supposed to uplift, inspire? I mean, how could a grown man in the pulpit expect me—a well-educated adult male—to buy into the notion that Eve actually talked to a snake? I got the meaning about obedience, but why was it being preached in such an unbelievable way? How could any serious individual take that as the gospel?

That led me to give a lot of thought about the difference between blind faith and knowing faith. I concluded that I couldn't just take another's word for it; I had to understand what I believed and why.

Many life experiences intervened before I began a serious study of the Bible. I still went to church regularly and left with the same empty feeling, asking myself what I got from being there. I concluded that I needed more. I further concluded that I would not get whatever I needed just by being in church. I needed to dig in and drill down.

Still I procrastinated, nagged by many questions. In 2002, after delivering a scorching, extemporaneous speech to the white powerbrokers in my community who had welcomed me into their midst, I knew I was in hot water. You probably know the joke about the two things that work best in hot water—a Christian in trouble and a tea bag. Anyway, I went to the Scriptures. I called on local black ministers. And I went to work, seeking a justification for many of my feelings about the church and, more importantly, about being born black. So far as I knew then, my black history was truncated, covering no more than about 393 years. Of course, we all know there is more—and there is.

The product of my study evolved as I did. Then in 2007, I published my very first book, *Entering The Promised Land*. I should note that this writing was shared with numerous ministers, whose response was muted. I don't know if that response was because it was a portal to a new way to decipher Scripture or because it challenged conventional biblical understanding. Either way, my work landed with a dull thud in certain circles.

Initially, I was disappointed that no one "got it". My book was either ignored, or I got a pat on the back as a neophyte. Later, I realized that maybe the challenge was too great, too revolutionary. Who knows?

I recall introducing *Entering The Promised Land* to an audience on a college campus with this challenge: Understanding my work requires you to go from a mind-set to a mind-change. I believe that is the imperative with any discovery that breaks new ground, and mine does.

In my biblical study that led to *Entering The Promised Land*, I literally stumbled upon a way to decipher biblical Scripture. For want of a better way to express it, I call it the Defined Word Approach to Biblical Scripture.

Let's be honest. I am not a scholar. I am simply a person of faith in search of a deeper meaning to Scripture, hopefully to put it into context with my life. Sometimes I think that very simplicity has revealed the Scripture to me.

My morning walks begin at four o'clock on the weekdays. Usually, the sky is an inky black, dotted with stars, an occasional moon, and sometimes clouds. I often think about how I am seeing the very heavens the ancients saw along the earth's same parallel. I live in Houston, Texas, and we very nearly share the 30N parallel with Cairo, Egypt. So I actually see what the pharaohs saw.

Sometimes I muse to myself about *National Geographic*'s February 2008 cover story, *The Black Pharaohs—Conquerors of Ancient Egypt*. Author Robert Draper tells the story of a black Nubian ruler by the name of Piye who invaded and conquered Lower Egypt. Draper's article said that Piye was the ruler of a robust African civilization that flourished on the southern banks of the Nile for twenty-five hundred years, going back at least as far as the first Egyptian dynasty.

I also think about the things that endure. We now know that the grains of sand in our deserts and on our beaches have been here for all time. The rocks—remember the movie *Grand Canyon*, where the family's vacation becomes a race against time, and when they finally get to the Grand Canyon, they begin to realize that the rocks have been there for millennia?

And I think about my Defined Word Approach to deciphering the Bible.

After publishing *Entering The Promised Land*, I called on a good friend and minister who had read my book and thought it was worthwhile. I considered that high praise. As I was leaving, he suggested I should investigate the Hebrew dictionary. Until then, I had relied on the *Oxford English Dictionary, Random House Webster's Unabridged Dictionary*, and other resources for my research, which were very good in leading me to conclude that the biblical Adam probably originated in Eastern Africa, which has now been confirmed by the scientific Adam thanks to the Y chromosome study conducted by Dr. Spencer Wells and revealed in his book, *The Journey of Man: A Genetic Odyssey*. His studies suggest humans left Africa sixty thousand years ago and journeyed throughout the world. It would be enlightening if Dr. Wells had his next study involve testing the DNA of black Jews living in Israel and Ethiopia and compare their DNA to African Americans living in the deep south, i.e., Alabama, Georgia and Mississippi. And while he's at it, perhaps he would conduct a DNA test on Jews and African Americans living in the USA.

There is more. Donald Johanson and Maitland Edey wrote in their 1981 book, *Lucy, the Beginning of Humankind*, about the discovery of 3.5 million-year-old human bones in Ethiopia, Africa. Their work reveals we now have archeological evidence that the scientific Adam is probably the same primitive man recorded in Genesis as Adam. Is it possible then that the opening chapters in *The Holy Bible*'s book of Genesis are providing us with the primitive history of humankind?

Think about that and about this: Words are symbols. Symbols are a means of expression. How many times a day do you look at a symbol and translate it into a word or words that have a meaning? You see a yellow circular sign with an X and RR. You translate it to "railroad crossing." Or you see a red circle with a bar drawn across it. You translate it to mean "no."

We know that the ancients communicated by depicting what they saw in coded language, the Rosetta Stone, or in pictures. We need go no further than the cliff dwellers' caves in Bandolier National Park outside Santa Fe, New Mexico, where we can see the images they drew to communicate.

So applying my various resource materials to words in biblical Scripture, I believe a way to decipher the meaning of the written word has been revealed. I realize this research could be dismissed as highly subjective. But isn't all interpretation of Scripture subjective? Further, I fully expect that it will be challenged along the lines that it does not address the historical social, economic and political context that may influence what was written. In that regard, I wish to make these points: I used a purist approach to the definitions of the words—there is no connotative meaning applied; for purposes of historical context, I recommend to the reader many other texts focused on the Holy Bible and the history of western civilization (notably, R.K. Harrison, to whom I refer in this work); and lastly, this reflects a story about people and the drive to procreate, neither of which has fundamentally changed through the millennia. Forgive this blunt reality, but the ways of the flesh—then and now—are no more or less than as reflected in the Scripture.

I commend this work to you with the hope that you understand my sincerity, and that you too will find with this reading comes a deeper understanding of ancient history and a deeper faith.

Finally, to my ever-patient wife, Carolyn, my children, Michael and Alexis, my family, colleagues, and friends, I thank you. My obsession has been sometimes troubling and disconcerting. Trust that it has caused me consternation too. If you find my deciphered Scripture offensive, please accept my very sincere apology. Know that I have tried to do my very best by all and that my love for you is boundless. Blessings!

CHAPTER 1

We Need to Get a Grip!

If you tuned into the news the week of August 7, 2011, you had to wonder if the world had gone mad. Pundits, news broadcasters, politicians, and some radio/TV ministers declared that Armageddon had arrived. Standard and Poor's had downgraded the United States' rating from triple A to double A-plus. The Dow Jones Industrials went into the wildest gyrations since the beginning of the New York Stock Exchange. The usual blame game and finger-pointing among US politicians was in overdrive.

Spain, France, and Italy were struggling to stay afloat. Greece and Ireland were already under financial water. There were street riots in England; young people in San Francisco were rioting against the Bay Area Rapid Transit Authority; Philadelphia, Denver, Chicago, and Milwaukee were on edge from recent turmoil. Flash mobs were taking to the malls and streets across the United States. Chaos reigned. The more sophisticated, tech-savvy among us declared that the culprit was the social media. With this new means of communicating to large numbers via Facebook, Twitter, and the now almost-archaic cell texting, people could be summoned to the streets in minutes. Unrest was bubbling like the old-fashioned percolator my mom heated up every morning. The universal, all-knowing "they" pronounced that it was anarchy.

Listening to the radio as I drove to work, the commentary rattled on. The only word that came to mind from the torrent of words spilling over me was *stop!*

I have never thought of my office as a refuge, but I'm now viewing it as a wonderful safe haven. In the quiet there, I am able to regroup my thoughts from the cacophony on the airwaves. I can look around my office to the young people who are professionals, working their way up. I can blot out the images of the kids (and very old hippies) encamped near Wall Street in New York, Oakland, Atlanta, and virtually across the country. Some have said these squatters are Woodstock wannabees. Not so. The Woodstock kids were happy—many of them under the influence of drugs—but they were happily participating in a music fest. Free sex and drugs were the side benefits. Today's group is into the sex, drugs, and street performances, but it is an angry group that rages about anything and everything. Some of their venting is incoherent, if not absurd, and some of it has merit. I am persuaded, however, that there are far more effective ways to communicate a message.

In my sophomore year in high school, I stood on the front lawn of my school in Montgomery, Alabama, and witnessed firsthand the Selma-to-Montgomery march led by Dr. Martin Luther King Jr. It was nonviolent and dignified and, by its quiet example, raised public awareness of the inhumanity and injustice to others in our society. My heart is heavy at attempts to compare the Occupy Wall Street movement to the civil rights movement. How on earth could anyone compare the civil rights movement to the fornication, use of illegal drugs, and indecency underway in New York City's public square? To the violence and obstructionism in Oakland? To the nonsensical reasoning that our country—the greatest nation in modern history—is a failure? How did we devolve into a society that no longer asks what it can do to help others, but rather demands gimme, gimme, gimme—it's all about me?

Famed World War II British journalist and writer Rebecca West wrote in *The Meaning of Treason* (1947) that a spiritual malaise had led people to abandon democratic values for utopian creeds. She continued to write about treason, her work culminating in 1964 with the release of *The New Meaning of Treason*. While she was not religious, West felt that the decline of Christianity had left men with no sense of limits. She felt that a modern evil had been unleashed, which made some men capable of performing great crimes for abstract ideals, while others betrayed their country for the same motives.

West's contemporary journalist and best friend, the American Dorothy Thompson, shared many of her views. Thompson had been the Berlin bureau chief for the *New York Post* newspaper. She was the first foreign journalist to interview Adolf Hitler in 1931, two years before his rise to power. Later, she said that Nazism was "a complete break with reason, with humanity, and Christian ethics that are at the basis of liberalism and democracy." Thompson wrote of her concern about the survival of democracy. "Once you let down the dams," she wrote, "once you relax in one direction, the floods sweep in."

The late great baseball player Satchel Paige advises not to look back because something might be gaining on us. But with all due respect to Mr. Paige, that's exactly what we need to do. Look back. Find out where we got it wrong. And try to figure out where we go from here.

The answers are really simple. What has gone wrong happened in that building with a pulpit and pews. The very fabric of our society—the church—is unraveling because the church has not evolved along with an enlightened population. There are four factors in play: First, the old faithful are literally dying. Second, many people are dropping out of church attendance because they feel the church is no longer relevant in their lives. Third, even for those who do attend church and have read the Bible, many admit they do not understand the text or the teachings. Then there's the younger generation that does not go to church or read the Bible at all.

Few among the under-thirty age group occupy a pew on Sunday. For many of them, that's the day to sleep in or hang with their buddies. God's not going to get ticked off if they are a no-show for church, they reason. Try the "God's wrath" threat on them and it will get laughed off or boomerang as a parental guilt trip. As a parent myself, I wonder where these New Age thinkers get their inspiration: The Internet? Twitter? Facebook? Do any of these sources provide the spiritual moorings that previous generations found in church? They obviously are hungry for something that will make their lives better. Yet church seems to be the very last stop in their journey for betterment. Regrettably, some live on their frustration and anger and take to the streets. Many times, they call themselves "anarchists." Others self-medicate with alcohol, drugs, or indiscriminate sex. Others resort to crime. Sum it up as "whatever."

We would welcome the luxury of being able to pass off the current turmoil as a sign of the times. Sadly, it is a spiral that has been winding downward for the past century. In business, a declining income statement foreshadows a decrease in sales and services and a disaffected client base. If not corrected, the business ultimately will fail. Think about this reality in terms of Christianity.

As corroboration of the decline, in an October 30, 2011 interview with Fox News, Father Jonathan Morris gave some startling statistics about the American Catholic church. Father Morris is a priest for a Catholic church in Manhattan's Soho and author of *God Wants You Happy: From Self-Help to God's Help*. He shared that in the 2011 survey of American Catholics, it was reported that only 30 percent of Catholics attend mass weekly. Father Morris mused that the largest religious group in America today is *former* Catholics. Today, 86 percent of Catholics—even lifelong Catholics—feel that it is appropriate to question the teachings of the church. He said that the younger people who do attend mass yearn for uplifting messages. His hope is that the church—which is now attempting to respond to the decline—will become more personable. Whether that will be achieved is problematic considering that the Vatican has directed the liturgy must become more complex. The reasoning is that the earlier liturgy was too easy, which allowed individuals to question and to draw their own conclusions. Time will test the wisdom of that new directive.

According to the *World Almanac* and the US Census Bureau, at the beginning of the twentieth century, Christians made up 40 percent of the world population and at the beginning of the twenty-first century that was down to 32.8 percent. In the United States, the Christian population dropped by 9 percent from 1990–2000. (You would be very worried if your savings took that kind of a sudden loss with no hope of recouping it.) A new report from the Pew Research Center shows that among "millennials"—those born after 1980 who became adults after 2000—25 percent, *one fourth* of them, are not affiliated with *any* religion. The bad news doesn't end there. The Pew forum on religion in public life finds about 20 percent of American adults say they have no particular ties to a given faith. That's up from about 15 percent just five years ago. And the data shows a generational change. Younger people are moving away from established religion. Obviously, in a country that has its founding principles based on a trust in God, that shift could shake the very underpinnings of government.

As I started this chapter, the apocalyptic view of the world was ringing in my ears, triggering my memory of a Denzel Washington movie about an apocalyptic world after the death of Christianity. The movie wasn't a box office hit, but it has merit in this context. *The Book of Eli*, released in theaters January 2010, is a movie about the Christian character Eli's journey to deliver a book, the Bible, to a West Coast location. The plot line is that this book will be the foundation for the new earth.

On his journey, Eli enters a lawless town where a man named Carnegie, played by Gary Oldman, wants the book at any cost. This includes murdering Eli, who sees the book as good. To Carnegie, the book is a way to control the citizens. The kicker is that both men see the Bible as the key to social regeneration.

The trend line is set, and Christianity has its work cut out. All the guitars, drums, stage lighting, and hoopla that a church could muster will not—I repeat, will not—bring the millennials into the fold. They are too educated, too worldly, and pragmatic for the buy-in. They are our children, our great joy. They also are not content to plod along in our footsteps. They, in particular, want and need more to sink their teeth into. It is my goal to serve up something for everyone to chew on.

*   *   *

The Bible is the accepted cornerstone for Christianity. Over the years, there have been attempts to modernize the language of the 1611 AD King James Version of the Bible, but it still is not an easy read. For even the most devout who use the original King James Version, the text can be full of stumbling blocks to understanding. A friend confided that trying to read the Bible so frustrated him that he put it down. I feel the difficulty in reading the Bible turns off many believers, so it's a stretch to think that nonbelievers would ever take on this reading.

Personally, I used to equate reading Scripture to reading Shakespeare—especially if I was reading a Study Bible with a multitude of footnotes. The fog index was very high. A breakthrough came when I started looking up the meanings of the Hebrew words that were used in the original biblical text. It was an eye-opener that I am sharing with you, and it begins with the very first verses in the Bible. *Let me emphasize that in no way have I changed any of the words in the Scripture. I have only sought to define them.*

Once you grasp the real message in those seemingly mundane, out-of-date words, my hope is that you will push on and discover for yourself that the Bible is a timeless blueprint for living.

CHAPTER 2

The Challenge:
Expanding Our Understanding

We live in an astounding world; a world where communication is almost instantaneous. Words and images are delivered to us via the Internet that wraps our globe. We see and hear and experience almost the very moment.

Our engineering and technical expertise creates new "wonders of the world"; a world that today has a skyscraper in Abu Dhabi that is twice the height of the famous Empire State Building. A cruise ship now sails the seas that dwarfs the Titanic two-fold, carrying over seven thousand passengers.

We look out in space and back in time. Our robots roam the surface of Mars. We study quasars, pulsars, and supernovas. In a sliver of time—within the one hundred years of the twentieth century—we put men on the moon and returned them safely to earth. We found that our universe is expanding. We now know that there are billions of galaxies with billions of stars each. In fact, we know there are more stars in our heavens than all the grains of sand on all the beaches and all the deserts on earth. And we have seen the very birth of our own universe almost fourteen billion years ago. Looking back, we can see a trillionth of a trillionth of a second from the creation of the universe.

We continue to search our heavens in order to learn about ourselves.

What is the stuff that makes up the universe, which still is 95 percent hidden from us? Other than on earth, is there life in our universe or beyond it? Is there a hidden universe out there we cannot see?

It is a world in constant pursuit of breakthrough knowledge that advances us. In medicine, the quest brings us new therapies and treatments. The heart and lung transplants that once held us in awe are now performed routinely. Surgery is performed in utero on an unborn baby. We have mapped the human genome and are using that knowledge to switch off genes carrying hereditary diseases. And we marry our technical and medical expertise to provide artificial devices to prolong life, enable mobility, and to give the surgeon new tools and capabilities.

Through genetic research, we also have scientific proof that billions of males through the millennia have carried the very same Y chromosome. To extrapolate, this means that almost all males through the modern ages have the very same super-ancestor. Scientists call this modern super-ancestor the scientific Adam, who was on earth sixty thousand years ago and is the father of all men on earth. The implication of this reality is that the Bible probably is the historical account of our ancestors, their lives, and their loves and failures.

And yet, despite what we know in a scientific sense, those who use the Bible to teach and instruct leave us wondering about the real truth of our beginning. With the human mind's ability to explore and learn, how is it feasible that very few, if any, of the religious scholars have ever related to us in practical terms what is written about our origin in the historical record of mankind?

Is it possible that religious scholars through the ages have known the truth but were reluctant to share it? But how can that be? Why would that be? Is the truth that, contrary to what is preached from the pulpit, there is a story-behind-the-story in biblical Scripture?

Writing as a black man and as a Christian, this is a question that, try as I might, I have not been able to put down for many years. Again and again, I have been pulled back to read and study, ponder, and then to study more.

The most puzzling aspect of my research is, again, to ask why it is that religious scholars throughout the years have not done the same?

And if they have, why have they not shared it with us? Why would they leave it for ministers to preach an allegory about a snake talking to Eve, when we all know that snakes cannot talk? And when and how did the forbidden fruit become an apple?

I realize these seem to be very elementary questions. But I believe they are fundamental to an understanding of "In the beginning ..."

CHAPTER 3

Revelations to New Thinking

Merely reading biblical Scripture can be difficult, but understanding it is even more challenging. Historians write about place and time. Theologians, who are the primary source for learning about Scripture, seldom point to the historical narrative. Perhaps that is because their mission is to teach, and the method they employ is biblical allegory. When we hear sermons about Moses parting the Red Sea, Shadrach, Meshach, and Abednego walking through the fiery furnace unharmed, or Daniel in the lion's den, the characters become almost fictionalized.

I am a self-taught biblical student, and I humble myself before those who have given their lives to theology and to the academic study of religion. In my view, however, taking biblical Scripture literally diminishes the import of the Word. Long before I started on the journey to understand Scripture, I was like many. It was good enough that I believed. I didn't need to think about what I believed or to know what I believed. I believed. Period!

When a subject or a problem seems to be very complex, we often step away from it. The combination of two forces—time and instant gratification—works like the law of inertia. If it takes too much time and effort, we are reluctant to tackle it. Sadly, I feel this happens to even the most devout churchgoers. They believe. Period! No need for anything beyond what's said in the pulpit every Sunday.

Then there are the mavericks like me. I just couldn't go to church any longer and hear the same sermons year after year and accept them at face value. Surely the biblical Scripture had more substance. How could I discern it? Was there anything that had not already been sermonized—maybe even sanitized? If I found it, would it change my fundamental belief?

I really didn't want to go on this very personal journey. I had a business to run. There were family and community obligations—all commitments on my time. And yet, in the early hours of the morning and in the solitude of my thoughts, I could not avoid thinking about Scripture and our ancient ancestors. So I began to read and research. Then I began to write and ultimately published *Entering The Promised Land*.

In *Entering The Promised Land*, I related how I literally stumbled onto a way to read and understand biblical Scripture. I had been studying Scripture for quite awhile and had already concluded that it is a written record of real people and their lives. *Random House Webster's Unabridged Dictionary* and the *Oxford English Dictionary* were useful resources to expand my understanding of the written word. I called my way of reading Scripture the Defined Word Approach to Biblical Scripture. With my work in print, it was time to focus on other obligations.

I probably should give up morning walks. After a very brief sabbatical, the questions were nagging me again. I would look up at the sky and think about how often the biblical Scripture references heaven, earth, and stars. What I found in my research and study is stunningly simple and is laid out before the reader with the opening Scriptures in Genesis.

CHAPTER 4

The Words Mean More Than We May Think

By nature, I have always been hyperactive and short on patience. My mind races ahead of my ability to give voice to my thoughts. In those moments, I tend to stammer, which only heightens my frustration in getting my point across. Sitting down to read and research for long periods of time has been one of the great challenges of my life. Writing has been an even greater challenge. But in reading, studying, and researching Scripture, I have achieved an unexpected discipline. I suppose this newfound patience is derived from my fascination with the subject matter.

It is somewhat amusing that noted sex researcher Alfred Kinsey's studies about human sexual appetites and behavior triggered the sexual revolution in the 1950s, as anyone truly interested in sexual proclivities needs only to pick up the Bible.

Most Christians are aware of the sexuality in the Scripture. We are familiar with the Song of Solomon. We have been taught to equate sinful behavior with Sodom and Gomorrah. If we have not read Scripture, we probably have seen the cinematic portrayal of Delilah in the bedchamber. Wielding shears, she cuts the sleeping Samson's hair, thereby robbing him of his phenomenal strength. Then there are David and Bathsheba, whose exploits can still make us blush. The explicit sex did not require using my Defined Word Approach! Seriously, while these accounts titillate, they lay down the marker for the dangers of succumbing to our baser instincts.

When I was researching my first book, *Entering The Promised Land*, I became intrigued by other stories involving sex—stories of debauchery, incest, deceit, homosexuality, infidelity, even prostitution. When I shared them with my friends, they jokingly suggested I should use *sex* as a word in the title of this book. And, of course, it all began with Adam and Eve and the temptation of Eve in the Garden of Eden. But we tend to overlook that Eve also gave birth to children. I think all would agree that motherhood is the noblest of callings.

A backtrack to *Genesis 1:1* in the *King James Version Holy Bible* brought me a startling revelation. It reads: "In the beginning, God created the heaven and the earth." One of the Old English definitions of *genesis* as found in the *Webster's New World College Dictionary* comes from the word *gignesthai*, which means "to be born." This word is related to *genos*, which means "race, birth, descent." As such, it is translated into the Hebrew word *bereshith*, or "in the beginning."

As I continued to study and look up Hebrew meanings to words in the book of Genesis, I was surprised at the generous use of words or phrases relative to birth, e.g., firstfruits, be fruitful, bear, bring forth, conceive, and so on. Was the author Moses writing about the creation of the universe, such as the planets, moon, and stars? Or was he writing about something much more basic, such as procreation? Viewed through this lens and employing the Hebrew meanings of various words, one can readily conclude that Scripture is a text about the male/female union, impregnation, and birth.

Keep in mind that the intention of Mosaic Law was to provide a code for moral conduct, and that the emphasis was on family. In Genesis, five times there is mentioned the encouragement to "be fruitful and multiply (*Genesis 1:22, 1:28, 8:17, 9:1, 35:11*)." The caveat is to fulfill the duty to procreate but not to indulge in the pleasures of the flesh. This duality is throughout Scripture—good and evil, heaven and earth, physical and spiritual, barren and fertile. The duality also goes to understanding the meaning of Scripture; it can be read literally and figuratively, where words may tell two stories.

Moses recognized that procreation is the foundation of humanity. On a more pragmatic level, the building of Israelite families also gave strength by virtue of their numbers. Procreate to populate obviously was the goal. For instance, in the fourth book of the Old Testament—Numbers—Moses and Aaron take a census of the children of Israel, numbering the young males twenty years of age and older who were able to go to war in Israel. From the 12 tribes, the young men who qualified totaled over six hundred thousand.

We can take a step further to see that the Scriptures correspond to the scientific proof that Adam was a black man. At least two of his distinctive physical features—a flat [wide] nose (*Leviticus 21:18*) and unshorn locks [nappy hair] (*Numbers 6:5*) are described in the Scriptures. This breakthrough may have occurred much later if a friend had not recommended the *Biblesoft Complete Reference Library PC Study Bible Version 5*. This tool proved invaluable in researching the definition of the Hebrew words "hair" and "locks." Thereafter, the *PC Study Bible* enhanced my study by allowing research of the Authorized English Version (translation) of the original Hebrew word, which then gave a direct path to *James Strong's Hebrew and Chaldee Dictionary and Greek Dictionary of the New Testament* for their definition(s). My earlier research had been a cumbersome process of manually searching in the KJV Concordance for the word in question in a Bible verse then maybe finding its appropriate number, and taking the last step to the *James Strong's Hebrew and Chaldee Dictionary* and *Greek Dictionary of the New Testament* for their definition(s).

The Hebrew definition of *hair* and its appropriate number 4748 in the *Hebrew and Chaldee Dictionary* reads: "From 7185 in the sense of knotting up round and hard; something turned (rounded), i.e. a curl (of tresses)—X well (set) hair." Now look at the Hebrew definition of *locks* and its appropriate number 4253, which reads, "A ringlet of hair (as gliding over each other)." Like many black men and women, if I did not keep my own hair close-cropped or treated with chemicals, it would resemble this description. A photograph appears on the following page.

Employing the Hebrew definition to a single word often led me through a maze of other related words. Because of the interconnectivity

The above photograph is an actual picture of a single strand of a black man's hair magnified 400 times (the hair's root appears in the upper right hand corner of the photograph). The strand resembles the Hebrew definition of hair, "knotting up round and hard," and the Hebrew definition of locks, "a ringlet of hair (as if gliding over each other)."

"Photograph is courtesy of Texas Children's Hospital Pathology Department" of the meanings, I soon began to cross-reference them. This is what I refer to as the "drill down." Or, for those who are familiar with Scripture, it is similar to tracing lineage. Sometimes a visual chart showing lineage is more effective. In this instance, the best I can offer is to visualize stair steps. One starts at the top and keeps stepping down until reaching the bottom. Let me explain by applying the Defined Word Approach to a Bible verse.

For example, when the Defined Word Approach is applied to the word *affliction* in the *Hebrew and Chaldee Dictionary*, it eventually provides a clearer meaning to *Genesis 29:32*, "And Leah conceived and bare a son, and she called his name Reuben for she said, Surely the LORD has looked upon my *affliction*; now therefore my husband will love me" (emphasis added).

It is clear that Leah, one of Jacob's wives, has given birth to a son. What is not clear is the meaning of her "affliction."[1] I contend an application of the Defined Word Approach reveals not one but multiple afflictions: 1) Depression that is misery. We can surmise depression and misery describes Leah's mental state; 2) looking down or browbeaten. We can surmise Jacob speaks unkind words to Leah; 3) family, daughter, homeborn, forth of, within; 4) to build, obtain children, make, set up. We can surmise Leah desperately wanted to have a family of her own; 5) bear, bring forth, grow, increase, and 6) be delivered of a child. We can surmise Leah has given birth to a baby.

From the biblical text, we learn from Leah's own words that she knew that Jacob did not love her, and that he did not want to be married to her (*Genesis 29:32–34*). From these statements, we can infer that she suffered from depression. Why did Jacob refuse to commit to her? Because he loved another woman, Leah's sister, Rachel. Jacob had worked seven years for her father, Laban, in order to have her sister Rachel's hand in marriage. On the morning after his presumed marriage to Rachel, he awoke to find he had slept with and was married to Leah (*Genesis 29:25*). One would logically think that not only did Jacob

---

[1] The word *affliction* is the Authorized English Version (translation) of the original Hebrew word. Application of the Defined Word Approach starts on page 64 and its use in Cross-Reference to Scripture starts on page 112.

not love Leah; he now actively hated her for her reprehensible actions. However, the Lord found favor with Leah. He opened her womb when He saw that Jacob hated her (*Genesis 29:31*). In a desperate attempt to gain Jacob's love, Leah bore not one but three children for him.

Leah is the example of the pitiful woman who knowingly gets pregnant, delivers a child, and thinks the man who impregnated her will then love and marry her. Of course, the reverse is also true when a woman gives a man a sexual favor, intentionally gets pregnant, delivers a baby, and the man wrongfully assumes the woman loves him. But in the end, he finds out money, not love, was her motivator.

Once again, we learn some things never change. Leah's "affliction" is twofold: 1) She and her sister, Rachel, are competing for the love of the same man, and 2) Leah suffers from depression because she bore children for a man she loves but who does not love her. Additional information can be found, starting on pages 64 and 112 respectively, in the Defined Word Approach and Cross-Reference to Scripture section.

Earlier in Genesis, we read of Hagar, Abram's concubine. Like Leah, Hagar loved a man who did not love her. Abram's barren wife, Sarai, gave him to Hagar to impregnate (*Genesis 16:3*), and the child she bore would be for Sarai and Abram. However, Hagar mistook the relationship as Abram's concubine to mean that he loved her and learned that Abram did not love her when he said to his wife, Sarai, "do to her as it pleaseth thee." Sarai then dealt harshly with Hagar, forcing her to run away (*Genesis 16:5–6*). Abram's willingness to allow the mother and his child to be driven away was a profound denial not only of Hagar but also of the moral code at the time.

Just as Leah's "affliction" was to birth children with the notion that Jacob would love her, Hagar birthed Abram's son, Ishmael, thinking Abram would love her. Then, as now, paternity does not necessarily lead to a committed relationship.

CHAPTER 5

The Bible: The Book of Life

There are numerous Bibles used in today's teaching and practice of Christianity. Most use as their basis the King James Version. I have studied various newer texts including the *New King James Version Holy Bible, Life Application Study Bible, New International Version Study Bible, The English Standard Version Study Bible,* and *King James Version Hebrew-Greek Key Word Study Bible.* I finally settled on the original King James Version, which is utilized by Strong, as the platform for exploring the Bible with the Defined Word Approach.

In truth, there were other Bibles that preceded the King James Version, although I suspect most Christian Americans are not aware of them. Probably the most widely known is the *Geneva Bible.* This Bible predates the King James Version by about five decades. The *Geneva Bible* is considered by most biblical scholars to be one of the most historically significant translations of the Bible into the English language. I emphasize the term *translation.* Keep in mind that biblical text is *translated* from the ancient Hebrew. I grant the religious scholars their due, but any body of work, by virtue of the human element, can be subject to external influences.

The *Geneva Bible* was the primary Bible of the sixteenth century Protestant movement. Notables in our history books who used it were William Shakespeare, Oliver Cromwell, John Milton, John Knox, John

Donne, and John Bunyan, author of *Pilgrim's Progress*. The Pilgrims who landed at Plymouth, Massachusetts carried with them the *Geneva Bible*.

Like most English translations of that period, the *Geneva Bible* was translated from scholarly editions of the Greek New Testament and the Hebrew Scriptures that comprise the Christian Old Testament. According to the online free encyclopedia Wikipedia, (see *Geneva Bible* @ www.Wikipedia.com for references) the English translation was principally based on the earlier translations by William Tyndale and Myles Coverdale; however, the *Geneva Bible* is the first where all of the Old Testament was translated directly from Hebrew.

In addition to its translation into English, the *Geneva Bible* stands out historically as the very first mechanically printed, mass-produced Bible. Biblical text left the chambers of the religious scholars to become available to the general public. And this particular Bible also encouraged study with its apparatus, which included a variety of study guides and aids. Students could cross-reference verse citations. Each chapter of the Bible had introductions that summarized the narrative. There were maps, tables, illustrations, and indexes—all of these made the *Geneva Bible* the very first Study Bible.

The *Geneva Bible* quickly became popular with readers and replaced the Bishops' Bible, the translation that previously had been authorized by the Church of England under Queen Elizabeth I.

The *Geneva Bible* was so named as the Protestant scholars who wrote it fled from England to Geneva, Switzerland, to work on the translation. In fact, the *Geneva Bible* was the very first Bible published in Scotland and had special appeal as both John Knox and John Calvin had been involved in its production.

The *Geneva Bible* was not without enemies. Early on, Elizabeth I had commissioned the production of the Bishops' Bible to replace it. The Catholic community's Douai Rheims edition came later. The Calvinist and Puritan movements had adopted the *Geneva Bible*, which made it disliked by the ruling pro-government Protestants of the Church of England. King James I—a Scot by birth but who now sat on the English throne—also disliked the *Geneva Bible*, so much so that he commissioned the Authorized Version, or King James Bible, in order to replace it. Despite the King James Version, the *Geneva Bible* remained popular among Puritans and was in widespread use until after the English Civil War.

James Charles Stuart was born to Mary, Queen of Scots, in Edinburgh Castle in 1566. His biography indicates that he grew under the direction of four tutors—among them was George Buchanan, a Calvinist. James had a long-distance relationship with his mother, whom he credited for not trying to convert him to Roman Catholicism. In fact, it was her religion and a Roman Catholic conspiracy to assassinate Queen Elizabeth I of England that led to her execution.

James was very learned and skilled in linguistics. He began to rule Scotland when just twelve years of age. His great goal to become the first king of both Scotland and England came to fruition in 1603 upon the death of Queen Elizabeth. He was forty-eight years old when he ascended to the throne, becoming King James VI of Scotland and King James I of England. As a Scotsman ruling over the English, he endured racism and slander.

Not only did he have enemies among his countrymen, King James was a Protestant who spoke of the Papists with contempt. The Papists (as Roman Catholics were then known) attempted to assassinate him several times. In 1605, for instance, Roman Catholic Guy Fawkes attempted to blow up Parliament when the king was to have been present. The plan was discovered, and Fawkes and his co-conspirators were executed.

Despite these many problems, King James was a successful monarch. He kept the kingdom from war and used his authority effectively. He also is remembered as the founding monarch of the United States. In 1607, colonists sent by the Virginia Company arrived in Jamestown, Virginia. Jamestown, his namesake, went on to become the first permanent English settlement on the American mainland.

Meanwhile, King James's crowning achievement was about to become a reality: the commission of what many consider to be the greatest piece of religious and literary work in the world—the Authorized King James Version of the Bible. His purpose was to give his subjects the greatest gift he could—*The Holy Bible*—so they could be saved and fed by the Word of God. The idea, however, was not his.

In January 1604, the king called the Hampton Court Conference regarding issues in the Church of England. At this conference, Dr. John Reynolds, a Puritan, requested of the king a new translation of the Bible. Reynolds alleged that translations during the reign of Henry VIII and Edward VI were corrupt. (Not to mention the *Geneva Bible* was not in favor among pro-government Protestants.)

King James bought into the idea and by mid-year had appointed fifty-four men to the translation committee. These men were considered to be the best linguists and scholars not only in the kingdom but also in the world. They were world-class scholars who were also Christians who lived holy lives as the heads of major universities, such as Cambridge, Oxford, and Westminster.

But there was opposition by the Catholic religion. According to the translator's notes in the preface of the King James Bible, the Catholic religion was adamant in its opposition to translating the Bible into the common tongue.

Obviously, the translators carried a heavy political burden with their work. Their final product continues as a marvel: It eclipsed all previous and subsequent versions of the Bible. Moreover, it remains the best-selling book of all time.

While we should pay our highest respect to the great accomplishment that is the King James Version of the Bible, we must also be aware that the translation into English was the effort of scholars working at the directive of their king. This is not to denigrate in any way the miraculous achievement; it is to remind us as we study that the original Word was written in ancient Hebrew—not English.

It is that simple fact that has led me to study the King James Version by searching out the Hebrew meaning of the words in the text, which I consider to be a step beyond translation. By using the Defined Word Approach to Biblical Study, I know—not believe, *know*—that there is a vastly deeper meaning to the King James Bible that generations of Christians have read in search of a higher purpose to our own lives.

CHAPTER 6

The Hebrew Language: The Root of Judaism, Christianity, and Islam

The original language of the Bible was classical Hebrew, meaning ancient Hebrew, and it is referred to as biblical Hebrew. The language in which the Bible was written had remarkably few words—eight thousand six hundred seventy four with seventeen hundred used only once.

In his research entitled *The Origin of the Hebrew Language*, Jeff A. Brenner of the Ancient Hebrew Research Center writes that Hebrew is classified as a Semitic language. Whether it was the root language for other Semitic languages, such as Canaanite, Akkadian, Phoenician, Aramaic, etc., is unknown. Its name is drawn from Shem (Shemitic), a son of Noah. According to the Bible, all people spoke the same language until the construction of the Tower of Babel in southern Mesopotamia, which occurred around 4000 BCE. *Genesis 11:5-9* relates that during the construction of the Tower, God confused the language of man and scattered the nations.

Thereafter, the Sumerians—known as Shinar in *Genesis 10:10*—appeared in southern Mesopotamia. They spoke in a non-Semitic language and are believed to have been ancestors of Japheth, another of Noah's sons. At about the same time, the Egyptians emerged in the south.

Their original language was Hamitic—from Noah's son, Ham—and was non-Semitic. During the time of the Sumerians and the Egyptians, those who spoke Semitic languages lived in Sumeria and traveled west to Canaan, now modern-day Israel.

Jewish tradition, which is supported by some Christian scholars, says that Hebrew was the original language of mankind. Brenner cites *Genesis 2:16* in which God spoke to Adam, giving him the language of God himself.

Hebrew was the spoken language of the ancient Israelites until the Roman destruction of the second temple in AD 135. After the destruction, Jewish people considered it blasphemous to speak Hebrew other than in prayer. Though Hebrew was not spoken, it was studied, read, and written.

Near the end of the nineteenth century in the last millennium— approximately eighteen hundred years after the Jews were run out of their homeland by the Romans—Hebrew was revived as a spoken language by a Jewish immigrant—Eliezer Ben Yehuda, who moved to Israel from Lithuania. Today, Modern Hebrew, which uses virtually the same alphabet as the Jews of two thousand years ago, has about one hundred thousand words. By comparison, modern English has about one million words.

The influence of the classical Hebrew extends beyond linguistics and religion. Hebrew words and phrases lifted from the Old Testament are in common use today. The Israel Ministry of Foreign Affairs carries on its web page an article by Norman Berdichevsky, who is a translator from Hebrew and Danish into English. Berdichevsky gives examples of how Hebrew has made the Bible the source for hundreds of expressions that are ingrained in the English language. He writes that English without them is as unthinkable as to imagine English without the influence of Shakespeare. For example: the writing on the wall (*Daniel 5:25*), the mark of Cain (*Genesis 4:15*), scapegoat (*Leviticus 16:26*), the meek shall inherit the earth (*Psalms 37:11*), the grapes of wrath (*Deuteronomy 32:32*), out of the mouths of babes and sucklings (*Psalms 8:2*), the good earth (*Deuteronomy 6:18*), the way of all flesh (*Genesis 6:12*), dust to dust (*Genesis 3:19*), how are the mighty fallen (*2 Samuel 1:19*), man shall not live by bread alone (*Deuteronomy 8:3*), and east of Eden (*Genesis 4:16*). In this small sample, four expressions were used by gifted writers to title their works: *The Good Earth* by Pearl Buck, *The Way of All Flesh* by Samuel Butler, and *East of Eden* and *The Grapes of Wrath*, both written by John Steinbeck.

Berdichevsky also notes that in some instances *mis*translations of Hebrew have entered English. After the destruction of the second temple, classical Hebrew was translated into Latin, the language of Rome. He writes that the most famous mistranslation is that of *keren*, which in classical Hebrew means ray, beam, or horn. As a result of the translation into Latin as "horn," generations of artists misrepresented Moses as possessing horns when his face should have been depicted as radiating rays of light.

Likewise, correctly translated, the Red Sea should have been the Reed Sea from the Hebrew *Yam Suf.* R. K. Harrison amplifies on this point in *Old Testament Times—A Social, Political, and Cultural Context.* Harrison writes that the names "Red Sea" (*Exodus 13:18*) and "the sea" (*Exodus 14:2*) may have indicated the Lake of Reeds, situated in the marsh lands between the Bitter Lakes and the town of Zilu (Thiel). Harrison makes the point that the Israelites were depicted as crossing a body of water that presented a natural obstacle to travel in the Sinai wilderness, and neither the Gulf of Suez nor the Gulf of Aqabah met that requirement. He adds that in antiquity the area north of the Gulf of Suez was a marshy ground where papyrus reeds grew in abundance. Harrison theorizes that these shallow waters would have been more easily parted by a wind in the manner described in *Exodus 14:21.*

In an August 13, 2011, news article titled *Scholars Trace Hebrew Bible's Evolution*, Matti Friedman reports about the Bible Project, which has been underway at the Hebrew University campus for fifty-three years. The project's purpose is to publish the authoritative edition of the Old Testament, also known as the Hebrew Bible, by tracking every single evolution of the text over centuries and millennia. The first shocker that would startle many readers of the Old Testament is this: "The sacred text that people revered in the past was not the same one we study today." Friedman writes that an ancient version of one book has an extra phrase. Another appears to have been revised to retroactively insert a prophecy after the events happened.

That the biblical text is considered inviolable has passed down through the generations. But the Bible Project is finding that there have been changes to biblical text contrary to the edicts of religion that hold that words of the Bible in the original Hebrew are divine, unaltered, and unalterable.

The Bible Project research, writes Friedman, shows that the transmission of this biblical text, which is at the root of Judaism, Christianity, and Islam, "was messier and more human than most of us imagine."

This is crucial for using the Defined Word Approach to Biblical Study. Key points to remember are that classical Hebrew had a limited vocabulary, which means that writers would employ the same word in several different contexts; that the translation of biblical text has provable *mis*translations; and that the final product, i.e., the King James Version of the Holy Bible, like its predecessors, was subject to external influences. In the case of the King James Version, the king assigned the team of translators. They worked at the pleasure of a monarch who was clearly at odds with the papacy in Rome. In fact, the monarch was so at odds that the papacy attempted to murder him.

Finally, the modern or Israeli Hebrew language is not the same as biblical or classical Hebrew. When Hebrew was revived as a spoken language in the late nineteenth century, Yiddish, the then-spoken language of the European Jewish people, was incorporated into Hebrew to create today's Hebrew. Also, it is commonplace that the words in living languages undergo change due to their usage. Connotation often plays a part in these changes. Outstanding examples that come to mind are Kelvinator, which came to mean refrigerator in the 1950s, and Coke, which became a generic term for a soft drink.

Deciphering biblical text using the Defined Word Approach is both challenging and rewarding. As with the mistranslation about Moses having horns, it opens the door to reconsider what the biblical writers really meant in their text and whether the translations we have relied on through the ages are accurate.

CHAPTER 7

Moses the Writer

Through the ages, the authorship of the first five books of the Old Testament—referred to by Christians as the Pentateuch and by Jews as the Torah—has been credited to Moses. In recent years, however, some academics have contended that there were several writers based on the difference in the writing style.

Based on my research, I agree. Yet others have gone so far as to suggest that Moses never existed. Notre Dame Professor Joseph Blenkinsopp stated in *The Pentateuch: An Introduction to the First Five Books of the Bible*,

> Here and there in the Pentateuch, Moses is said to have written certain things ... but nowhere is it affirmed that the Pentateuch was authored by Moses ... One would therefore think that what calls for an explanation is not why most people stopped believing in the dogma of Mosaic authorship, but rather why anyone believed it in the first place.

Irrespective of the spectrum of viewpoints, the reality is that the Old Testament exists, and that Moses remains an important prophet in Judaism, Christianity, Islam, the Baha'i Faith, Rastafarian, and many other faiths.

According to Jewish tradition, the Torah was revealed to Moses in 1312 BCE at Mount Sinai (another date given for this event is 1233

BCE). At that point, Moses was middle-aged and had led the Israelites and other slaves out of bondage in Egypt.

Many scholars have attempted to disprove the biblical narrative about the over four hundred years of captivity in Egypt. R. K. Harrison writes in *Old Testament Times: A Social, Political, and Cultural Context* that the historical conditions that existed from the nineteenth century BC in the Near East and Egypt are in full accord with the biblical tradition. With that in mind, he maintains that the rise of Semitic influence would have made it possible for the Hebrew Joseph's rise to political prominence. The Hyksos, who had invaded and occupied parts of Egypt from the eighteenth to the sixteenth century BC, were tolerant of the Hebrews. That relationship enabled the Hebrews to be firmly established in Goshen, in the eastern part of the Nile delta, where the Hyksos had their capital. But these fortunes were reversed with the expulsion of the Hyksos by Ahmosis I, which was when the Semites were enslaved and made to work as peasants.

Harrison notes, "This situation appears to correspond with that described in the first chapter of Exodus, though the identity of the 'pharaoh who knew not Joseph' is by no means clear." He offers that the enslavement of the Hebrews could have started with Ahmosis, but their greatest hardship was probably associated with the construction at Pithom and Raameses under Seti I and Ramses II.

Despite their difficult lives, the Hebrew population grew, which prompted the Egyptians to pass a law providing for the elimination of all male children born to Semitic women. Exodus recounts how the infant Moses was placed in a boat and set afloat on the river that was used for bathing by a daughter of the pharaoh, who found the baby and adopted him into the royal household, where his birth mother, Jochebed, was her handmaiden. According to Exodus, Moses was the son of Amram, a member of the Levite tribe of Israel descended from Jacob. Jochebed was kin to Amram's father Kehath. Moses had an older brother and sister, Aaron and Miriam.

In the years prior to Moses' birth, Pharaoh Amenhotep IV, husband of Nefertiti, forsook political and administrative pursuits to pursue religion. As such, he eliminated the Egyptian system of deities and revived solar monotheism by making the sun deity Re supreme. This action also included suppression of the Amun cult. The new religion was named Aton, which was a revival of an ancient solar title. When Amenhotep IV's son, Tutankhamen, ascended to the throne, he immediately eradicated Aton and restored the complex system of deities and the Amun priesthood. At the young Tut's death, the Amun priests honored him with a lavish burial.

Mythology, mysticism, and rituals all shaped the belief system of the time. Moses grew up in the royal palaces. His education was probably in the priestly circle of Heliopolis, where the complex motifs of Re formed his instruction. Harrison writes that there is little doubt that Moses became familiar with the religious beliefs and practices of ancient Canaan. He was in touch with the dialects of Canaan as well as with Babylonian cuneiform, which was used for diplomatic communication. Further, he probably knew a wide range of priest craft, which would be included in royal household education.

The religion of the Canaanite people was a crude, ritualistic polytheism. In the Near East, it was associated with fertility cult worship that was especially debased. The principal deity was El. His consort was Asherat, the counselor of the gods, and known to the Israelites as Asherah. These two—El and Asherat—produced the fertility deity Baal, who later succeeded El as the king of the Canaanite pantheon.

The Canaanite religion was in marked contrast to the high ethical ideals of Israelites. The Canaanite deities were, in today's vernacular, lowlifes. Child sacrifice, polygamy, ritual prostitution, and licentious worship were the ways of their religion. Obviously, there could be no common ground between their debased beliefs and the morality of the God of Israel.

Being part of the Egyptian royal household did not preclude Moses from having contact with Semites. The pharaohs had residences in the Delta region during the New Kingdom period in which he lived. Children of concubines were educated in the royal harems.

In his adult travels, Moses visited the Hebrews to see how they were faring. In an outrage, he killed an Egyptian in an effort to stop the beating of a Hebrew. Moses then buried the body, hoping his act would not be discovered. But he learned the next day that his deed was known. In fear for his life, he fled over the Sinai Peninsula to Midian, where he met and married Zipporah, the daughter of a Midianite priest (*Exodus 2:11-21*). For the next forty years, he lived there as a superintendent of her father Jethro's herds.

It was while tending flocks at Mount Horeb that he had a theophany, or vision, in which Jehovah appeared to him in a burning bush. Under divine instruction in that encounter, he and his brother Aaron were to return to Egypt to deliver the descendants of the patriarchs Abraham, Isaac, and Jacob from the shame of forced labor. Their ultimate destination would be the Promised Land. In biblical times, this area—now known as Israel—was the land of Canaan (*Exodus 3:1-8*).

The Exodus narrative contained in the Bible portrays Moses as a man of strong conviction and deep spiritual insight whose disappointment brought him ever closer to God. Imagine for a moment what it would have been for one tasked with his divine assignment. *Exodus 12:37–38* relates that there were on foot about six hundred thousand men *beside* children and that a mixed multitude went with them. The "mixed multitude" refers to the non-Semitic slave groups who joined the Israelite exodus.

For the next forty years, this sometimes-unruly mob wandered the desert. With the discipline and personal spiritual reserve of Moses, these people eventually emerged from their hardships in the wilderness as a people united in their loyalty to God.

The genius of Moses was his role as lawgiver. He was the divinely appointed agent to form the legislative system that became fundamental to Israelite life. The corpus of this covenant with the people was the Decalogue, or the Ten Commandments. In the recent past, there were scholars who held that Moses could not have written this legislation. But archaeological discoveries in the Sinai Peninsula and Transjordan give contrary evidence.

Inscriptions in the turquoise mines of Serabit el Khadem in the Sinai, once controlled by the Egyptians, show that prior to the Mosaic period there was an alphabetic script. These inscriptions were discovered in 1904 by Sir Flinders Petrie and were later deciphered and traced to the alphabetic script used by Semitic slaves from Canaan who had worked in the turquoise mines for Thotmes III. Other scholars contend that they were from an earlier period in Egyptian history. No one argues, however, that their discovery proves there was written communication in the Mosaic period.

Debate about the authorship of the Pentateuch or Torah will no doubt continue. Whether it was the work of one man, Moses, or a compilation of writings by others, the Pentateuch or Torah nonetheless endures. This simple reality should bring some agreement: By some means, the Word was written, and the Word became the law that civilized people through the millennia have relied on as the moral code by which the family of man should live.

CHAPTER 8

Five Steps to Biblical Understanding

The Bible is the book of the Christian faith. To believers, it is the Word of God as presented to the spiritually inspired prophets and culminates in the teachings and resurrection of God's Son, Jesus Christ, which they accept as the path to eternal truth. While the Bible reflects this truth, I contend that biblical interpretation over the centuries has altered the actual meaning of some biblical text.

Over the past four hundred years, conventional biblical teaching sometimes has inferred meaning other than that intended by biblical language. One of the most outstanding examples of this point occurs in the early verses of Genesis. Conventional teaching maintains that the writer is describing the creation of the *universe*—the earth, sun, moon, stars, and galaxies. But upon closer examination of biblical or classical Hebrew, the language of the Pentateuch, the term *universe* does not even exist! This may explain why the 1611 King James Version of the Holy Bible never uses the word *universe*. It may also explain why despite centuries of conventional teaching the word *universe* is not used in the computerized *Biblesoft Complete Reference Library PC Study Bible Version 5*. The term both of these versions use is *world*.

The 1611 King James Version predates the Bibles in use today, such as the, *New International Version Study Bible, Life Application Study Bible, and The English Standard Version Study Bible*, etc. These Bibles are the ones that employ the translated term *universe* in place of the original term *world*.

There is a vast difference between the terms *world* and *universe*. In the Hebrew language, the language of the Pentateuch, *world* means *earth*. It means the same in the Greek language as well. This is a far more limited in scope than *universe*, which refers to "the totality of all things that exist," including the solar system and galaxies. This point is raised to emphasize the influence of religious scholars and translators on religious education and belief.

Please understand I am *not* saying that God did not create the *universe*. What I am saying is there is no biblical evidence to support the thesis that God created the *universe*. So the question that needs answering is, where did the interpretation of God creating the *universe* originate? Research dating back to a publication in 1953, *The Interpreter's Bible*, reveals not one book but twelve volumes. The authors describe *The Interpreter's Bible* methodology as having two sides. One is a picture of biblical facts as seen by the exegete (interpreter). The other side is the same picture as seen by the expositor (storyteller) who then recasts the interpreted Scripture. In their practice, this two-sided view provides the truth from two perspectives. In my view, this lends itself to possible misinterpretation over time. Let's remember a key point. The foundation of *The Interpreter's Bible* is based on the word *universe*. It's worth repeating: The word *universe* does not appear in the 1611 King James Version of the Bible nor does it have an ancient Hebrew origin.

From my research, it appears that over the past sixty years other publications have adopted the *universe* terminology in *The Interpreter's Bible*. To be more direct, what other discipline or field of study populated by scholars would remain unchallenged for so long?

We can agree that Moses was describing creation in the first books of Genesis. But Jewish tradition teaches that he was explaining the origin of the Hebrew people. The key to confirming that Moses was explaining the origin of the Hebrew people as recorded in *Genesis 1:1–5* is to apply the Defined Word Approach to each word in the story of creation as recorded in the King James Version of *The Holy Bible*. This approach was first revealed in my 2007 book, *Entering The Promised Land*.

The Defined Word Approach first requires the reader to change his or her mind when reading the modern language used in the Bible. Second, it focuses on what the ancient writer saw in daily life—was written in the language of the day—without reaching beyond into the historical social, economic and moral context. In that regard, and I realize this is an extremely simplistic example—but these were people with a much smaller vocabulary—take a sentence in our elementary school books: "Johnny's dog is gone." It does not say if a law had been passed to pick up dogs, if Johnny could not afford to have a dog, or how Johnny felt about it. All the reader knows is the simple statement. That is the "purist" method used in the Defined Word Approach. For other context on the period of Biblical writing, I suggest study of western civilization history. Third, it analyzes what the words mean in the Bible as defined in *James Strong's Hebrew Chaldee Dictionary and Greek Dictionary of the New Testament*. Fourth, it cross-references the individual defined word to its usage in other biblical text. And fifth, it uses logic and common sense.

With the application of these five steps, it is clear that the metaphors or figurative speech in *Genesis 1:1-5* actually represents the male and a female union as the source of procreation. With the human union there is the birth of a baby, the highest known form of life. Thus the beginning of the Hebrew people!

The story of creation and other biblical stories are important for the following reasons: 1) The stories about ancient biblical characters are very similar to our daily lives. Their stories, if deciphered accurately, provide a template for daily living. They delineate how our actions positively or negatively impact our family. From their stories, we learn, as stated in *Ecclesiastes 1:9*, "There is no new thing under the sun." If we learn from their mistakes, our lives would be better; 2) Inaccurate interpretations destroy the Bible's credibility as a history book, which, as such, I believe there's appropriate subject matter to be taught in public schools. The biblical stories were written by humans in ancient times about everyday occurrences. And that's how we record history today. When theologians insist Eve talked to a snake, all credibility of the Bible as a history book evaporates. With this background, let's begin our journey to a brand-new biblical understanding.

As previously mentioned, the first step in deciphering Scripture requires a willingness to suspend mind-set for a possible mind-change. Over the years, biblical interpretations have seldom changed. Truth is, they have been repeated so often that they are almost rote.

Many years ago, I was trying to teach my father a new concept, when, in exasperation, he blurted out, "Willie James, I'm too old to learn this!" For some, like my father, it will be difficult or impossible to embrace a new concept that is contrary to an ingrained belief. So I ask you, why, then, is the Bible today considered irrelevant to so many people?

The second step in deciphering biblical Scripture is to let our imagination travel back in time to the days of the ancients. We then can see the very same symbols dotting the sky and the landscape, e.g., the sun, moon, stars, darkness, night, day, rain, trees, rivers, ground, etc. The differences being, however, that back then they were synonymous or associated in a metaphoric way with the ancient Homo sapiens. These symbols were used to: 1) identify who they were, 2) describe their physical appearance, 3) describe features of their body, 4) describe bodily functions, and 5) describe daily activities. I contend these symbols were used by the ancient writers to paint a picture with the words found in the book of Genesis and throughout the Bible.

The third step analyzes individual words found in Scripture, which includes tracing their etymology. This step alone may reveal the biblical story.

The fourth step looks at how the word being defined is used by cross-referencing Scripture as recorded in the *King James Version Hebrew-Greek Key Word Study Bible*.

The fifth and final step involves the application of logic and common sense, which inspires me to note the following about this treatise. A review of Hebrew words found specifically in *Genesis 1:1–5* and throughout the Bible reveals both literal and figurative meanings. This leads me to think that ancient writers, like modern writers, used both literal and figurative language to communicate their messages. However, even with many Hebrew definitions conveying both literal and figurative meanings, *The Holy Bible* is interpreted literally, which necessitates applied logic.

That being said, the combination of all five steps reveals the story. I truly believe that by changing one's mind-set, viewing the world through the eyes of ancient people, applying the Defined Word Approach, applying Cross-Reference to Scripture, and applying logic and common sense lays the foundation for deciphering other biblical Scripture in the Old and New Testaments. Application of this approach allows the reader to decipher biblical Scripture that reveals a story never before told about the creation.

By itself, the Defined Word Approach lays out the path with various nouns, verbs, adjectives, adverbs, and prepositional phrases that frequently lead to the exact equivalent in English letters of the original Hebrew word *yalad* and its appropriate number 3205 in *James Strong's Hebrew and Chaldee Dictionary*.

The term *yalad* describes a woman in labor who delivers a baby. Interestingly, the revelation about *yalad* aligns with the biblical stories about married couples and their son(s): Adam and Eve and their sons, Cain and Seth; Abraham and Sarah and their son, Isaac; Isaac and Rebekah and their sons, Jacob and Esau. The two exceptions are Noah and his sons, Shem, Ham, and Japheth, as Noah's wife is never mentioned by name. Jacob and his wives, Leah and Rachel, along with their maids Zilpah and Bilhah, had twelve sons. The many births in these stories and others throughout the Old Testament establish the biblical lineage to Joseph and Mary and their son, Jesus Christ.

Another aspect of the Defined Word Approach amplifies the reader's understanding of the story of creation by examining the role that metaphors or figurative speech play. Frequently, the Hebrew definition of words includes both a literal and figurative meaning as they relate to ancient writings. I contend many interpretations using the literal meanings should have been used figuratively.

Fast-forward to today, and we can see literal and figurative meanings showing up in our culture as written lyrics of songs. You may recall Elvis Presley's famous hit tune *Hound Dog*. According to writers Jerry Leiber and Mike Stoller, they didn't like the way Elvis sang it in 1956 because he was referring to a literal hound dog. On the other hand, they preferred the way blues vocalist Big Mama Thornton sang the same song in 1952. Her version of the hound dog was a man.

Another example of figurative meanings shows up in legendary blues singer B. B. King's song *Sweet Little Angel* in the lyrics, "I've got a sweet little angel, I love the way she spread her wings." Use your imagination and you can figure out he's not singing about wings literally but figuratively—and it has nothing to do with angels or flying.

Here's another example: the singing group The Temptations and their hit tune *Papa Was a Rollin' Stone*. This papa had many women in his life other than the children's mother. And how about the late great Marvin Gaye and his hit tune *Flying High (In the Friendly Sky) without ever leavin' the ground?* Here, he sings euphemistically about illegal drugs—an addiction that eventually led to his untimely death.

Let's take a look at sports, starting with basketball and football legends *Clyde the Glide* and *Air McNair*, respectively. The first describes former National Basketball Association and University of Houston player Clyde Drexler, who appeared to defy gravity as he floated through the air toward the hoop before delivering a thunderous dunk. The second, Tennessee Titans/Houston Oilers and Alcorn State University quarterback, the late Steve McNair, who many times brought his teams from the brink of defeat with pinpoint scoring passes deftly delivered to scampering receivers.

Finally, let's review nicknames of everyday individuals. Back in college, my roommate's nickname was *Flyweight*. This name was playfully given to him due to his slender frame and actual weight at the time being around 125 pounds although he claimed to be 130. Flyweight was the football team's cameraman who lived and worked in an environment where the average weight of a football player was 230 pounds. And then there's my favorite nickname, *Blue*, which affectionately describes an African American with very dark skin.

I share this use of figurative speech or metaphors to show how even today their usage is common and the true meanings often can be missed. If you read these lyrics or nicknames literally, it would be possible to miss the communicator's message. If the censors had known or could prove that the songs of the 1960s had lyrics with sexual connotations, those like The Rolling Stones' first hit, *(I Can't Get No) Satisfaction*, probably never would have made the airwaves.

CHAPTER 9

Defined Word Approach: A Key That Unlocks the Bible

While refining what I call the Defined Word Approach, a unique opportunity to test its application was presented. A junior class of high school students was to participate in a weekend retreat on entrepreneurship, and the coordinators invited me to speak on the subject of networking. It dawned on me as I prepared my speech that application of the Defined Word Approach to the term *networking* might be validation of how this approach works. I went to work, employing the "drill down" process:

Step 1—Find the definition of the word *networking* in the *Random House Webster's Unabridged Dictionary* where it is defined as "a supportive system of sharing information and services among individuals and groups having a common interest."

Step 2—Look up the meaning of each word used in the definition of *networking*: 1) *a*, 2) *supportive*, 3) *system*, 4) *of*, 5) *sharing*, 6) *information*, 7) *services*, 8) *among*, 9) *individuals*, 10) *and*, 11) *groups*, 12) *having*, 13) *common*, and 14) *interest*.

Step 3—Continue drilling down by repeating step two. Look up the meaning of each word in the definition of *networking*. At this point, we are three levels deep. The definition of the first key word, *supportive*, is defined as "providing support." Next, look up the definition of the key words that define *supportive*: 1) *providing*, and 2) *support*.

Amazingly, each drill-down provided more information and clarity to the word *networking*, which gave me the basis for a speech on networking. (See the Addendum for an abbreviated drill-down.)

If the word *networking* had been a Hebrew word, the next step would have been to search the Bible to find its usage in biblical Scripture, which would support the definition of the word in question. This is called Cross-Reference to Scripture.

Based on application of the Defined Word Approach, I have concluded that there is a deeper meaning in words, hence the possibility of a greater story than the obvious. With this in mind, I am confident that the Defined Word Approach, when applied to Hebrew words found in biblical Scripture, reveals ancient stories as originally communicated by the author. This may shed light on what the apostle John says in *John 1:1*, "In the beginning was the Word." And I'd like to add that there is a story in every word.

When deciphering biblical Scripture, one must be willing to suspend their mind-set for a mind-change when presented with compelling evidence. View the world through the eyes of ancient people. Analyze each key word by applying the Defined Word Approach and cross-reference individual words found in Scripture. Lastly, employ logic and common sense. I contend that the combination of all the above reveals ancient biblical stories that are undeniable.

*   *   *

Let's start the process by deciphering the following biblical Scripture that's found in the *King James Version Hebrew-Greek Key Word Study Bible, Genesis 1:1–5*. The application of the Defined Word Approach, the accompanying Cross-Reference to Scripture associated with footnotes one through thirty-nine, and an understanding that the book of Genesis, Chapters one, two and three and *The Lord's Prayer* when read *primarily as figurative rather than literal* gives a new understanding of Scripture. This process also confirms my thesis that the story of creation reveals a newly married male and female and the building of their family with the birth of their first of six children. Lastly, keep in mind there is no biblical or classical Hebrew word for *universe*, as the term *universe* does not exist in *Genesis 1:1*, "In the beginning God created the heaven and the earth." Another bit of information I offer for consideration: Based on accepted biblical teachings that the story of creation is about God creating the *universe*, it appears God made a logistical error. He created light (*Genesis 1:3*) *after* creating the heaven and the earth (*Genesis 1:1*). How could vegetation like plants and trees on the earth exist without light?

According to biblical scholars and the *King James Version Hebrew-Greek Key Word Study Bible*, "The Hebrews often identified the books of the Old Testament by the first word of the text. In this way when a scroll was unrolled they were able to tell immediately which book it contained." As a result, this merits an examination of the phrase "In the beginning," with a focus on the Authorized English Version (translation) of the original Hebrew word *beginning*.[2] An application of the Defined Word Approach to the word *beginning* reveals a story about the birth of a couple's first baby. This disclosure immediately follows the revelation that *God*,[3] also known as the supreme God or Holy Spirit, *created*"[4] or made a union between an adult male named *heaven*[5] and a female named *earth*.[6] Today, this union is called "marriage" and is consummated by the male and female in their physical union. Read what Jesus says in *Mark 10:6–7*. I find His words rather enlightening. "But from the beginning of the creation, God made them male and female. For this cause shall a man leave his father and mother, and cleave to his wife." You can read nearly identical Scripture in *Matthew 19:4–9*.

See Defined Word Approach, footnote 4h, where the definition of *created* means *cut down*" I could not find a Cross-Reference to Scripture that is associated with the phrase *cut down* in a human way. However, I think it is noteworthy because in the drill-down, the word *divorce* and its appropriate number 3748 traces its etymology to the phrase *cut down*. The appropriate number 3772 is associated with the phrase *cut down*" which means, "Make an alliance or bargain, originally by cutting

---

[2] The word *beginning* and others that follow are the Authorized English Version (translation) of the original Hebrew words. Application of the Defined Word Approach starts on page 69 and their use in Cross-Reference to Scripture starts on page 117. The Defined Word Approach and Cross- Reference of Scripture also apply to footnotes 3 through 85.

flesh and passing between the pieces." In addition, the word *covenant* is defined as *cut down*" and it means "a compact (made by passing between pieces of flesh)." I am led to believe these definitions are associated with a male and female engaged in coitus.

In *Genesis 17:2*, a covenant is made between God and Abram where He would multiply Abram's seed. Fulfillment of the covenant begins with Abraham (formerly named Abram) and Sarah engaging in coitus to create their son, Isaac. In ancient days, prior to the birth of Adam and Eve, this male and female were metaphorically called the *heaven* and the *earth*.

We know that waters from the heavens give and sustain life as we know it on Earth. Just as the rain from heaven falls on the earth, penetrates it, and subsequently a plant springs forth, the human male version of *heaven* rains on or impregnates a human female version of *earth* that births a baby. One validation of *earth* as a female can be found in the *James Strong's Hebrew and Chaldee Dictionary's* definition of the phrase *thing of naught*,[7] which is defined as "an end (especially of the earth)." Common sense dictates the earth literally does not and will not end. Rather the earth ending refers to the *earth* metaphorically as a female that dies. Based on the Bible's theme of family, this female likely died during or shortly after giving childbirth.

The second validation of the *earth* metaphorically being a female can be found by applying the Defined Word Approach to the word *giants*[8] found in *Genesis 6:4*, which reads,

> There were giants *in the earth* (emphasis added) in those days; and also after that, when the sons of God came in unto the daughters of men, and they bare children to them, the same became mighty men which were of old, men of renown.

The application of the Defined Word Approach to the word *giants* reveals these *giants* came from a family of *giants* who metaphorically were bullies or tyrants. Of course, we know that families start with babies. These *giants* "in the earth" are referring to babies or giants in the mother's womb, and their mother is the *earth*. Conversely, the preceding verse, *Genesis 6:1* literally reads, "And it came to pass, when men began to multiply *on the face of the earth, and daughters were born unto them,"* (emphasis added). This indicates that after these *giants* were born, they birthed babies who became *giants* and literally walked *on the earth*.

There is one final observation about the female metaphorically being called *earth*. Consider the roundness of a pregnant woman's belly in the days just before delivery, and then compare her belly to photos of the earth taken from outer space. Wow!

To understand the metaphor for the word *heaven* as being a male requires analyzing biblical verses *Genesis 2:1, 4*. *Genesis 2:1* reads, "Thus the heavens and earth *were finished,*[9] and all the *host*[10] of them." Unlike in *Genesis 1:1* where the word *heaven* is singular, notice how the word *heavens* in *Genesis 2:1* is plural. This indicates more than one *heaven* or that *heaven* is more than one place. At the same time, the word *earth*, metaphorically a female, is both singular and plural, depending on how the word *earth* is used in a sentence.

Many think of *heaven* as being a singular place that we will go to in our next life. So the logical question is, what does the plural word *heavens* mean? An application of the Defined Word Approach reveals that the plural word *heavens* means that in the beginning, contrary to popular belief, the biblical Adam was not the first male on earth. There were many *heavens* or males on earth who preceded Adam. Likewise, the biblical Eve was not the first female. For biblical purpose, Adam and Eve established the lineage to King David who is the forbearer to Jesus, which is revealed later in the New Testament. Although marriage was not a ceremony as we know it, the males and females who populated the earth were couples, which is what's reflected in the story of Adam and Eve. The male and female, head of household were called *host* (a mass of persons). Interestingly, *The Brown-Driver-Briggs Hebrew and English Lexicon* defines *host* as "figuratively of great numbers." This would suggest there were a great number of males and females.

Naturally, these married couples birth children who also numbered in size like an army. Like their parent's *heaven, earth* and *host* the children would one day become adults, marry, and continue populating the Earth. For each set of parents, the act of bearing children and rearing them to adulthood is a part of their own lives that is complete and is passed on to their children. As we look at our own ancestry, we see that this is like a connective tissue that links family units from one generation to the next. Thus we have the continuity of creation.

Next, review the word *generations*[11] as found in *Genesis 2:4*, which reads, "These are the *generations of the heavens and of the earth* when they were created, in the day that the LORD God made the earth and the heavens," (emphasis added). Now that God had populated the Earth with married humans, the subsequent biblical stories will be about the married Adam and Eve's ancestors who preceded them in the —Garden of Eden and their descendants. These ancestors and descendants trace their heritage from the heavens and earth as noted by the key word *of* in the phrase "generations of the heavens and of the earth." Of course, it is commonly accepted that the generations written about in the Bible end with the betrothed Joseph and Mary and the birth of the baby Jesus (*Matthew 1:18-25*).

There is more on the definition of *heaven*, which is also defined as "the dual" (see Defined Word Approach, footnote 5). Duality plays a central role in biblical writings. Remember how the creation reveals a story about the marriage of a male and a female and the birth of their first baby? Duality is associated with everyone and everything as opposites—*male and female, boy and girl, heaven and earth*, and *darkness and light*. You will also find the term associated with the synonyms *without form* and *void* and *let there be and there was*.

The instructions God gave to the *male* called *heaven* and the *female* called *earth* after their creation or marriage is found in *Genesis 1:28* where He ordered them, "Be fruitful, and multiply, and replenish the earth, and subdue it." In other words, He instructed the male and female to produce many children and their children to produce many children. This knowledge lays the foundation for deciphering the upcoming verses, *Genesis 1:2–5*.

I have three final comments on the word *heaven* being a metaphor for a *male*. First, an examination of the word *heaven* and its appropriate number 8064, along with its exact equivalent in English letters, *shamayim*, are found in the *James Strong's Hebrew and Chaldee Dictionary*. The comparative of Noah's oldest son Shem's name along with its appropriate numbers 8034 and 8035 is the word *heaven* or its exact equivalent in English letters, *shamayim*. See Defined Word Approach #5b. Second, according to Jeff A. Brenner of the Ancient Hebrew Research Center, Hebrew is classified as a Semitic language drawn from the word Shem, the name of Noah's oldest son. This makes me ponder if there's a connection between Hebrew being a Semitic language and the association of the Hebrew word "shamayim," its Authorized English Version *Shem* and metaphoric meaning *heaven*. Think of it as *Shem* being number one or above everybody and everything. If you're the author, this could be very likely. Third, the Authorized English Version of the Greek word for *heaven* and its exact equivalent in English letters, *airo*, along with its appropriate numbers 142, are found in the *James Strong's Greek Dictionary of the New Testament*. The comparative of its appropriate Hebrew number 5375, and its exact equivalent in English letters, *nasa*, is defined as *an honourable man*.

Conversely, an application of the Defined Word Approach to the word *earth*, its appropriate number 776, and its exact equivalent in English letters, *erets,* drills down to a female who gives birth to a baby (see footnote 6b and the same numbered Cross-Reference to Scripture).

I have spent considerable time on the words *heaven* and *earth* because they—along with the word *beginning*—lay the foundation for my thesis. I have tried to describe in a scholarly and logical way that the application of the Defined Word Approach reveals their ancient biblical secrets.

Jesus spoke in parables, which contained metaphoric language. Once again, a notable exception—which is crucial to my contention that the book of Genesis is a metaphoric account of creation—is when Jesus spoke to the Pharisees in *Mark 10:6*, where he says, "But from the beginning of creation, God made them male and female. For this cause shall a man leave his father and mother, and cleave to his wife." There, Jesus specifically referenced the creation laid out in *Genesis 1:1* as the creation of *male* and *female*, i.e., *heaven* and *earth*. I encourage the reader to read the entirety of *Mark 10:1–12*.

My deciphering of Scripture continues with "And the earth was without form, and void; and darkness was upon the face of the deep.

And the Spirit of God moved upon the face of the waters" (*Genesis 1:2*). The conjunction *and* at the beginning of *Genesis 1:2* signals a continuation of the story from *Genesis 1:1* over an unknown period of time. Interestingly, the word *and* appears at the beginning of every verse beginning with *Genesis 1:2* through *Genesis 1:31*, which indicates *Genesis 1:1–31* is one continuous story over an unknown period of time. The best correlation is like that of a small child stringing a story together with a series of *ands*. Incorporated in these *ands* is the use of nature as a way to identify humans metaphorically.

The author begins to describe anatomically the condition or the appearance of the female's body. "The earth *was*[12] *without form*[13] and *void*"[14] means the *female* had delivered a baby. An examination of the words *without*[15] and *form*[16] individually means the same thing. It appears the writer was trying to drive home a point. Logically, it makes sense that immediately after God *created/married* the male and female, they would engage in coitus, and the female would become pregnant. Stated differently, the male and female were created as dual entities that would unite to create a new life.

The phrase "*darkness*[17] was upon the *face*[18] of the *deep*"[19] indicates the female had experienced a miscarriage. Her stillborn baby's eyes never opened to see the light of day, another indication of death. The lifeless face of this stillborn baby is described as *darkness*. The *baby*, or *face*, is delivered from the womb, or *deep*, and falls lifelessly to the ground. There is no sign of life on the face or in the body in general. This story often plays out today as young and older married couples experience the pain of their baby being stillborn.

Remember the word *and* signals a continuation of the story over an unknown period of time. It is unknown whether the female's labor continues during this pregnancy or much later when another *baby* or *face*, starts movement toward birth. This story continues with a baby being born. Once again, the amniotic fluids preceded this birth with the prior stillborn birth or this birth many months later as a single birth. In the not too distant past, a newborn would have been spanked on the buttocks to stimulate the first breath. The baby's reaction is seen on its little face—there frequently is a cry with the first breath, the eyes squint against the bright lights, and the chin quivers in a chatter. Those who have witnessed a birth will recall the picture that I have described.

In summary, "the *Spirit*[20] of God *moved*[21] *upon*[22] the *face* of the *waters*."[23] These *waters*, or amniotic fluids, cushion the fetus in the womb, which is the metaphoric *deep*. When they begin to leak, the baby's birth is imminent. Today, like in ancient times, these *waters* also represent a new spiritual life.

More clarity comes to this deciphered Scripture when the Hebrew definition of the word *upon* reveals itself (see footnote 22). These four definitions from start to finish are associated with childbirth.

I find it rather interesting that *darkness* means death and that one of the Hebrew definitions of *waters* mean *conceive again*, which coincides with the first baby being born dead and the second birth but first live child of the male and female. Any mother who has given birth knows about the amniotic fluids that precede the birth. Also, anyone who has witnessed a birth may recall that when the baby first appears, the crown of the head shows, and the face is normally in a skyward position.

The face provides lifelong recognition. During our life, it becomes synonymous with who we are. Thus the baby is called the *face* of the waters or amniotic fluids.

The birthing process is described in the following Scripture: "And God said, Let there be light: and there was light" (*Genesis 1:3*). The story continues when God *said*,[24] or commanded, the newly born baby to open its eyes, or *let there be*[25] a birth, and behold *there was*[26] a birth. The baby opens his or her eyes and sees the *light*,[27] which signals a second time to the parents that the baby is alive.

The child has entered the world and it is a live birth: "And God saw the light, that it was good: and God divided the light from the darkness" (*Genesis 1:4*). God witnessed or *saw*[28] the newborn baby, or *light*, and was pleased by proclaiming, "it was *good*."[29] Earlier in *Genesis 1:2*, we learned that the *darkness* represents death.

When God *divided*[30] the *light* from *darkness*, we learned there was a second birth. The female was either pregnant with twins or the second birth occurred many months later. Again, we see an example of duality at work. While the couple was very sad with the loss of their first newborn infant, shortly thereafter they experienced joy with the second baby being a live birth.

The use of "light," *Day* as a metaphor for life and "darkness," *Night* as death is conveyed in the following Scripture: "And God called the light Day, and the darkness he called Night. And the evening and the morning were the first day" (*Genesis 1:5*). When God *called*[31] the *light Day*,[32] He was referring to the baby's birth[day] as a symbol for *light* and the *Night*[33] as a symbol for death. Like the *night*, a baby that never sees the *light* is stillborn, or has died prior to birth. Fast-forward to *Exodus 12:29* where it is revealed that during the *night*, the Lord killed the firstborn of Pharaoh.

The *evening*[34] in ancient days reminds us of today when males and females start the courting process. At this special time, the male and female met at the well for a cold drink of water. Many young and old today call the end of the workday or start of the evening "Happy Hour." The meeting occurs at the local tavern for a cold, intoxicating beverage.

With the approach of evening, the ritualistic mating dance of males and females begins, culminating in their physical union. The combination of the courtship, the *evening* and the *morning*[35]—when the male sows his seed—results in the ultimate outcome, a baby. The *evening* and *morning were*[36] and still is the beginning of creation. The *first*[37] *day*[38] represents the first baby born in the male and female's family.

A look back at the Old English definition of the word *genesis*, which comes from the word *gignesthai*, means, "to be born." This definition fits perfectly with the story of creation, representing the birth of a baby and the marriage of a male and female.

Remember the earlier comments on page 35 about the married couples and their sons? We can now add one more: *Heaven* and *Earth* and their son—the *Face.*

The revelation that the creation includes the birth of a baby leads me to a popular story found in the New Testament (*John 3:1–21*) about a man name Nicodemus. In summation, Nicodemus asked Jesus how to attain everlasting life or to ascend to heaven. Jesus explains that he must be *born again.*[39] Rightfully so, Nicodemus thinks Jesus is talking about going back into his mother's womb and coming from the immersed waters or amniotic fluids found there. However, Jesus was speaking metaphorically, as the birth He was referring to was being baptized or immersed in water and receiving the Holy Spirit. Baptism cleanses an individual of all sins. Just as a baby comes into this world free of sin from the mother's womb where he or she was surrounded in water or amniotic fluid, metaphorically the same thing occurs when baptized.

Based on the previous information, I contend that the Old and New Testaments of the Bible mirror each other. First, *Genesis 1:3* begins with the birth of the firstborn baby of *Heaven* and *Earth*, and *Matthew 1:25* starts with the birth of Joseph and Mary's firstborn son named Jesus, who represents *the beginning* of life everlasting. Second, *Genesis 1:1* begins with the creation or marriage of the *heaven* and the *earth*, and *Matthew 1:18* begins with the betrothed couple, Joseph and Mary. Let's remember that both marriages were created and ordained by God.

If conventional biblical interpretation has taken us in a different direction as indicated by usage of the word *universe* versus *world*, it is plausible that this could have happened in other instances. With regard to creation, we have no absolute scientific or even religious proof that it happened as described in the early chapters of Genesis. Our belief is based on religious theories associated with literal doctrine preached from the pulpit throughout the centuries. With that in mind, people of faith are led to believe:

- Adam and Eve were the first man and woman on earth as opposed to their being the first named humans in Jesus' lineage.
- God took a rib out of Adam to make Eve as opposed to their marriage being consummated.
- Eve talked to a snake as opposed to another man who was convincing her to commit adultery.

So I ask the reader: Does this make any sense? Even with blind faith, the literal interpretation of the above-referenced biblical stories and the story of creation stretch the imagination. On the other hand, with a knowing faith, the metaphoric deciphering of the stories based on the application of the Defined Word Approach does not ask us to suspend our common sense.

CHAPTER 10

Adam, Eve, and the S-s-s-serpent

In the Deep South, Sunday is more than a holy day. Going to a black church is the social event of the week; it is a time to see and be seen. It is also a time to dress up. Three-piece suits topped off with a fedora and a long watch chain. Lavish headgear with bright, fanciful-colored plumage and the dress and shoes to match. It doesn't get any better.

Of course, Sunday is also a time for worship. Congregants raise their voices in song and in praise of the Lord, giving the minister voluble "Amen's." Sometimes it can become so loud that it seems like a shouting contest between the minister and his flock. There is no lack of theatrics.

In this environment, the Word is preached, often quite literally. It still flourishes in churches across the country, irrespective of the denomination and the predominant ethnicity of the congregations, and on some of the more colorful teleministry programs.

As I think back, even today I can hear the minister hiss "s-s-s-serpent" in his sermon about Adam and Eve and the fall. Doubtful it ever occurred to any of us so wrapped up in the hissing that it was highly unlikely that a serpent could talk to Eve or she speak to it.

The imagery is vivid: In the midst of Shangri-la is a huge tree. At its base are Adam and Eve, naked. Eve's hand is outstretched to Adam, offering him a bite of an apple (how this became the forbidden fruit is unknown). Coiled above leering down at them is the serpent. It boggles the mind that many ministers have been content to limit the lesson of Adam and Eve to this depiction even as churchgoers have become more educated and have more information at their disposal. However, there is much more to the story when the Scripture is deciphered.

A point that needs to be reemphasized: Early on, the book of Genesis was a narrative about primitive people who were polytheistic and pagan in their worship. The title *Genesis*—defined by *Random House College Dictionary* as "an origin, creation, or beginning"—underscores that primitivism.

There is ample scientific evidence that humankind existed prior to the writing of any biblical text. I wrote about the primitive Adam in the Preface and described two of his physical features on page 14. Add to the discovery of Adam by geneticist Spencer Wells the *Mitochondrial Eve*, which the March 2006 issue of *National Geographic* featured in an article entitled *The Greatest Journey Ever Told—The Trail of Our DNA.*

Mitochondrial Eve lived roughly 150,000 years ago in Africa. Scientists say she was not the only woman alive at the time, but if geneticists are correct, all of humanity is linked to Eve through an unbroken chain of mothers. Reaching back even further is Lucy found in Addis Ababa, Ethiopia, which is also in Africa. Lucy is the oldest, most complete, and best-preserved skeleton of humankind ever found. *Lucy—the Beginning of Humankind*, written by Donald Johanson and Maitland Edey, documents her as 3.5 million years old.

All biblical text, by comparison, is very, very young. In fact, the Hebrew Bible, considered by scholars to be the very first Bible, was written in about 500 BC, which makes biblical text only about twenty-five hundred years old!

So how should we look at the Hebrew Bible?

First, it serves as an historical account about mankind. Secondly, the fundamental religious purpose was to establish monotheism, the worship of one almighty God, and to establish a code of conduct for a more enlightened people.

We see this in *Genesis 1, 2, and 3.* The accounts of creation, or the *marriage of* a *male* and *female* in Chapter 1 and early in Chapter 2, morph from the primitive people into a new level of awareness later in Chapters 2 and 3. We read about the primitive people who preceded Adam and Eve (that's right, Adam and Eve were *not* the very first people on Earth) in *Genesis 1:26–28.*

> And God said, Let us make man in our image, after our likeness... So God created man in his *own* image, in the image of God created he him: male and female created he them. And God blessed them, and God said unto them, Be fruitful and multiply, and replenish the earth.

And it all started in the Garden of Eden with the *tree* and the *river.* Just as Adam and Eve were not the first humans on earth, they also were not the first to live in the Garden of Eden. In my book, *Entering The Promised Land,* I first made reference to man being created in a place other than the Garden of Eden and later being placed or put there. The premise for my reasoning is based on the metaphoric meaning of the tree first mentioned in *Genesis 2:9.* Metaphorically speaking, the *tree* [40] and the *river* [41] in *Genesis 2:10* were Adam and Eve's ancestors.

Based on the application of the Defined Word Approach and Cross-Reference to Scripture, you may recall Adam's first ancestors were *heaven* and *earth.* I contend the writings in *Genesis 1, 2, and 3* reflect an earlier writing style where symbols or objects were used to depict characters. This writing style predates Adam and Eve in the Garden of Eden.

For the following Scripture, the Defined Word Approach and Cross-Reference to Scripture start on pages 93 and 254, respectively. An examination of the Authorized English Version (translation) of the original Hebrew word *tree* reveals a male or female born in a geographical location that they never leave. Think of a tree and its roots.

On the other hand, the *river,* which denotes movement, reveals a male or female constantly walking from one location to another. Logically, it makes sense to use a *river* as a symbol for humans that express movement. The ancient writer was well aware of rivers, as there were at least four, which included the world-famous Jordan River where

Jesus was baptized by John the Baptist. The Jordan River is located on the eastern border of Israel (Canaan) and is 156 miles long with fast-moving currents in certain areas.

This leads me to *Genesis 2:10*, my very first interpretation back in 2006, which reads, "And a river[41] *went*[42] *out*[43] of *Eden*[44] to *water*[45] the *garden*;[46] and from *thence*[47] it was *parted*,[48] and *became*[49] into *four*[50] *heads*."[51] Back then, the interpretation was based solely on looking at the definition of each word in the *Random House Webster's Unabridged Dictionary* and the *Oxford English Dictionary* and drilling down the definitions. At the time, I concluded that Adam was the *river* who was banished from the Garden of Eden. He later impregnated his wife, Eve. After the great flood, his descendant, Noah, had three sons, Shem, Ham, and Japheth, who would be three of the four heads. The fourth head was Jesus, who was a descendant of Noah's son Ham.

Five years have passed since I first promulgated my interpretation of *Genesis 2:10*. Based on the application of the Defined Word Approach since then, which has given me a clearer and better understanding of the Garden of Eden story, I now conclude the *river* was Adam's ancestor who left the Garden of Eden and impregnated his wife when he watered the garden. Notice the Hebrew definition for *water* is euphemistically defined as *semen*. (See Defined Word Approach footnote 45 and the accompanying Cross-Reference to Scripture.) The four heads of humankind were Adam before the great flood and Noah's three sons, Shem, Ham and Japheth, afterward.

Remember the comments on pages 35 and 46 about the married couples and their sons? We can now add one more couple in addition to *Heaven* and *Earth* and their son, *Face*. The next two ancestors in Jesus' lineage are *Tree* and *River* and their son, *Man*. They along with *Heaven* and *Earth* were the predecessors to Adam and Eve in the Garden of Eden.

Genesis 2:4 reiterates the account of creation of the primitive people, "These are the generations of the heavens and of the earth when they were created," and continues in *Genesis 2:6–7*, "But there went up a mist from the earth, and watered the whole face of the ground. And the Lord God formed man of the dust of the ground, and breathed into his nostrils the breath of life; and man became a living soul." In this Scripture, Moses is describing the birth of a baby.

In *Exodus 1:16*, birthing is described as a woman sitting on a stool and the baby then drops to the ground. Prior to birth, the placenta ruptures and the amniotic fluid is released (we refer to that as the mother's water breaking, which is the immediate precursor to birth). Assuming a mother was on a birthing stool when her water broke, a mist would go up from the earth and water the whole face of the ground, meaning the newborn's face, as the baby leaves the womb. The breath of life is the baby's first intake of air followed by a cry. "...and man became a living soul (*Genesis 2:7*)." This is an interesting note that again raises questions about traditional biblical interpretations.

Also in *Exodus 1:16*, midwives are given instructions about killing a newborn son and allowing a daughter to live. In this verse, it refers to the birth stool that a mother sat on during delivery, and it seems reasonable to assume that a mother had to sit in the squat position. With that in mind, the newborn probably was very close to the ground, if not on it. And that leads us to *Genesis 3:19* that says, "For dust thou art, and unto dust shalt thou return." Or to Job's statement (*Job 33:6*) that he also has been made of clay. Or Isaiah's petition to God (*Isaiah 64:8*), "But now, O LORD, thou art our Father; we are the clay, and thou our potter."

It's ironic that some modern American mothers-to-be are opting for the squat-birth in midwife-attended birthing centers instead of hospitals. In the birthing centers, these mothers use a standing squat position to birth. The reason is that gravity reportedly makes the delivery easier. Mothers who have tried both the traditional and the ancient birthing positions say that the ancient method is far less stressful.

So man became a living soul in *Genesis 2:7*. Later, in the same chapter, the Lord God decides that Adam (the first man named in Jesus' lineage—not the first man on Earth) needed a helpmeet, or wife. He caused a *deep*[52] *sleep*[53] to fall upon Adam, and he slept: and he *took*[54] one of his *ribs*,[55] *closed*[56] up the *flesh*[57] and *made*[58] a woman. The deep sleep, taking of Adam's rib and closing up the flesh, is the consummation of their physical union.

Notice the Defined Word Approach footnote 56 defines *closed* as "to plump, i.e., fill up hollows." The next footnote, 57, euphemistically defines *flesh* as "the pudenda of a man." It appears ancient and modern-day societal norms are identical. A female's introduction to sexual intercourse is considered a rite of passage to womanhood. Once again, some things never change.

All our lives, we have been taught that God literally took a rib out of Adam and made Eve (*Genesis 2:21–22*). However, I described above that the taking of Adam's rib was a consummation of their marriage. Further, in *Genesis 2:23*, Adam tells Eve, "This is now." In today's language, that would be akin to the late great Motown singer Marvin Gaye singing, "Let's Get It On." If this appears far-fetched and you are not convinced, consider this. According to believers of the literal interpretation of the story of creation, God created a female back in *Genesis 1:27*, which reads, "So God created *man* (emphasis added) in his own image, in the image of God created he him; male and female created he them."

That noted, let's return to deciphering the Scripture.

And Adam said: This is now *bone*[59] of my bones and flesh of my flesh: she shall be called Woman, because she was taken out of Man. Therefore shall a man leave his father and his mother, and shall *cleave*[60] unto his wife: and they shall be one flesh. And they were both naked, the man and his wife, and were not ashamed (*Genesis 2:23–25*).

At the conclusion of their consummation, Eve "was taken out of Man." She removed herself from Adam, and their union was ordained by God. Once again, Scripture confirms their sexual union.

Moses sets the conduct for marriage: The union of a man and a woman is a bond (marriage) in which they forsake all others, even their parents. Moreover, their union—although expressed physically—is elevated to a much higher level where they "were not ashamed." Moses is also laying the predicate for faithfulness. We know throughout the early chapters of Genesis, as it is repeated again and again, that adultery and murder are the two most grievous errors, i.e., sins, in behavior.

Enter the s-s-s-serpent. The use of the *serpent*[61] as a literary device is not surprising. Animals, especially dragons, were large players in pagan religions. One Hebrew legend gives animals the gift of smooth talk. And the Hebrew word for serpent, *nahash*, as defined by the *Oxford English-Hebrew Dictionary* means figuratively "a snake or a deceitful person." The serpent is also defined as "the name of two persons." See Defined Word Approach, footnote 61c. Interestingly, in later Scripture, the selfsame serpent becomes personified as Satan.

In the story of Adam and Eve, we are told that the serpent is more *subtle*[62] (crafty) than any *beast*[63] of the field (*Genesis 3:1*). In other words, the serpent is a *beguiling*[64] sweet-talker. In reality, the serpent is a womanizer who deceives Eve into thinking he really cares about her. If necessary, he will pull out the old "I think I may love you" line. Even today in virtually every socioeconomic stratum, there are men who are smooth-talking "players" and women who have heard it all.

The biblical serpent is so smooth that Eve, contrary to instruction, acknowledges his presence, which gives him the opening to "hit" on her. She then engages in conversation with him. These were her initial mistakes. Then, he tells her straightaway that if she *eats*[65] or *touches*[66] the forbidden fruit, she will have a new knowledge (*Genesis 3:1–7*). Translation: "Eat of what I have to offer; there will be no consequences other than you'll know all about what I'm about to introduce to you."

The seduction continues until Eve gives in. She eats the *fruit*,[67] meaning she has sex with this smooth-talking womanizer—and she likes it. In fact, she likes it so much that she introduces Adam to the pleasure. By presenting him with this *fruit*, or another woman, that Eve *gave*[68] to him, she also is excusing her adulterous behavior (*Genesis 3:6*).

Women throughout the ages have been tempted and/or seduced similarly. And there are consequences. In today's world, it can range from a sexually transmitted disease to an unwanted pregnancy to abandonment—or all three.

At first, Adam hides from the Lord God because he now has carnal knowledge and is ashamed, as this has demeaned his "marriage" to Woman. But try as he might to hide, God knows what has happened. Adam tries to escape blame for his own conduct, pointing out to God that it was the Woman whom God gave to him who convinced him to eat the forbidden fruit (to pleasure himself in sex) (*Genesis 3:12*). The Woman, when questioned by God, did not deny her fault, but justified her behavior by explaining that the serpent had talked her into committing adultery (*Genesis 3:13*).

Because of their newfound carnal knowledge, God meted out the consequences: The Woman would suffer travail and pain in childbirth, and Adam would sire bad seeds or children. For both, the children's growth and development would also be a source of pain. As for the serpent, he would always be considered a lowlife whose seed would be at enmity with Woman's, meaning that any relations they would have would be unfulfilling for both.

Only after God had meted out his punishment did Adam name his wife Eve. She was the mother of all living in Jesus' lineage after giving birth to her son Seth who was fathered by Adam. Later in Genesis, we come to suspect that Eve was a Canaanite, as I believe Eden was in Canaan or modern-day Israel. We hear from Abraham (*Genesis 24:3*), who is living among the Canaanites and in search of a wife for his son Isaac, that his servant is not to bring him a Canaanite wife for Isaac. We could surmise that his directive was based on the precedent Eve set as a Canaanite.

Here's an interesting point: Even though God was unhappy with Adam and Eve's adulterous behavior and ultimately banished Adam from the Garden of Eden (*Genesis 3:23*), he clothed them with coats of skins (*Genesis 3:7*) or figuratively covered their newly realized nakedness / disgrace. Here's how I concluded that Adam and Eve were adulterous. I base my theory on the definition of the word "naked" as written in *Genesis 2:25*; "And they were both naked, the man and his wife, and were not ashamed." The Hebrew definition of *naked* and its appropriate number 6174 is derived from the appropriate number 6191, which is defined as "to be cunning (usually in a bad sense);—take crafty [counsel], be prudent, deal subtilly." In addition, the appropriate number 6175 is a passive participle of the appropriate number 6191 which is defined as "cunning (usually in a bad sense)—crafty, prudent, subtil." Even though Adam and Eve strayed off the narrow path, the lesson to take away is God was still their protector, their Redeemer.

Deciphering the Hebrew words in this story gives it extraordinary significance. Once again, the application of the Defined Word Approach and the Cross-Reference to Scripture, which start on pages 93 and 254 respectively, provides unmistakable evidence. Over the years, we have heard preachments about *the fall, original sin, and the need for obedience to God*. Why could the clergy not put it in simple language? The story about Adam and Eve is about adulterous sex. Infidelity to your spiritual commitment to another—marriage—is a destructive force that leads to *The Fall*, or breakup of the husband and wife, which often has catastrophic effects on the children. When God drove out Adam from the Garden of Eden, it was a scene from modern day. Adam divorced Eve. Yes, Adam divorced Eve! Of course, just like today, his family was broken up (*Genesis 3:24*). I know this may sound far-fetched. However, I rest my interpretation on the Hebrew definition of *drove out*,[69] as defined in *James Strong's Hebrew and Chaldee Dictionary*, which means, "divorced woman."

Even more, our infidelity to our relationship with God is destructive, as it damages and reduces our spiritual bond. If we do partake, whether our mistake is reversible depends on our ability to accept responsibility for our actions and to seek redemption.

Instead, we are served prose about this being the first time man grapples with external forces—sin, etc.—and how we must resist temptation in obedience to God. In my view, the writer of the Adam and Eve story is telling us, simply: 1) Before you do something contrary to what you inherently know is right, 2) be aware of the consequences, for 3) there is a price to be paid, and you *will* pay it whether through redemption or long-suffering. Consider this as the first and most enduring biblical lesson.

CHAPTER 11

The Next Step

A friend who has known me through my spiritual journey called with exciting news. At least that was how it was presented to me. While my friend was at the gym, others were talking about the Bible and the story of creation. Both were very mature adults. Voices lowered, they agreed that they did not believe in "The Creation" as presented in the Bible and from the pulpit. The statement my friend brought to me was, "There has to be more to it." Of course! This has been the prime mover in my study. *There is more to it. And this is but a phase of my research, which will continue in the months and years ahead.*

The year 2011 was the four hundredth anniversary of the first publication of the King James Version of the Holy Bible. As noted earlier, this was not the first translation into the English language. And as noted, according to classical Hebrew linguists, not all of the translation into English was correct. Over the course of the past four centuries, in an attempt to update the King James biblical language, the meaning of even the original text has been changed.

With the application of the Defined Word Approach, we can see the impact on our understanding. One of the best examples of this point is in the Lord's Prayer. The Defined Word Approach reveals a prayer to the Father about the birthing of children who become His kingdom. The Authorized English Version (translation) of the original

Greek words in the King James Version reads in *Matthew 6:9,10*: "*Our*[70] *Father,*[71] *which*[72] *art*[73] *in*[74] *Heaven,*[75] *Hallowed*[76] *be*[77] *thy*[78] *name.*[79] *Thy Kingdom*[80] *come.*[81] *Thy will*[82] *be done,*[83] *in*[74] *earth,*[84] as it is in heaven." (emphasis added).

The New King James Version, produced in an attempt to modernize the language, reads, "Our Father, in heaven, Hallowed be Your name. Your kingdom come. Your will be done *On* earth as it is in heaven" (emphasis added).

The emphasis focuses on the phrase, *in earth*. The translations that follow change the phrase *in earth* to *on earth*. There is a significant difference between the meanings of the word *in*,[74] which is used to indicate inclusion within a space or a place, and *on*,[85] which means being supported by something. If the translation from the original Hebrew by the King James translators is *in earth*, this gives credibility to my thesis that the original writer was referring to something happening inside the earth as opposed to on it. Thus, *in earth* metaphorically refers to a female's womb. This fits with the story of creation revealing the birth of a baby.

The applications of the Defined Word Approach and Cross-Reference to Scripture to the opening lines of the Lord's Prayer start on pages 105 and 299, respectively. They support my thesis that the opening lines of the Lord's Prayer are about birthing children.

Moving forward, an examination of the meaning of the words *in earth* versus *on earth* and the disparity is obvious. In the original King James Version, the use of the words *in earth* and the subsequent verse suggests that the prayer is a blessing about procreation. *On earth* takes away that very important meaning. As established in the story of creation, heaven is a metaphor for a male and earth, a female. In ancient days, children were considered the strength of a family as noted by *Genesis 49:3*: "Reuben, thou art my firstborn, my might, and the beginning of my strength, the excellency of dignity, and the excellency of power." Common sense dictates, for an ancient family, there's inherent strength in numbers for survival in general, etc.

I also contend the Lord's Prayer is about our heavenly Father, whose kingdom starts with children and is established on Earth. Naturally, this kingdom starts in the female's (earth) womb. With this in mind, I believe the prayer should be read: Our Father which art in heaven, hallowed be thy name, thy kingdom come will be done in earth, as it is in heaven. As opposed to two sentences—*Thy kingdom come* and *Thy will be done*—there is now one sentence; *Thy kingdom come will be done in earth*. The key word *will* now becomes a verb just like the word *come*. Both words denote action instead of the word *will* being a noun.

This rendition of "thy kingdom come will be done in earth" provides a clearer meaning. The kingdom coming is the birthing of children. And to emphasize the message, it is repeated that the coming of children will in fact be done or will take place. *Mark 10:15* reads, "Verily I say unto you, Whosoever shall not receive the kingdom of God as a little child, he shall not enter therein." Remember, *Genesis 1:1* is about the birth of the first baby. It appears that with the innocence of a child we will enter the kingdom of heaven.

I am somewhat bemused by the admonition in *Revelation 22:18–19*, which warns against changing words in the Bible. The King James Version of these verses homes in on the message.

> For I testify unto every man that heareth the words of the prophecy of this book, If any man shall add unto these things, God shall add unto him the plagues that are written in this book: And if any man shall take away from the words of the book of this prophecy, God shall take away his part out of the book of life, and out of the holy city, and from the things which are written in this book.

Presumably that was to protect the meaning of the sacred Scripture. And yet it is provable that in many instances the words have been changed and hence the meaning.

I remind the reader once again that the Defined Word Approach to understanding biblical text has not altered a single word in Scripture. The only tool to a new understanding is examination of the classical Hebrew vocabulary that was employed to write the original biblical manuscripts.

CHAPTER 12

Parting Words

Maybe you are where I once was. In other words, your spiritual life appears to be heading nowhere. You may attend church on Sunday and walk away empty as I once did. The Bible seems like a riddle and makes no sense. Maybe you long for the days when you knew Jesus was alive and God was real in the way I now feel. Maybe you long for the days when someone near to you would talk about going home and being with Jesus. Maybe you long for the day when you had someone in your life whose faith inspired you.

It is not my desire to give you my testimonial to hear you respond, "Amen!" or "That's right, brother!" or even say, "Yes! Yes! Yes!" Rather, I want to give you some food for your soul. I want to give you something that will make you think. I want to give you something that will allow you to enrich your life and continue your journey or even to begin one. *My research is ongoing, and the deciphering of biblical Scripture will be shared as an expanding body of work.*

It is my sincere hope that my research is received as new insight that will stimulate your thinking. It is my heartfelt wish that the faith of those who believe in God be deepened. I also hope that those who have doubts about God will experience a renewed interest in spirituality, that the scholars who maintain or defend certain dogma about the Bible will reexamine old assumptions, and that nonbelievers will be curious enough to take a look at the Bible and what it really teaches.

Let me close with this message or warning. According to research, Christianity is dying! (Lights flashing while sirens blare.) The reason is quite simple. The more educated humans become, the less likely they believe the literal biblical messages coming from the pulpit: 1) Eve talked to a snake; 2) God opened Adam's flesh, removed a rib, and made Eve; 3) Moses parted the Red Sea; and 4) the walls of Jericho came tumbling down. The same can be said of many other interpretations. I concur with others who claim these stories are allegories. By substituting metaphors for the literal, the stories' real meaning is revealed. Fundamentally, these are stories about real people in real-life situations.

To recap, and I cannot emphasize this point enough, there is no ancient Hebrew word that means *universe*. The word *universe* cannot be found in the text of the King James Version, which was written in 1611. Bibles, such as the *Life Application Study Bible*, *NIV Study Bible*, *English Standard Version Study Bible*, etc., were all translated from the King James Version and have changed the word *world*, first found in *1 Samuel 2:8* of the King James Version, to *universe*. It is common knowledge that the book of Samuel was written long after Moses wrote the story of creation in the book of Genesis.

As I stated in the beginning of my work, I am a believer. And as I continue to research, I am more spiritually grounded than at any time in my life. Please understand that my intention is to point out how translation can affect meaning, hence our understanding. The translators wrote of a *universe* while the original writers wrote of a *world*. Through the lens of the Hubble Telescope, scientists are going back in time to translate the origin of the *universe*. They are revealing to us the utter simplicity at the edge of the physical universe, which is a conglomeration of stars and gases—matter. By contrast, and coming forward in time, biblical translators have done the very opposite. Translations have become so complex it is difficult to find the real meaning of Scripture.

The salvation of Christianity is in our hands *right now, today*. Simply, it is to search for, to understand, and then pass along the true messages left to us by the prophets and by Jesus. These were not complicated, esoterical lessons that would lend themselves to pontification. Jesus called for a simplistic faith in *Matthew 18:4* when he brought forward a child from the crowd and said, "Whosoever therefore shall humble himself as this little child, the same is greatest in the kingdom of heaven."

Throughout my writing, I have returned many times to the very basic message that the earliest metaphorical story about the creation is about the male and female bonding for purposes of creating a family. What follows throughout the Scripture are examples of how choices we make can either build the family generation upon generation or can tear it asunder through self-absorption, deceit, envy, and revenge—and those only skim the surface of the havoc that can be wrought by bad choices.

As I reflect on my life, I feel so fortunate. No matter the difficulty of the moment or the challenge before me, the Bible, my grounding in the church and my spiritual awareness are the constants that have sustained me. While I have made my share of mistakes, faith has given me the courage to be honest with others and myself. It can be scary to face oneself and all the messy stuff that goes on around us. I cannot fathom how anyone can navigate the sometimes-troubled waters of life without the navigational aids provided by the Bible.

The irony is that the Bible tells us straight up what may come from our choices. Clearly delineated is this very basic choice: We can navigate through life by using the Bible as our guide or we can drift through it without any spiritual moorings.

In Chapter One, I wrote about the millennials. One can assume they represent the future and the salvation of Christianity. That so, they must be brought into the fold and need to be aware that the fundamental choices life offers are laid out in the Bible. With this awareness, they will make the Bible their guide for living. The secularism in entertainment or in the various other media, partying, or in self-aggrandizement will be known for what they are—illusory and unfulfilling.

I pray for the day when others are inspired to become engaged in understanding the true meaning of the Bible and to use it not for preachments but as a reality-based primer on life and living. Virtually every lesson in life is contained *in the Word*.

An Application of the Defined Word Approach

Jacob and His Two Wives

If one does not understand a communication, be it written or spoken, the logical action is to pull out a dictionary to find the meanings of the words. We cannot learn without understanding the words presented to us.

"In the beginning was the Word, and the Word was with God, and the Word was God. The same was in the beginning with God" (*John 1:1*). So wrote the apostle John who, interestingly, was not only a follower of Jesus, but also was his cousin who grew up with him. In fact, their mothers were pregnant at the same time. And it was John who baptized Jesus. By all accounts, they were best friends in addition to being blood relatives. I believe John's words reveal the key to deciphering Scripture. By finding the meanings of the words and applying them to the Bible, we can have a much more expansive understanding of Scripture.

Applying the Defined Word Approach is like walking down stairs until you reach the ground floor. This is how the process works: The following is associated with the Authorized English Version (translation) of the Hebrew word for *affliction* as written about and deciphered in the biblical story *Jacob Works to Pay for Two Wives*.

With the application of the Defined Word Approach, the Word is thoroughly examined. Below, see the words and definitions that come from the *James Strong's Hebrew and Chaldee Dictionary* and *Greek Dictionary of the New Testament* as an appendix to the *King James Version Hebrew-Greek Key Word Study Bible*. The following words are arranged to allow the reader to use the Defined Word Approach to understand the meaning of translated Hebrew and Greek words that lead to deciphering biblical Scripture. Eventually, in this drill-down process, the definitions reveal the meaning of the biblical verse or story.

In bold type, you will find the deciphering of Scripture starting with footnote 1a followed by the Authorized English Version of the word *affliction* that has been translated from Hebrew. The translated word *affliction* is followed by its exact equivalent in English letters, *oiny*, which is enclosed in parentheses and followed by its appropriate number, 6040. Continuing on the same line, the word *oiny* traces its etymology from the appropriate number 6031. The Authorized English Version (translation) of *oiny* as defined in the *King James Version Hebrew-Greek Key Word Study Bible — Hebrew and Chaldee Dictionary* defines it as "depression, that is, misery."

1a. affliction (*oniy*). 6040. From 6031; "depression, i.e., misery."

In descending order, proceed to the next line in bold type that starts with the appropriate number 6031, which is followed by its exact equivalent in English letters, *anah*. The word *anah* is followed by its Authorized English Version (translation) that defines it as "rather identical with 6030 through the idea of looking down or browbeating."

6031 (*anah*); a primitive root. Possibly rather identical with 6030 through the idea of looking down or browbeating.

In descending order, proceed to the next line in bold type that starts with the appropriate number 6030, which is followed by its exact equivalent in English letters, *anah*, in parentheses. The reader is instructed to see the appropriate number 1042.

6030 (*anah*). See also 1042.

In descending order, proceed to the next line in bold type that starts with the appropriate number 1042, which is followed by its exact equivalent in English letters, *Beth Anowth*, in parentheses. The phrase *Beth Anowth* traces its etymology from the appropriate number 1004.

1042 (*Beth Anowth*). From 1004.

In descending order, proceed to the next line in bold type that starts with the appropriate number 1004, which is followed by its exact equivalent in English letters, *bayith*, in parentheses. The word *bayith* traces its etymology from the appropriate number 1129. Its Authorized English Version (translation) defines it as "family, daughter, homeborn, forth of, and within."

1004 (*bayith*). From 1129; "family, daughter, homeborn, forth of, within."

In descending order, proceed to the next line in bold type that starts with the appropriate number 1129, which is followed by its exact equivalent in English letters, *banah*, in parentheses. The word *banah* in its Authorized English Version (translation) defines it as "to build, obtain children, make, and set up."

1129 (*banah*); "to build, obtain children, make, set up."

In descending order, proceed to the next line in bold type that starts with the Authorized English Version (translation) of the word *make*, which is immediately followed by its exact equivalent in English letters, *parah*, in parentheses. The word *parah* is followed by its appropriate number 6509, and its Authorized English Version (translation) literally or figuratively means, "bear, bring forth, grow, and increase."

make (*parah*). 6509; "bear, bring forth, grow, increase."

In descending order, proceed to the next line in bold type that starts with the Authorized English Version (translation) of the words *bear*, *bring forth*, *grow*, and *increase*. These words are immediately followed by their exact equivalent in English letters, *yalad*, in parentheses, which is followed by its appropriate number 3205. The appropriate number 3205 is followed by its Authorized English Version (translation) that defines it as "be delivered of a child."

bear, bring forth, grow, increase (*yalad*), 3205; "be delivered (of a child)."

From the definition, "be delivered (of a child)," I conclude Rachel's "affliction" was birthing a baby for Jacob.

The next step is to find biblical Scripture where the words: 1) *affliction*, 2) *make*, 3) *bear*, 4) *bring forth*, 5) *grow*, 6) *increase*, and 7) *be delivered* are found in biblical verses that support this thesis. You will find this information in the Cross-Reference to Scripture section that starts on page 112.

Please note I did not find cross-reference Scriptures for the following definitions of *affliction*: 1) depression, that is, misery; 2) through the idea of looking down or browbeating; 3) a female rival; 4) an opponent; and 5) brokenhearted. I am including these definitions because they are unmistakable in describing Leah's feelings when you read the story of Jacob and his two wives, Rachel and Leah.

Apply the same steps to the following footnoted words appearing as numbers 1a to 85:

1a.   **affliction** (*oniy*). 6040. From 6031; "depression, i.e., misery."

       6031 (*anah*); a primitive root. Possibly rather identical with 6030 through the idea of looking down or browbeating.

       6030 (*anah*). See also 1042.

       1042 (Beth Anowth). From 1004 and a plural from 6030.

       1004 (*bayith*). Probably from 1129; "family, daughter, forth of, homeborn, within."

       1129 (*banah*); "obtain children, make, set up."

       make (*parah*). 6509; "(lit. or fig.) bear; bring forth; grow; increase."

       bear, bring forth, grow, increase (*yalad*). 3205; "be delivered (of a child)."

1b. **affliction** (*sheber*). 7667. From 7665.

7665 (*shabar*); "bring to the birth."

1c. **affliction** (*tsarah*). 6869. Fem. of 6862; "a female rival."

6862 (*tsar*); "an opponent."

1d. **affliction** (*sheber*). 7667. From 7665.

7665 (*shabar*); "(lit. or fig.) brokenhearted."

Defined Word Approach: A Key That Unlocks the Bible

2a. **beginning** (*reshiyth*). 7225; "first." "(first product) of my manly vigour."[86]

first (*ben*). 1121. From 1129; "a son (as the builder of the family name)."

1129 (*banah*); "to build (lit. or fig.), obtain children, make."

make (*parah*). 6509; "bear; bring forth."

bear, bring forth (*yalad*). 3205; "born; be delivered (of a child); be the son of (travailing woman)."

2b. **beginning** (*tchillah*). 8462. From 2490; "in the sense of opening; a commencement; first (time)."

2490 (*chalal*). A primitive root. Compare 2470.

2470 (*chalah*). A primitive root. Compare 2342; "woman in travail."

2342 (*chuwl*) (*chiyl*); "to writhe in pain (esp. of parturition); (fig.) bear, (make to) bring forth, travail (with pain)."

2a With the definitions of "born," "be delivered of a child," and "be the son of travailing woman," my thesis of the "beginning" being about the birth of a child as opposed to the beginning of the universe is confirmed. The next step is to find biblical Scripture where the words in the drill down—1) *beginning*, 2) *first*, 3) *a son*, 4) *make*, 5) *bear, bring forth*, 6) *born, be delivered*, and 7) *son of a travailing woman* are found in the text and support my thesis. This process further validates the beginning being a story about the birth of a male and female's first baby and is called cross-referencing. These words used in Scripture start on page 117.

[86] The Brown-Driver-Briggs Hebrew and English Lexicon - Hendrickson Publishers - 2010

bear, bring forth, travail. 3205 (*yalad*); "born; be delivered (of a child); be the son of (travailing woman, woman that travail -eth, -ing woman)."

3.   **God** (*'elohiym*). 430; "the supreme God."

4a.   **created** (*bara*). 1254; "make."

make (*nathan*). 5414; "lie."

lie (*shakab*). 7901; "to lie down (sexual connection)."

4b.   **created** (*bara*). 1254; "make fat."

make fat (*chalats*). 2502; "deliver."

deliver (*nathan*). 5414; "to give."

to give (*chazaq*). 2388; "cleave."

cleave (*dabaq*). 1692; "be joined."

be joined (*yachad*). 3161; "to be."

to be (*chamad*). 2530; "desire."

4c.   **created** (*bara*). 1254; "make fat."

make fat (*chalats*). 2502.

2504 (*chalats*). From 2502; "the loins (as the seat of vigor)."

the loins (*yarek*). 3409; "(by euphemism) the generative parts."

4d.   **created** (*bara*). 1254; "do."

do (*nathan*). 5414; "to give."

to give (*chazaq*). 2388; "cleave."

cleave (*dabaq*). 1692; "be joined."

be joined (*yachad*). 3161; "to be."

to be (*chamad*). 2530; "covet."

covet (*avah*). 183; "lust (after)."

4e.   **created** (*bara*). 1254; "do."

do (*nathan*). 5414; "lay; lie."

lay, lie (*shakab*). 7901; "to lie down (for sexual connection)."

4f.   **created** (*bara*). 1254; "do."

do (*nathan*). 5414; "take."

take (*dabaq*). 1692; "be joined."

be joined (*yachad*); "to be."

4g.   **created** (*bara*). 1254; "do."

do (*nathan*). 5414; "take."

take (*laqach*). 3947; "mingle."

mingle (*arab*). 6151. Corresponding to 6148.

6148 (*arab*); "surety."

surety (*yada*). 3045; "lie by man."

3046 (*yda*). Corresponding to 3045; "know."

4h. **created** (*bara*). 1254; "cut down."

cut down (*karath*). 3772; "to covenant (i.e., make an alliance or bargain, originally by cutting flesh and passing between the pieces);" "**covenant**."

divorce (*kerithuth*). 3748. From 3772; "a cutting (of the matrimonial bond);" "divorcement."[87]

covenant (*berith*). 1285; "a compact (because made by passing between pieces of flesh)."

1286 (*Briyth*). The same as 1285; "alliance of marriage." [100]

4i. **created** (*bara*). 1254; "choose."

choose (*bachar*). 977; "join."

join (*yacaph*). 3254; "increase; conceive again."

4j. **created** (*bara*). 1254; "choose."

choose (*bachar*). 977; "join."

join (*qarab*). 7126; "come near."

come near (*nagash*). 5066; "(euphemistically) to lie with a woman."

[87, 100] 4h. The Brown-Driver-Briggs Hebrew and English Lexicon - Hendrickson Publishers - 2010

5a. **heaven** (*shamayim*). 8064; dual of an unused singular.

name (*shem*). 8034. Perhaps rather from 7760 through the idea of definite and conspicuous position. Comparative 8064; "an appellation, as a mark or memorial of individuality."

7760 (*sum*); "set up."

set up (*banah*). 1129; "make."

make (*parah*). 6509; "to bear fruit; (lit. or fig.) bear, bring forth."

bear, bring forth (*yalad*). 3205; "born; be delivered (of a child); be the son of (travailing woman)."

5b. **heaven** (*shamayim*). 8064; dual of an unused singular.

name (*shem*). 8034. Perhaps rather from 7760 through the idea of definite and conspicuous position. Comparative 8064; "an appellation, as a mark or memorial of individuality."

Shem (*Shem*). 8035. Same as 8034; a son of Noah.

a son (*ben*). 1121 from 1129.

1129 (*banah*); "to build; (lit. or fig.) "obtain children, make."

make (*parah*). 6509; "to bear fruit"; (lit. or fig.) "bear, bring forth."

bear, bring forth (*yalad*). 3205; "born; be delivered (of a child); be the son of (travailing woman)."

5c.   **heaven** (*shamayim*). 8064; dual of an unused singular.

name (*shem*). 8034. Perhaps rather from 7760 through the idea of definite and conspicuous position. Comparative 8064; "an appellation, as a mark or memorial of individuality."

Shem (*Shem*). 8035. Same as 8034; a son of Noah.

a son (*ben*). 1121. From 1129.

1129 (*banah*); "make."

do (*nathan*). 5414; "take."

take (*laqach*). 3947; "mingle."

mingle (*arab*). 6151. Corresponding to 6148.

6148 (*arab*); "surety."

surety (*yada*). 3045; "lie by man."

3046 (*yda*). Corresponding to 3045; "know."

5d.   **heaven** (*ouranos*). Greek. 3772. Perhaps from the same as 3735.

3735 (*oros*); "rear". Perhaps akin to 142.

142 (*airo*) by Hebraism. Comparative 5375.

5375 (*nasa'*); (lit. and fig.) bear, bring forth."

bear, bring forth (*yalad*). 3205; "born; be delivered (of a child); be the son of (travailing woman)."

6a. **earth** (*aphar*). 6083. See 1035.

1035 (*Beyth Lechem*). From 1004.

1004 (*bayith*); "homeborn."

homeborn (*yaliyd*). 3211. From 3205.

bear, bring forth (*yalad*). 3205; "born; be delivered (of a child); be the son of (travailing woman)."

6b. **earth** (*erets*). 776; "nations,"

nations (*ummah*). Aramaic. 524. Corresponding to 523.

523 (*ummah*). From the same as 517.

517 (*'em*); "a mother (as the bond of the family)." Like 1.

1 (*ab*); "father."

father (*aman*). 1121.

a son (*ben*). 1121. From 1129.

1129 (*banah*); "make."

make (*parah*). 6509; "to bear fruit (lit. or fig.): bear; bring forth."

bear, bring forth (*yalad*). 3205; "born; be delivered (of a child); be the son of (travailing woman)."

6c. **earth** (*aphar*). 6083. See 1035.

1035 (*Beyth Lechem*). From 1004.

1004 (*bayith*); "family."

family (*mishpachah*). 4940. Comparative 8198; "a family, i.e., circle of relatives, kindred."

kindred (*mowledeth*). 4138. From 3205; "nativity (plural birthplace); by implication lineage, native country; also offspring, family: begotten, born, issue, kindred, native (-ity)."

bear, bring forth (*yalad*). 3205; "born; be delivered (of a child); be the son of (travailing woman)."

6d. **earth** (*adamah*). 127. From 119.

119 (*adam*); "to show blood (in the face)."

7. **thing of nought** (*ephes*). 657; "an end (especially of the earth)."

658 (*Ephec Dammiym*). From 657 and the plural of 1818.

1818 (*dam*); "blood (as that which, when shed, causes death)."

8a. **giants** (*nphiyl*). 5303 properly.; "a feller, i.e., a bully or tyrant."

8b. **giants** (*rapha*). 7497. See also 1051.

1051 (*Beyth Rapha*). From 1004 and 7497; "house of (the) giants."

1004 (*bayith*). Probably from 1129; "daughter, forth of, within."

1129 (*banah*); "obtain children, make, set up."

make (*parah*). 6509; "to bear fruit (lit. or fig.): bear, bring forth, grow, increase."

bear, bring forth (*yalad*). 3205. "born; be delivered (of a child); be the son of (travailing woman)."

9.   **were finished** (*kalah*). 3615; "fulfil."

fulfil (male). 4390; "to fill or be full of."

4392 (male). From 4390; "she that was with child."

10a.   **host** (*chel*). 2426. See 2342.

2342 (*chuwl*); "to writhe in pain (especially of parturition); (fig.) bear; bring forth."

bear, bring forth (*yalad*). 3205; "born; be delivered (of a child); be the son of (travailing woman)."

10b.   **host** (*tsbaah*). 6635; "a mass of persons."

10c.   **host** (*machaneh*). 4264 "The basic idea of this word is that of a multitude of people who have gathered together."[88]

11a.   **generations** (*towldah*). 8435. From 3205.

bear, bring forth [children] (*yalad*). 3205; "born; be delivered (of a child); be the son of (travailing woman)."

---

[88] 10c. Spiros Zodhiates, *King James Version Hebrew-Greek Key Word Study Bible—Old Testament Dictionary*, (Chattanooga, TN: AMG Publishing, 2008).

11b. **generations** (*towldah*). 8435; "(fig.) birth."

birth (*mishber*). 4866; "the orifice of the womb (from which the fetus breaks forth); breaking forth."

breaking forth (*perets*). 6556; "(lit. or fig.) forth."

forth, bear, bring forth (*yalad*). 3205; "born; be delivered (of a child); be the son of (travailing woman)."

12. **was** (*haya*). 1961. Comparative 1933; "to exist."

1933 (*hava*); "to breathe; to be."

to be, bear, bring forth (*yalad*). 3205; "born; be delivered (of a child); be the son of (travailing woman)."

13a. **without form** (*tohuw*). 8414; "desert."

desert (*yshiymown*). 3452. See 1020.

1020 (*Beth ha-Yshiy-mowth*). The plural of 3451.

3451 (*yshiymah*); "desolation: let death seize."

13b. **without form** (*tohuw*). 8414; "desert."

desert (*yshiymown*). 3452. See 1020.

1020 (*Beth ha-Yshiy-mowth*). From 1004.

1004 (*bayith*); "homeborn."

homeborn (*yaliyd*). 3211 (*yalid*). From 3205.

bear, bring forth (*yalad*). 3205; "born; be delivered (of a child); be the son of (travailing woman)."

13c.   **without form** (*tohuw*). 8414; "thing of nought."

thing of nought (*ephes*). 657; "an end (especially of the earth)."

658 (*Ephec Dammiym*). From 657 and the plural of 1818.

1818 (*dam*); "blood (as that which, when shed, causes death)."

14.   **void** (*parar*). 6565; "come to nought."

come to nought (*hayah*). 1961 primitive root. Comparative 1933.

1933 (*hava*); "to breathe; to be."

to be, bear, bring forth (*yalad*). 3205; "born; be delivered (of a child); be the son of (travailing woman)."

15a.   **without** (*ayin*). 369; "to be nothing or not exist; to nought."

to nought (*aven*). 205; "to pant (hence to exert oneself, usually in vain)."

206 (*Aven*). The same as 205. See also 1007.

1007 (*Beth Aven*). From 1004.

1004 (*bayith*); "homeborn."

homeborn (*yaliyd*). 3211 (*yalid*). From 3205.

bear, bring forth (*yalad*). 3205; "born; be delivered (of a child); be the son of (travailing woman)."

15b.   **without** (*tayiym*). 8549. From 8552.

8552 (*tamam*); "(lit. or fig., transitive or intransitive) cease."

cease (*chadal*). 2308.

2309 (*chedel*). From 2308; "the state of the dead."

15c.   **without** (*tohuw*). 8414; "thing of nought."

thing of nought (*ephes*). 657; "an end (especially of the earth)."

658 (*Ephec Dammiym*). From 657 and the plural of 1818.

1818 (*dam*); "blood (as that which, when shed, causes death)."

15d.   **without** (*tohuw*). 8414; "desert."

desert (*yshiymown*). 3452. See 1020.

1020 (*Beth ha-Yshiy-mowth*). The plural of 3451.

3451 (*yshiymah*); "desolation: let death seize."

15e.   **without** (*ayin*). 369; "to be nothing or not exist; to nought."

to nought (*aven*). 205; "to pant (hence to exert oneself, usually in vain)."

1126 (*Ben-Owniy*). From 1121 and 205; "son of my sorrow; Ben-Oni, the original name of Benjamin: Ben-oni."

15f. **without** (chuwts) 2351 from an unused root meaning to sever; properly separate by a wall, i.e. outside:

16. **form** (*yatsar*). 3335. Probably identical with 3334.

3336 (*yetser*). From 3335; "(figuratively) conception."

conception (*herayown*). 2032 from 2029; "pregnancy."

2029 (*harah*); "(lit. or fig.) conceive."

conceive (*zara*). 2232; "(fig.) bear."

bear, bring forth (*yalad*). 3205; "born; be delivered (of a child); be the son of (travailing woman)."

17a. **darkness** (*choshek*). 2822; "(fig.) death."

death (*mavet*). 4194. From 4191.

4191 (*muwth*); "to die."

4192 (*Muwth*). From 4191 and 1121.

first, a son (*ben*). 1121. From 1129; "a son (as the builder of the family name)."

1129 (*banah*); "make; to build up."

make (*parah*). 6509; "to bear fruit (lit. or fig.), bear, bring forth."

bear, bring forth (*yalad*). 3205; "born; be delivered (of a child); be the son of (travailing woman)."

17b.   **darkness** (*choshek*). 2822; "(fig.) destruction; death."

destruction (*chebel*). 2256; "a noose (as of cords); (fig.) a throe [agony of death] (especially of parturition); sorrow."

sorrow (*chuwl*) or (*chiyl*). 2342; "to writhe in pain (especially of parturition); (fig.) bear, bring forth, travail."

bear, bring forth, travail (*yalad*). 3205; "born; be delivered (of a child); be the son of (travailing woman)."

17c.   **darkness** (*choshek*). 2822; "(fig.) misery, death, destruction."

misery (*amal*). 5999; "labor or travail."

labor, bear, bring forth, travail (*yalad*). 3205; "be delivered (of a child); be the son of (travailing woman)."

18a.   **face** (*paniym*). 6440. "form."

form (*yatsar*). 3335. Probably identical with 3334.

3336 (*yetser*). From 3335; "(figuratively) conception."

conception (*herayown*). 2032 from 2029; "pregnancy."

2029 (*harah*); "(lit. or fig.) conceive."

conceive (*zara*). 2232; "(fig.) bear."

bear, bring forth (*yalad*). 3205; "born; be delivered (of a child); be the son of (travailing woman)."

18b.   **face** (*aph*). 639; "properly the nose or nostril; hence the face, and occasionally a person."

18c. **face** (*paniym*). **6440 upside down**

19a. **deep** (*thowm*). 8415. From 1949; "an abyss (as a surging mass of water)."

    1949 (*huwm*). Comparative 2000.

    2000 (*hamam*). See 1995.

    1995 (*humown*); "multiply."

    multiply (*rabah*). 7235; "be full of."

    be full of (male). 4390.

    4392 (male). From 4390; "she that was with child."

19b. **deep** (*amaq*). 6009.

    6010 (*emeq*). From 6009. See also 1025.

    1025 (*Beyth ha-Emeq*). From 1004.

    1004 (*bayith*); "homeborn."

    homeborn (*yaliyd*). 3211. From 3205.

    bear, bring forth (*yalad*). 3205; "born; be delivered (of a child); be the son of (travailing woman)."

20. **spirit** (*ruwach*). 7307; "(fig.) life."

    life (*nephesh*). 5315. From 5314; "a breathing creature."

    5314 (*naphash*); "to breathe."

to breathe (*nshamah*). 5397; "soul."

21a.   **moved** (*huwm*). 1949. Comparative 2000.

2000 (*hamam*). See 1995.

1995 (*humown*); "multiply."

multiply (*rabah*). 7235; "be full of."

be full of (male). 4390.

4392 (male). From 4390; "she that was with child."

21b.   **moved** (*huwm*). 1949. Comparative 2000.

2000 (*hamam*). See 1995.

1995 (*humown*); "many."

many (*yacaph*). 3254; "conceive again."

3255 (*ycaph*). Corresponding to 3254: "add."

22a.   **upon** (*al*). 5921; "out of."

out of (*meah*). 4578; "womb."

22b.   **upon** (*al*). 5921; "forth of."

forth of (*yatsa*). 3318; "begotten; bring forth."

begotten, bring forth, travail (*yalad*). 3205; "born; be delivered (of a child); be the son of (travailing woman)."

22c.   **upon** (*al*). 5921; "forth of."

forth of (*mishber*). 4866. From 7665; "the orifice of the womb (from which the fetus breaks forth), birth."

7665 (*shabar*); "bring to the birth."

22d.   **upon** (*kol*). 3605; "the whole."

the whole (*Chaviylah*). 2341. From 2342.

2342 (*chuwl*); "to writhe in pain (especially of parturition); (fig.) bear (make to) bring forth."

bear, bring forth (*yalad*). 3205; "born; be delivered (of a child); be the son of (travailing woman)."

23a.   **waters** (*mayim*). 4325; dual of a primitive noun (but used in a singular sense); "water; (fig.) juice; (by euphemism) semen: spring."

Spring, fountain (*maqowr*). 4726; "(by euphemism) of the female pudenda; (fig.) of progeny; fountain, issue."

issue (*mowledeth*). 4138. From 3205; "nativity (plural birthplace); by implication lineage, offspring, family: begotten, born, issue, kindred, native (-ity)."

begotten, bring forth, travail (*yalad*). 3205. "born; be delivered (of a child); be the son of (travailing woman)."

23b.   **waters** (*mayim*). 4325; dual of a primitive noun (but used in a singular sense): "(by euphemism) semen: water."

water (*zarziyph*). 2222. See 2220.

2220 (*zrowa*). From 2232.

2232 (*zara*); "(fig.) bear."

bear (*yalad*). 3205; "born; be delivered (of a child); be the son of (travailing woman)."

23c. **waters** (*mayim*). 4325; dual of a primitive noun (but used in a singular sense): "(by euphemism) semen: water."

water (*shaqah*). 8248; "cause to."

cause to (*qarab*). 7126; "bring forth."

bring forth (*yalad*). 3205; "born; be delivered (of a child); be the son of (travailing woman)."

23d. **waters** (*mayim*). 4325; dual of a primitive noun (but used in a singular sense): "(by euphemism) semen: water."

water (*zarziyph*). 2222. See 2220.

2220 (*zrowa*). From 2232.

2232 (*zara*); "(fig.) bear."

2233 (*zera*). From 2232; "seed; (fig.) fruit, posterity: child."

child (*yeled*). 3206. From 3205; "something born, i.e., offspring."

bear, bring forth (*yalad*). 3205; "born; be delivered (of a child); be the son of (travailing woman)."

23e.   **waters** (*mayim*). 4325; figuratively of a bride; enjoyment of one's own wife; of harlotry.[89]

24.   **said** (*amar*). 559; "command."

command (*tsavah*). 6680; "appoint."

appoint (*naqab*). 5344.

female (*nqebah*). 5347. From 5344; "woman."

woman (*ishshah*). 802; "wife."

25.   **let there be** (*haya*). 1961 a primitive root (comparative 1933); "to exist."

1933 (*hava*); "to breathe; to be; become; have."

be, bear, bring forth (*yalad*). 3205; "born; be delivered (of a child); be the son of (travailing woman)."

26.   **there was** (*haya*). 1961 a primitive root (comparative 1933); "to exist."

1933 (*hava*); "to breathe; to be; become; have."

be, become, have, bear, bring forth (*yalad*). 3205; "born; be delivered (of a child); be the son of (travailing woman)."

27.   **light** (*owr*). 216; "morning."

morning (*boqer*). 1242. From 1239.

---

[89] 23e. The Brown-Driver-Briggs Hebrew and English Lexicon — Hendrickson Publishers — 2010

to plough (*baqar*). 1239; "break forth."

break [broken] forth (*parats*). 6555; "grow."

grow (*tsamach*). 6779; "to sprout (transitive or intransitive, lit. or fig.): bear, bring forth."

bear, bring forth (*yalad*). 3205; "born; be delivered (of a child); be the son of (travailing woman)."

28.   **saw** (*chazah*). 2372; "behold."

behold (Reuben). 7205. From the imperative of 1121; "see ye a son; Reuben, a son of Jacob."

first (*ben*). 1121. From 1129; "a son (as the builder of the family name)."

1129 (*banah*); "make; to build up."

make (*parah*). 6509; "to bear fruit (lit. or fig.): bear, bring forth."

bear, bring forth (*yalad*). 3205; "born; be delivered (of a child); be the son of (travailing woman)."

29.   **good** (*towb*). 2896; "precious."

precious (*meshek*). 4901.

4902 (*Meshek*). The same in form as 4901; a son of Japheth.

30.   **divided** (*baqa*). 1234; "break forth."

break forth, broken forth (*parats*). 6555; "breach; grow."

breach (*perets*). 6556. From 6555; "forth."

6557 (*Perets*). The same as 6556; Pharez.

bear, bring forth (*yalad*). 3205; "born; be delivered (of a child); be the son of (travailing woman)."

31a.   **called** (*qara*). 7121; "address by name."

31b.   **called** (*bow*). 935; "bring forth."

bring forth (*yalad*). 3205; "born; be delivered (of a child); be the son of (travailing woman)."

32.   **day,** waters (*yowm*). 3117; "birth."

birth, bring forth (*yalad*). 3205; "be delivered (of a child); be the son of (travailing woman)."

33a.   **night** (*layil*). 3915; (fig.) "midnight."

midnight (*chatsoth*). 2676. From 2673.

2673 (*chatsah*); "divide."

33b.   **night** (*layil*). 3915; "(fig.) adversity."

adversity (*ra*). 7451; "affliction."

affliction (*sheber*). 7667. From 7665.

7665 (*shabar*); "bring to the birth."

34.   **evening** (*ereb*). 6153. From 6150.

6150 (*arab*). Rather identical with 6148.

6148 (*arab*); "surety."

surety (*yada*). 3045; "lie by man."

3046 (*yda*). Corresponding to 3045; "know."

know (*yada*). 3045; "lie by man."

35.　　**morning** (*boqer*). 1242. From 1239.

to plough (*baqar*). 1239; "break forth."

break [broken] forth (*parats*). 6555; "breach; grow."

grow (*tsamach*). 6779; "to sprout (transitively or intransitively, lit. or fig.): bear, bring forth."

bear, bring forth (*yalad*). 3205; "born; be delivered (of a child); be the son of (travailing woman)."

36.　　**were** (*haya*). 1961 a primitive root (comparative 1933); "to exist."

1933 (*hava*); "to breathe; to be."

to be, bear, bring forth (*yalad*). 3205; "born; be delivered (of a child); be the son of (travailing woman)."

37.　　**first** (*ben*). 1121. From 1129; "a son (as the builder of the family name)."

1129 (*banah*). A primitive root; "to build (lit. and fig.): obtain children, make, set up."

make (*parah*). 6509; "to bear fruit (lit. or fig.): bear; bring forth."

bear, bring forth (*yalad*). 3205; "born; be delivered (of a child); be the son of (travailing woman)."

38. **day** (*yowm*). 3117; "birth."

birth (*yalad*). 3205; "born; be delivered (of a child); be the son of (travailing woman)."

39a. **born again** (*gennao*). Greek. 1080; "to procreate (properly of the **father**, but by extension of the mother)."

1 (*ab*); "father."

father (*aman*). 1121.

a son (*ben*). 1121. From 1129.

1129 (*banah*); "make."

make (*parah*). 6509; "to bear fruit (lit. or fig.): bear; bring forth."

bear, bring forth (*yalad*). 3205; "born; be delivered (of a child); be the son of (travailing woman)."

39b. **born again** (*gennao*). Greek. 1080; "to procreate (properly of the father, but by extension of the **mother**)."

mother (*em*). 517; "a mother (as the bond of the family)."

523 (*ummah*). From the same as 517; "nation."

nation (*gowy*). 1471. From the same root as 1465.

1465 (*gevah*); "body."

body (*beten*). 990; "the womb; as they be born."

Adam, Eve, and the S-s-s-serpent

40.   **tree** (*ezrach*). 249; "native (persons); homeborn." "A native (one arising from the soil; = 'free tribesman'RS Sem. 1.75)"[90]

native (*mowledeth*). 4138. From 3205; "birthplace."

homeborn (*yaliyd*). 3211. From 3205.

3205; "born; be delivered (of a child); be the son of (travailing woman)."

41a.   **river** (*peleg*). 6388.

6389 (*Peleg*). The same as 6388; Peleg, a son of Shem. "son of Eber"[91]

41b.   **river** (*nachal*). 5158. From 5157.

5157 (*nachal*); "to inherit as a (fig.) mode of descent."

---

[90] 40. The Brown-Driver-Briggs Hebrew and English Lexicon — Hendrickson Publishers — 2010

40. The combined definitions of *native* and *homeborn* confirm my thesis that the "tree" metaphorically is a male or female. This male or female is born in a particular geographical area. Because the male or female metaphorically have roots, they never leave this area during their lifetime. At some point in the female's life, she will be impregnated by the male and deliver a baby. The next step is to find biblical Scripture where the words: 1) *tree*, 2) *native*, 3) *homeborn*, 4) *born*, and 5) *be delivered* are found in the text and support the thesis. This is called Cross-Reference to Scripture, which starts on page 254.

[91] 41a. The Brown-Driver-Briggs Hebrew and English Lexicon — Hendrickson Publishers — 2010

41a. The Authorized English Version (translation) of the original Hebrew word *Peleg* metaphorically is a river, which is a symbol for humans walking. Also the "river" as "a mode of descent" refers to the descendants of Adam, which includes Noah and his descendants, Shem and Peleg. These words used in Cross-Reference to Scripture start on page 254.

5159 (*nachalah*). From 5157; "patrimony."

patrimony (*al*). 5921; "forth of."

forth of (*yatsa*). 3318; "begotten."

begotten (*yalad*). 3205; "born; be delivered (of a child); be the son of (travailing woman)."

41c.   **river** (*uwbal*). 180. From 2986. In the sense of 2988.

2986 (*yabal*). A primitive root; prop. "to flow; causative to bring (especially with pomp): bring (forth.")

41d.   **river** (*nachal*). 5158. "simile of glory of nations." "figurative of invaders or foes[92]

42.   **went** (*bow*). 935. "to go."

to go (*halak*). 1980; "to walk."

43.   **out** (*min*). 4480; "out of."

44a.   **Eden** (Eden). 5731. The same as 5730.

5730 (eden); from 5727; "pleasure."

5727 (adan) a primitive root; to be soft or pleasant; figuratively and reflexively to live voluptuously: — delight self.

44b.   **Eden** (Eden). 5731. The same as 5730.

5730 (eden). See also 1040.

---

[92] 41d. The Brown-Driver-Briggs Hebrew and English Lexicon — Hendrickson Publishers — 2010

1040 (*Beyth Eden*). From 1004.

1004 (*bayith*); "homeborn."

homeborn (*yaliyd*). 3211 (*yalid*). From 3205.

bear, bring forth [children] (*yalad*). 3205; "born; be delivered (of a child); be the son of (travailing woman)."

45a.   **water** (*mayim*). 4325; dual of a primitive noun (but used in a sing. sense); "water; (by euphemism) semen."

water (*zarziyph*). 2222. See 2220.

2220 (*zrowa*). From 2232.

2232 (*zara*); "(fig.) bear."

bear (*yalad*). 3205; "born; be delivered (of a child); be the son of (travailing woman)."

45b.   **water** (*mayim*). 4325; dual of a primitive noun (but used in a sing. sense); "water; (by euphemism) semen."

water (*shaqah*). 8248; "cause to."

cause to (*qarab*). 7126; "come near; bring forth."

bring forth (*yalad*). 3205; "born; be delivered (of a child); be the son of (travailing woman)."

46.   **garden** (*gan*). 1588 "(figuratively of a bride)."[93]

---

[93] 46. The Brown-Driver-Briggs Hebrew and English Lexicon — Hendrickson Publishers — 2010

bride (*kallah*). 3618; "daughter-in-law, spouse."

47.   **thence** (*sham*). 8033; "there; (transf. to time) then."

48.   **parted** (*parad*). 6504; "separate (oneself), divide." "of sons of Rebekah representing nations"[94]

divide (*baqa*). 1234; "break forth."

break forth, broken forth (*parats*). 6555; "breach."

breach (*perets*). 6556. From 6555; "forth."

6557 (*Perets*). The same as 6556; Pharez.

forth, bear, bring forth [children] (*yalad*). 3205; "born; be delivered (of a child); be the son of (travailing woman)."

49.   **became** (*haya*). 1961. A primitive root (comparative 1933); "to exist."

1933 (*hava*); "to breathe; to be."

to be, bear, bring forth (*yalad*). 3205; "born; be delivered (of a child); be the son of (travailing woman)."

50.   **four** (*arba*). 702. From 7251; "four."

7251 (*raba*). Rather identical with 7250 through the idea of sprawling "at all fours."

7250 (*raba'*); "to squat or lie out flat in copulation; lie down."

---

[94] 48. The Brown-Driver-Briggs Hebrew and English Lexicon — Hendrickson Publishers — 2010

lie down (*shkab*); "to lie down for sexual connection."

7902 (*shkabah*). From 7901; "seed."

seed (*zera*). 2233; "(fig.) fruit."

fruit (*bakar*). 1069; "to burst the womb; bear or make early fruit of woman."

51.   **heads** (*rosh*). 7218; "first."

first, a son (*ben*). 1121. From 1129.

1129 (*banah*); "make."

make (*parah*). 6509; "to bear fruit (lit. or fig.): bear; bring forth."

bear, bring forth (*yalad*). 3205; "born; be delivered (of a child); be the son of (travailing woman)."

52a.   **deep** (*thowm*). 8415 from 1949; "an abyss (as a surging mass of water)."

1949 (*huwm*). Comparative 2000.

2000 (*hamam*). See 1995.

1995 (*humown*); "multiply."

multiply (*rabah*). 7235; "be full of."

be full of (male). 4390.

4392 (male). From 4390; "she that was with child."

52b. **deep** (*amaq*). 6009.

6010 (*emeq*). From 6009. See also 1025.

1025 (*Beyth ha-Emeq*). From 1004.

1004 (*bayith*); "homeborn."

homeborn (*yaliyd*). 3211. From 3205.

bear, bring forth (*yalad*). 3205; "born; be delivered (of a child); be the son of (travailing woman)."

53. **sleep** (*shakab*). 7901; "to lie down (for sexual connection)."

54a. **took** (*laqach*). 3947; "to take; mingle."

mingle (*arab*). 6151. Corresponding to 6148.

6148 (*arab*); "surety."

surety (*yada*). 3045; "lie by man."

3046 (*yda*). Corresponding to 3045; "know."

know (*yada*). 3045; "to know; lie by man."

54b. **took** (*laqach*). 3947; "be taken in marriage."[95]

55. **rib** (*tsela*). 6763. From 6760.

6760 (*tsala*); "to curve."

---

[95] 54b. The Brown-Driver-Briggs Hebrew and English Lexicon — Hendrickson Publishers — 2010

6761 (*tsela*). From 6760; "fall."

fall (*naphal*). 5307; "lie down."

56a.   **closed** (*kacah*). 3680; "to plump, i.e., fill up hollows."

56b.   **closed** (*zuwr*). 2115. A primitive root; "to press together: thrust together."

57.   **flesh** (*basar*). 1320; "(by euphemism) the pudenda of a man; kin, nakedness."

kin (*sheer*). 7607. From 7604; "flesh as swelling out; kinsman."

kinsman (*gaal*). 1350; "marry his widow."

nakedness (ervah). 6172; "nudity, literally (especiallythe pudenda) or figuratively disgrace."[96] "implying shameful exposure; mostly of woman."[97]

Editors Note: If someone sees the nakedness of another, he or she has engaged or will engage in inappropriate sexual conduct.

58a.   **made** (asah). 6213. "to do." "Provocatively, the word appears twice in Ezekiel to imply the intimate action of caressing or fondling the female breast."[98] "Do something (in relation or intercourse) with person."[99]

make (*asah*). 6213; "to do."

---

[96] 57. Spiros Zodhiates, *King James Version Hebrew-Greek Key Word Study Bible,* (Chattanooga, TN: AMG Publishing, 2008).

[97] 57. The Brown–Driver–Briggs Hebrew and English Lexicon – Hendrickson Publishers – 2010

[98] 58a. Spiros Zodhiates, *King James Version Hebrew-Greek Key Word Study Bible,* (Chattanooga, TN: AMG Publishing, 2008).

[99] 58a. The Brown–Driver–Briggs Hebrew and English Lexicon – Hendrickson Publishers – 2010

58b. **made** (*karath*). 3772; "to covenant (i.e., make an alliance or bargain, originally by cutting flesh and passing between the pieces);" "**covenant.**"

divorce (*kerithuth*). 3748. From 3772; "a cutting (of the matrimonial bond);" "divorcement."[87]

covenant (*berith*). 1285; "a compact (because made by passing between pieces of flesh)".

1286 (*Briyth*). The same as 1285; "alliance of marriage."[100]

59. **bone** (*etsem*). 6106. From 6105.

6105 (*atsam*); "close."

close (*dabaq*). 1692; "(fig.) to catch by pursuit; take."

take, taken (*laqach*). 3947; "to take."

60a. **cleave** (*dabaq*). 1692; "be joined."

be joined (*yachad*). 3161; "to be."

to be (*chamad*). 2530; "desire."

60b. **cleave** (*dabaq*). 1692; "be joined."

be joined (*yachad*). 3161; "to be."

to be (*chamad*). 2530; "covet."

covet (*avah*). 183; "lust (after)."

[87, 100] 58b. The Brown-Driver-Briggs Hebrew and English Lexicon — Hendrickson Publishers — 2010

61a. **serpent** (*Nahash*) A deceitful person.[101]

61b. **serpent** (nachash). 5175 As a crafty tempter.[102]

61c. **serpent** (*nachash*). 5175; "a snake (from its hiss): serpent.

5176. (Nachash) The same as 5175; Nachash, the name of two persons.

62. **subtle** (*aruwm*). 6175; "cunning (usually in a bad sense)."

63. **beast** (*chay*). 2416; "strong."

strong (*chazaq*). 2389; "violent."

violent (*chamac*). 2555; "cruel."

64. **beguiled** (*nasha*). 5377; "to lead astray; i.e. (morally) to seduce."[103]

65a. **eat** (*chala*). 2490; "prostitute." "reflexive pollute, defile oneself; sexually"[108]

65b. **eat** (*okel*). 400; "prey."

prey (*malqowach*). 4455. From 3947.

take (*laqach*). 3947; "mingle."

mingle (*arab*). 6151. Corresponding to 6148.

---

[101] 61a. Oxford English-Hebrew Dictionary – Oxford NY – Oxford University Press – 1996

[102] 61b. The Brown-Driver-Briggs Hebrew and English Lexicon — Hendrickson Publishers — 2010

[103] 64. Spiros Zodhiates, *King James Version Hebrew-Greek Key Word Study Bible*, (Chattanooga, TN: AMG Publishing, 2008).

[108] 65a. The Brown-Driver-Briggs Hebrew and English Lexicon — Hendrickson Publishers — 2010

6148 (*arab*); "surety."

surety (*yada*). 3045; "lie by man."

3046 (*yda*). Corresponding to 3045; "know."

66.   **touch** (*naga*). 5060; "euphemistically, to lie with a woman."

67a.   **fruit** (*priy*). 6529; "from 6509."

6509 (parah) (be, cause to be, make) fruitful.

67b.   **fruit** (*priy*). 6529; "reward."

reward (*shachad*). 7810; "gift."

gift (*mattan*). 4976. From 5414.

to give (*nathan*). 5414; "do." "of sexual relation"[104]

67c.   **fruit** (*priy*). 6529; "reward."

reward (*shachad*). 7810; "gift."

gift (*mattan*). 4976. From 5414.

to give (*nathan*). 5414; "lay." "of sexual relation"[104]

67d.   **fruit** (*priy*). 6529; "reward."

reward (*shachad*). 7810; "gift."

gift (*mattan*). 4976. From 5414.

---

[104] 67b.,c.,d. The Brown–Driver–Briggs Hebrew and English Lexicon – Hendrickson Publishers – 2010

to give (*nathan*). 5414; "lie." "of sexual relation"[104]

67e. **fruit** (*priy*). 6529; "reward."

reward (*shachad*). 7810; "gift."

gift (*mattan*). 4976. From 5414.

to give (*nathan*). 5414; "take." "of sexual relation"[104]

67f. **fruit**[105] (*karpos*). 2590. from base of 726.

726 (*harpazo*). from a derivative of 138.

138 (*haireomai*). "probably akin to 142; to take for oneself."

142 (*airo*). By Hebrew [compare 5375]

5375 (*nasa*). A verb; "to take a wife or to get married."[106]

68. **gave** (*nathan*). 5414; "to give." "of sexual relation."[104]

to give (*chazaq*). 2388; "cleave."

cleave (*dabaq*). 1692; "be joined."

be joined (*yachad*). 3161; "to be."

to be (*chamad*). 2530; "desire;" "of lustful desire." "desirable young men = fine, attractive young men."[107]

---

[104] 67e., [107] 68. The Brown–Driver–Briggs Hebrew and English Lexicon – Hendrickson Publishers – 2010

[105,106] 67f. Spiros Zodhiates, *King James Version Hebrew-Greek Key Word Study Bible—Key Insights Into God's Word*—Old Testament Dictionary—New Testament Dictionary, (Chattanooga, TN: AMG Publishing, 2008).

69.   **drove out** (*garash*). 1644; "to drive out from a possession; esp. to expatriate or **divorce: divorced woman."**

divorce (*kerithuth*). 3748. From 3772; "a cutting (of the matrimonial bond)."

3772 (*karath*); "to covenant; (i.e., make an alliance or bargain, originally by cutting flesh and passing between the pieces)."

The Lord's Prayer

Unless otherwise noted, all words being defined are assumed to be Greek.

70.   **our** (*hemon*). 2257; "of us."

71.   **father** (*pater*). 3962; "(lit. or fig.) father."

       3965 (*patria*). As if feminine of a derivation of 3962; "lineage."

       lineage (*mowledeth*). Hebrew. 4138. From 3205.
       3205; "born; be delivered (of a child); be the son of (travailing woman)."

72.   **which** (*hos*). 3739. See also 3757.

       3757 (*hou*); "at which place, i.e., where."

73.   **art** (*hareh*). Hebrew. 2030. From 2029.

       2029 (*harah*); "(lit. or fig.) progenitor [the foundation of a family]."

74.   **in** (*en*). 1722. A primary preposition denoting (fixed) position (in place, time, or state) and (by implication) instrumentality (medially or constructively), i.e., a relation of rest.

---

71. From the definitions of "father," "lineage," "born," "be delivered," "son of travailing woman" and their usage in biblical Scripture, I conclude the Authorized English Version for the word *father* and its Greek equilivant *pater* reveals a story about the descendants/children of the Creator/Father who is known by Christians as God. This supports my thesis that the Lord's Prayer is a prayer about the birthing of children also known as a kingdom. These words used in Cross-Reference to Scripture start on page 299.

75a.   **heaven** (*ouranos*). 3772. Perhaps from the same as 3735.

3735 (*oros*); "rear." Perhaps akin to 142.

142 (*airo*) by Hebraism. Comparative 5375.

5375 (*nasa*); Hebrew. "(lit. and fig.) bear, bring forth."

bear, bring forth (*yalad*). 3205; "born; be delivered (of a child); be the son of (travailing woman)."

75b.   **heaven** (*shamayim*). Hebrew. 8064.

name (*shem*). 8034. Perhaps rather from 7760. Comparative 8064.

7760 (*sum*); "set up."

set up (*banah*). 1129; "make."

make (*parah*). 6509; "to bear fruit (lit. or fig.): bear, bring forth."

bear, bring forth (*yalad*). 3205; "born; be delivered (of a child); be the son of (travailing woman)."

75c.   **heaven** (*shamayim*). Hebrew. 8064.

name (*shem*). 8034. Perhaps rather from 7760. Comparative 8064.

Shem (Shem). 8035. The same as 8034; a son of Noah.

a son (*ben*). 1121. From 1129.

1129 (*banah*); "make."

make (*parah*). 6509; "to bear fruit (lit. or fig.): bear, bring forth."

bear, bring forth (*yalad*). 3205; "born; be delivered (of a child); be the son of (travailing woman)."

76.   **hallowed** (*hagiazo*). 37; "to make holy, ceremonially purify; (mentally) to venerate: hallow, be holy, sanctification."

77.   **be** (*pleroo*). 4137. From 4134; "to make replete, i.e., level up (a hollow)."

78.   **thy** (*sou*). 4675; "thine own."

79a.   **name** (*onoma*). 3686. From a presumed derivation of the base of 1097; a "name" (lit. or fig.) [authority, character].

1097 (*ginosko*); "to know."

know (*eido*). 1492; "behold."

79b.   **name** (*shem*). Hebrew. 8034. Perhaps rather from 7760 through the idea of definite and conspicuous position. Comparative 8064; "an appellation, as a mark or memorial of individuality."

heaven (*shamayim*). 8064; dual of an unused singular.

80.   **kingdom** (*basileia*). 932. From 935.

935 (*basileus*). Probably from 939; "foundation."

foundation (basis); "(fig.) conceive."

conceive (*katabolé*). 2602. From 2598; "(fig.) conceive."

81.   **come** (*exerchomai*). 1831; "(lit. or fig.) come forth."

come forth (*ekporeuomai*). 1607; "issue."

issue (*haimorroeó*). 131. From 129.

129 (*haima*); "kindred."

kindred (*genos*). 1085; "(lit. or fig.) born."

born (*gennaó*). 1080; "to procreate; (fig.) bear, beget, be born, bring forth, conceive."

82a.   **will** (*melló*). 3195; "shall (begin)."

shall (*tiktó*). 5088; "to produce from seed, as a mother; (lit. or fig.) bear, be born, bring forth, be delivered."

82b.   **will** (*melló*). 3195; "shall (begin)."

shall begin (*chala*). Hebrew. 2490. A primitive root. Comparative 2470.

2470 (*chalah*); "woman in travail."

woman in travail (*yalad*). 3205; "born; be delivered (of a child); be the son of (travailing woman)."

77.   **be** (*pleroo*). 4137. From 4134; "to make replete, i.e., level up (a hollow)."

83.   **done** (*ginomai*). 1096; "to become (come into being); (lit., fig., intensive, etc.) be."

be (*echō*). 2192; "(lit. or fig.) conceive."

conceive (*katabolē*). 2602. From 2598; "(fig.) conceive."

74.   **in** (*en*). 1722. A primary preposition denoting (fixed) position (in place, time, or state) and (by implication) instrumentality (medially or constructively), i.e., a relation of rest.

84a.   **earth** (*aphar*). Hebrew. 6083. See 1035.

1035 (*Beyth Lechem*). From 1004.

1004 (*bayith*); "homeborn."

homeborn (*yaliyd*). 3211. From 3205.

bear, bring forth (*yalad*). 3205; "born; be delivered (of a child); be the son of (travailing woman)."

84b.   **earth** (*erets*). Hebrew. 776; "nations."

nations (*ummah*). Aramaic. 524. Corresponding to 523.

523 (*ummah*). From the same as 517.

517 (*'em*); "a mother (as the bond of the family)." Like 1.

1 (*ab*); "father."

father (*aman*). 1121.

a son (*ben*). 1121. From 1129.

1129 (*banah*); "make."

make (*parah*). 6509; "to bear fruit (lit. or fig.): bear, bring forth."

bear, bring forth (*yalad*). 3205; "born; be delivered (of a child); be the son of (travailing woman)."

84c. **earth** (*adamah*). Hebrew. 127. From 119.

119 (*adam*); "to show blood (in the face)."

85. **on** (*epano*); "up above, i.e., over or on."

An Application of Cross-Reference to Scripture

Jacob and His Two Wives

The following footnotes relate to those found in the text of *Jacob and His Two Wives*. The key word *affliction* is found in *Genesis 29:32* and utilized again in other Scripture as noted by the appropriate biblical reference. Italics are for added emphasis on the term *affliction* and other defined key words also italicized along with the chapter and verse(s). The footnotes show how these words used in the context of the Bible verse agree with the definitions revealed by the Defined Word Approach.

1a.   And the angel of the Lord said unto her, Behold, thou art with child, and shalt bear a son, and shalt call his name Ishmael; because the Lord hath heard thy *affliction*. And he will be a wild man; his hand will be against every man, and every man's hand against him; and he shall dwell in the presence of all his brethren. And she called the name of the Lord that spake unto her, Thou God seest me: for she said, Have I also here looked after him that seeth me? Wherefore the well was called Beer-lahai-roi; behold, it is between Kadesh and Bered. And Hagar bare Abram a son: and Abram called his son's name, which Hagar bare, Ishmael. And Abram was fourscore and six years old, when Hagar bare Ishmael to Abram (*Genesis 16:11–16*).

And she vowed a vow, and said, O Lord of hosts, if thou wilt indeed look on the *affliction* of thine handmaid, and remember me, and not forget thine handmaid, but wilt give unto thine handmaid a man child, then I will give him unto the Lord all the days of his life, and there shall no razor come upon his head (*1 Samuel 1:11*).

And Abraham said, Because I thought, Surely the fear of God is not in this place; and they will slay me for my wife's sake. And yet indeed she is my sister; she is the *daughter* of my father, but not the *daughter* of my mother; and she became my wife (*Genesis 20:11–12*).

And Leah said, God hath endued me with a good dowry; now will my husband dwell with me, because I have born him six sons: and she called his name Zebulun. And afterwards she bare a *daughter*, and called her name Dinah (*Genesis 30:20–21*).

And David said to Abishai, and to all his servants, Behold, my son, which came *forth of* my bowels, seeketh my life: how much more now may this Benjamite do it? let him alone, and let him curse; for the LORD hath bidden him (*2 Samuel 16:11*).

As he came *forth of* his mother's womb, naked shall he return to go as he came, and shall take nothing of his labour, which he may carry away in his hand" (*Ecclesiastes 5:15*).

The sorrows of a travailing woman shall come upon him: he is an unwise son; for he should not stay long in the place of the breaking *forth of* children (*Hosea 13:13*).

And when a stranger shall sojourn with thee, and will keep the passover to the LORD, let all his males be circumcised, and then let him come near and keep it; and he shall be as one that is born in the land: for no uncircumcised person shall eat thereof. One law shall be to him that is *homeborn*, and unto the stranger that sojourneth among you. Thus did all the children of Israel; as the LORD commanded Moses and Aaron, so did they. And it came to pass the selfsame day, that the LORD did bring the children of Israel out of the land of Egypt by their armies (*Exodus 12:48–51*).

And Isaac entreated the LORD for his wife, because she was barren: and the LORD was entreated of him, and Rebekah his wife conceived. And the children struggled together *within* her; and she said, If it be so, why am I thus? And she went to inquire of the LORD. And the LORD said unto her, Two nations are in thy womb, and two manner of people shall be separated from thy bowels; and the one people shall be stronger than the other people; and the elder shall serve the younger. And when her days to be delivered were fulfilled, behold, there were twins in her womb. And the first came out red, all over like a hairy garment; and they called his name Esau. And after that came his brother out, and his hand took hold on Esau's heel; and his name was called Jacob: and Isaac was threescore years old when she bare them (*Genesis 25:21–26*).

And the LORD said unto Abram, after that Lot was separated from him, Lift up now thine eyes, and look from the place where thou art northward, and southward, and eastward, and westward: For all the land which thou seest, to thee will I give it, and to thy seed for ever. And I will *make* thy seed as the dust of the earth: so that if a man can number the dust of the earth, then shall thy seed also be numbered (*Genesis 13:14–16*).

And when thy days be fulfilled, and thou shalt sleep with thy fathers, I will *set up* thy seed after thee, which shall proceed out of thy bowels, and I will establish his kingdom (*2 Samuel 7:12*).

Nevertheless for David's sake did the LORD his God give him a lamp in Jerusalem, to *set up* his son after him, and to establish Jerusalem (*1 Kings 15:4*).

And the angel of the LORD said unto her, Behold, thou art with child, and shalt *bear* a son, and shalt call his name Ishmael; because the Lord hath heard thy affliction (*Genesis 16:11*).

But the angel said unto him, Fear not, Zacharias: for thy prayer is heard; and thy wife Elisabeth shall *bear* thee a son, and thou shalt call his name John (*Luke 1:13*).

Unto the woman he said, I will greatly multiply thy sorrow and thy conception; in sorrow thou shalt *bring forth* children; and thy desire shall be to thy husband, and he shall rule over thee (*Genesis 3:16*).

And she shall *bring forth* a son, and thou shalt call his name JESUS: for he shall save his people from their sins. Now all this was done, that it might be fulfilled which was spoken of the Lord by the prophet, saying, Behold, a virgin shall be with child, and shall *bring forth* a son, and they shall call his name Emmanuel, which being interpreted is, God with us. Then Joseph being raised from sleep did as the angel of the Lord had bidden him, and took unto him his wife: And knew her not till she had brought forth her firstborn son: and he called his name JESUS (*Matthew 1:21–25*).

And Joseph brought them out from between his knees, and he bowed himself with his face to the earth. And Joseph took them both, Ephraim in his right hand toward Israel's left hand, and

Manasseh in his left hand toward Israel's right hand, and brought them near unto him. And Israel stretched out his right hand, and laid it upon Ephraim's head, who was the younger, and his left hand upon Manasseh's head, guiding his hands wittingly; for Manasseh was the firstborn. And he blessed Joseph, and said, God, before whom my fathers Abraham and Isaac did walk, the God which fed me all my life long unto this day, The Angel which redeemed me from all evil, bless the lads; and let my name be named on them, and the name of my fathers Abraham and Isaac; and let them *grow* into a multitude in the midst of the earth (*Genesis 48:12–16*).

As thou knowest not what is the way of the spirit, nor how the bones do *grow* in the womb of her that is with child: even so thou knowest not the works of God who maketh all (*Ecclesiastes 11:5*).

But David took not the number of them from twenty years old and under: because the LORD had said he would *increase* Israel like to the stars of the heavens (*1 Chronicles 27:23*).

And when her days to *be delivered* were fulfilled, behold, there were twins in her womb (*Genesis 25:24*).

And his daughter in law, Phinehas' wife, was with child, near to *be delivered*: and when she heard the tidings that the ark of God was taken, and that her father in law and her husband were dead, she bowed herself and travailed; for her pains came upon her (*1 Samuel 4:19*).

1b.   And the angel of the LORD said unto her, Behold, thou art with child, and shalt bear a son, and shalt call his name Ishmael; because the LORD hath heard thy *affliction*. And he will be a wild man; his hand will be against every man, and every man's hand against him; and he shall dwell in the presence of all his brethren. And she called the name of the LORD that spake unto her, Thou God seest me: for she said, Have I also here looked after him that seeth me? Wherefore the well was called Beer-lahai-roi; behold, it is between Kadesh and Bered. And *Hagar bare Abram a son*: and Abram called his son's name, which Hagar bare, Ishmael. And Abram was fourscore and six years old, when Hagar bare Ishmael to Abram (*Genesis 16:11–16*).

And she vowed a vow, and said, O LORD of hosts, if thou wilt indeed look on the *affliction* of thine handmaid, and remember me, and not forget thine handmaid, but wilt give unto thine handmaid a man child, then I will give him unto the LORD all the days of his life, and there shall no razor come upon his head (*1 Samuel 1:11*).

Before she travailed, she brought forth; before her pain came, she was delivered of a man child. Who hath heard such a thing? who hath seen such things? Shall the earth be made to bring forth in one day? or shall a nation be born at once? for as soon as Zion travailed, she brought forth her children. Shall I *bring to the birth*, and not cause to bring forth? saith the LORD: shall I cause to bring forth, and shut the womb? saith thy God (*Isaiah 66:7-9*).

Defined Word Approach: A Key That Unlocks the Bible

The following footnotes relate to those found in the text of *Defined Word Approach: A Key That Unlocks the Bible.* The author has italicized the key words for purposes of discussion. The key words are also found in *Genesis 1:1-5* and appear in other supporting Scripture as follows:

2a. Reuben, thou art my firstborn, my might, and the *beginning* of my strength, the excellency of dignity, and the excellency of power (*Genesis 49:3*).

If a man have two wives, one beloved, and another hated, and they have born him children, both the beloved and the hated; and if the firstborn son be hers that was hated: Then it shall be, when he maketh his sons to inherit that which he hath, that he may not make the son of the beloved firstborn before the son of the hated, which is indeed the firstborn: But he shall acknowledge the son of the hated for the firstborn, by giving him a double portion of all that he hath: for he is the *beginning* of his strength; the right of the firstborn is his (*Deuteronomy 21:15-17*).

And the LORD said unto her, Two nations are in thy womb, and two manner of people shall be separated from thy bowels; and the one people shall be stronger than the other people; and the elder shall serve the younger. And when her days to be delivered were fulfilled, behold, there were twins in her womb. And the *first* came out red, all over like a hairy garment; and they called his name Esau. And after that came his brother out, and his hand took hold on Esau's heel; and his name was called Jacob: and Isaac was threescore years old when she bare them (*Genesis 25:23-26*).

And it came to pass in the time of her travail, that, behold, twins were in her womb. And it came to pass, when she travailed, that the one put out his hand: and the midwife took and bound upon his hand a scarlet thread, saying, This came out *first*, And it came to pass, as he drew back his hand, that, behold, his brother came out: and she said, How hast thou broken forth? this breach be upon thee: therefore his name was called Pharez. And afterward came out his brother, that had the scarlet thread upon his hand: and his name was called Zarah (*Genesis 38:27-30*).

And Adam knew his wife again; and she bare *a son*, and called his name Seth: For God, said she, hath appointed me another seed instead of Abel, whom Cain slew. And to Seth, to him also there was born *a son*; and he called his name Enos: then began men to call upon the name of the LORD (*Genesis 4:25-26*).

Then Joseph her husband, being a just man, and not willing to make her a public example, was minded to put her away privily. But while he thought on these things, behold, the angel of the Lord appeared unto him in a dream, saying, Joseph, thou son of David, fear not to take unto thee Mary thy wife: for that which is conceived in her is of the Holy Ghost. And she shall bring forth *a son*, and thou shalt call his name JESUS: for he shall save his people from their sins. Now all this was done, that it might be fulfilled which was spoken of the Lord by the prophet, saying, Behold, a virgin shall be with child, and shall bring forth *a son*, and they shall call his name Emmanuel, which being interpreted is, God with us. Then Joseph being raised from sleep did as the angel of the Lord had bidden him, and took unto him his wife: And knew her not till she had brought forth her firstborn son: and he called his name JESUS (*Matthew 1:19-25*).

And, behold, I purpose *to build* an house unto the name of the LORD my God, as the LORD spake unto David my father, saying, Thy son, whom I will set upon thy throne in thy room, he shall build an house unto my name. (*1 Kings 5:5*).

Now Sarai Abram's wife bare him no children: and she had a handmaid, an Egyptian, whose name was Hagar. And Sarai said unto Abram, Behold now, the LORD hath restrained me from bearing: I pray thee, go in unto my maid; it may be that I may *obtain children* by her. And Abram hearkened to the voice of Sarai (*Genesis 16:1-2*).

118

And the LORD said unto Abram, after that Lot was separated from him, Lift up now thine eyes, and look from the place where thou art northward, and southward, and eastward, and westward: For all the land which thou seest, to thee will I give it, and to thy seed for ever. And I will *make* thy seed as the dust of the earth: so that if a man can number the dust of the earth, then shall thy seed also be numbered (*Genesis 13:14-16*).

And the angel of the LORD said unto her, Behold, thou art with child, and shalt *bear* a son, and shalt call his name Ishmael; because the LORD hath heard thy affliction (*Genesis 16:11*).

But the angel said unto him, Fear not, Zacharias: for thy prayer is heard; and thy wife Elisabeth shall *bear* thee a son, and thou shalt call his name John (*Luke 1:13*).

Unto the woman he said, I will greatly multiply thy sorrow and thy conception; in sorrow thou shalt *bring forth* children; and thy desire shall be to thy husband, and he shall rule over thee (*Genesis 3:16*).

And she shall *bring forth* a son, and thou shalt call his name JESUS: for he shall save his people from their sins. Now all this was done, that it might be fulfilled which was spoken of the Lord by the prophet, saying, Behold, a virgin shall be with child, and shall *bring forth* a son, and they shall call his name Emmanuel, which being interpreted is, God with us. Then Joseph being raised from sleep did as the angel of the Lord had bidden him, and took unto him his wife: And knew her not till she had brought forth her firstborn son: and he called his name JESUS (*Matthew 1:21-25*).

Now these are the generations of the sons of Noah, Shem, Ham, and Japheth: and unto them were sons *born* after the flood (*Genesis 10:1*).

And Abraham was an hundred years old, when his son Isaac was born unto him. And Sarah said, God hath made me to laugh, so that all that hear will laugh with me. And she said, Who would have said unto Abraham, that Sarah should have given children suck? for I have *born* him a son in his old age (*Genesis 21:5-7*).

And Jacob begat Joseph the husband of Mary, of whom was *born* Jesus, who is called Christ (*Matthew 1:16*).

And his daughter in law, Phinehas' wife, was with child, near to *be delivered*: and when she heard the tidings that the ark of God was taken, and that her father in law and her husband were dead, she bowed herself and travailed; for her pains came upon her (*1 Samuel 4:19*).

A woman when she is in travail hath sorrow, because her hour is come: but as soon as she is delivered of the child, she remembereth no more the anguish, for joy that a man is born into the world (*John 16:21*).

2b. Reuben, thou art my firstborn, my might, and the *beginning* of my strength, the excellency of dignity, and the excellency of power (*Genesis 49:3*).

If a man have two wives, one beloved, and another hated, and they have born him children, both the beloved and the hated; and if the firstborn son be hers that was hated: Then it shall be, when he maketh his sons to inherit that which he hath, that he may not make the son of the beloved firstborn before the son of the hated, which is indeed the firstborn: But he shall acknowledge the son of the hated for the firstborn, by giving him a double portion of all that he hath: for he is the *beginning* of his strength; the right of the firstborn is his (*Deuteronomy 21:15-17*).

And the LORD said unto her, Two nations are in thy womb, and two manner of people shall be separated from thy bowels; and the one people shall be stronger than the other people; and the elder shall serve the younger. And when her days to be delivered were fulfilled, behold, there were twins in her womb. And the *first* came out red, all over like a hairy garment; and they called his name Esau. And after that came his brother out, and his hand took hold on Esau's heel; and his name was called Jacob: and Isaac was threescore years old when she bare them (*Genesis 25:23-26*).

And it came to pass in the time of her travail, that, behold, twins were in her womb. And it came to pass, when she travailed, that the one put out his hand: and the midwife took and bound upon his hand a scarlet thread, saying, This came out *first*, And it came to pass, as he drew back his hand, that, behold, his brother came out: and she said, How hast thou broken forth? this breach be upon thee: therefore his name was called Pharez. And afterward came out his brother, that had the scarlet thread upon his hand: and his name was called Zarah (*Genesis 38:27-30*).

A woman when she is in travail hath sorrow, because her hour is come: but as soon as she is delivered of the child, she remembereth no more the anguish, for joy that a man is born into the world (*John 16:21*).

Fear took hold upon them there, and *pain*, as of a woman in travail (*Psalm 48:6*).

And the angel of the LORD said unto her, Behold, thou art with child, and shalt *bear* a son, and shalt call his name Ishmael; because the LORD hath heard thy affliction (*Genesis 16:11*).

But the angel said unto him, Fear not, Zacharias: for thy prayer is heard; and thy wife Elisabeth shall *bear* thee a son, and thou shalt call his name John (*Luke 1:13*).

Unto the woman he said, I will greatly multiply thy sorrow and thy conception; in sorrow thou shalt *bring forth* children; and thy desire shall be to thy husband, and he shall rule over thee (*Genesis 3:16*).

And she shall *bring forth* a son, and thou shalt call his name JESUS: for he shall save his people from their sins. Now all this was done, that it might be fulfilled which was spoken of the Lord by the prophet, saying, Behold, a virgin shall be with child, and shall *bring forth* a son, and they shall call his name Emmanuel, which being interpreted is, God with us. Then Joseph being raised from sleep did as the angel of the Lord had bidden him, and took unto him his wife: And knew her not till she had brought forth her firstborn son: and he called his name JESUS (*Matthew 1:21-25*).

And it came to pass in the time of her *travail*, that, behold, twins were in her womb. And it came to pass, when she travailed, that the one put out his hand: and the midwife took and bound upon his hand a scarlet thread, saying, This came out first, And it came to pass, as he drew back his hand, that, behold, his brother came out: and she said, How hast thou broken forth? this breach be upon thee: therefore his name was called Pharez. And afterward came out his brother, that had the scarlet thread upon his hand: and his name was called Zarah (*Genesis 38:27-30*).

Now these are the generations of the sons of Noah, Shem, Ham, and Japheth: and unto them were sons *born* after the flood (*Genesis 10:1*).

And Abraham was an hundred years old, when his son Isaac was born unto him. And Sarah said, God hath made me to laugh, so that all that hear will laugh with me. And she said, Who would have said unto Abraham, that Sarah should have given children suck? for I have *born* him a son in his old age (*Genesis 21:5-7*).

And when her days to *be delivered* were fulfilled, behold, there were twins in her womb (*Genesis 25:24*).

And his daughter in law, Phinehas' wife, was with child, near to *be delivered*: and when she heard the tidings that the ark of God was taken, and that her father in law and her husband were dead, she bowed herself and travailed; for her pains came upon her (*1 Samuel 4:19*).

3.   In the beginning *God* created the heaven and the earth (*Genesis 1:1*).

But from the beginning of the creation *God* made them male and female (*Mark 10:6*).

4a. So God *created* man in his own image, in the image of God *created* he him; male and female *created* he them (*Genesis 1:27*).

This is the book of the generations of Adam. In the day that God *created* man, in the likeness of God made he him; Male and female *created* he them; and blessed them, and called their name Adam, in the day when they were *created* (*Genesis 5:1-2*).

How long wilt thou go about, O thou backsliding daughter? for the LORD hath *created* a new thing in the earth, A woman shall compass a man (*Jeremiah 31:22*).

And he arose from thence, and cometh into the coasts of Judaea by the farther side of Jordan: and the people resort unto him again; and, as he was wont, he taught them again. And the Pharisees came to him, and asked him, Is it lawful for a man to put away his wife? tempting him. And he answered and said unto them, What did Moses command you? And they said, Moses suffered to write a bill of divorcement, and to put her away. And Jesus answered and said unto them, For the hardness of your heart he wrote you this precept. But *from the beginning of the creation* **God made them male and female**. For this cause shall a man leave his father and mother, and cleave to his wife; And they twain shall be one flesh: so then they are no more twain, but one flesh. **What therefore God hath joined together, let not man put asunder**. And in the house his disciples asked him again of the same matter. And he saith unto them, Whosoever shall put away his wife, and marry another, committeth adultery against her. And if a woman shall put away her husband, and be married to another, she committeth adultery (*Mark 10:1-12*).

And the LORD God said, It is not good that the man should be alone; I will *make* him a help meet for him (*Genesis 2:18*).

And the LORD said unto Abram, after that Lot was separated from him, Lift up now thine eyes, and look from the place where thou art northward, and southward, and eastward, and westward: For all the land which thou seest, to thee will I give it, and to thy seed for ever. And I will *make* thy seed as the dust of the earth: so that if a man can number the dust of the earth, then shall thy seed also be numbered (*Genesis 13:14-16*).

And I will *make* thee exceeding fruitful, and I will make nations of thee, and kings shall come out of thee. And I will establish my covenant between me and thee and thy seed after thee in their generations for an everlasting covenant, to be a God unto thee, and to thy seed after thee (*Genesis 17:6-7*).

And Hamor communed with them, saying, The soul of my son Shechem longeth for your daughter: I pray you give her him to wife. And *make* ye marriages with us, and give your daughters unto us, and take our daughters unto you (*Genesis 34:8-9*).

And if a man entice a maid that is not betrothed, and *lie* with her, he shall surely endow her to be his wife (*Exodus 22:16*).

4b. So God *created* man in his own image, in the image of God *created* he him; male and female *created* he them (*Genesis 1:27*).

This is the book of the generations of Adam. In the day that God *created* man, in the likeness of God made he him; Male and female *created* he them; and blessed them, and called their name Adam, in the day when they were *created* (*Genesis 5:1-2*).

How long wilt thou go about, O thou backsliding daughter? for the LORD hath *created* a new thing in the earth, A woman shall compass a man (*Jeremiah 31:22*).

And he arose from thence, and cometh into the coasts of Judaea by the farther side of Jordan: and the people resort unto him again; and, as he was wont, he taught them again. And the Pharisees came to him, and asked him, Is it lawful for a man to put away his wife? tempting him. And he answered and said unto them, What did Moses command you? And they said, Moses suffered to write a bill of divorcement, and to put her away. And Jesus answered and said unto them, For the hardness of your heart he wrote you this precept. But *from the beginning of the creation **God made them male and female**. For this cause shall a man leave his father and mother, and cleave to his wife; And they twain shall be one flesh: so then they are no more twain, but one flesh. **What therefore God hath joined together, let not man put asunder**. And in the house his disciples asked him again of the same matter. And he saith unto them, Whosoever shall put away his wife, and marry another, committeth adultery against her. And if a woman shall put away her husband, and be married to another, she committeth adultery (*Mark 10:1-12*).

And the LORD shall guide thee continually, and satisfy thy soul in drought, and *make fat* thy bones: and thou shalt be like a watered garden, and like a spring of water, whose waters fail not. And they that shall be of thee shall build the old waste places: ***thou shalt raise up the foundations of many generations; and thou shalt be called, The repairer of the breach***, The restorer of paths to dwell in (*Isaiah 58:11-12*).

And he said, Well; I will make a league with thee: but one thing I require of thee, that is, Thou shalt not see my face, except thou first bring Michal Saul's daughter, when thou comest to see my face. And David sent messengers to Ish-bosheth Saul's son, saying, *Deliver* me my wife Michal, which I espoused to me for an hundred foreskins of the Philistines. And Ish-bosheth sent, and took her from her husband, even from Phaltiel the son of Laish (*2 Samuel 3:13-15*).

And it came to pass, that in the morning, behold, it was Leah: and he said to Laban, What is this thou hast done unto me? did not I serve with thee for Rachel? wherefore then hast thou beguiled me? And Laban said, It must not be so done in our country, *to give* the younger before the firstborn. Fulfill her week, and we will give thee this also for the service which thou shalt serve with me yet seven other years. And Jacob did so, and fulfilled her week: and he gave him Rachel his daughter to wife also. And Laban gave to Rachel his daughter Bilhah his handmaid to be her maid. And he went in also unto Rachel, and he loved also Rachel more than Leah, and served with him yet seven other years. And when the Lord saw that Leah was hated, he opened her womb: but Rachel was barren. And Leah conceived, and bare a son, and she called his name Reuben: for she said, Surely the Lord hath looked upon my affliction; now therefore my husband will love me. And she conceived again, and bare a son; and said, Because the Lord hath heard that I was hated, he hath therefore given me this son also: and she called his name Simeon. And she conceived again, and bare a son; and said, Now this time will my husband be joined unto me, because I have born him three sons: therefore was his name called Levi. And she conceived again, and bare a son: and she said, Now will I praise the Lord: therefore she called his name Judah; and left bearing (*Genesis 29:25-35*).

Therefore shall a man leave his father and his mother, and shall *cleave* unto his wife: and they shall be one flesh (*Genesis 2:24*).

And she conceived again, and bare a son; and said, Now this time will my husband *be joined* unto me, because I have born him three sons: therefore was his name called Levi (*Genesis 29:34*).

And Sarai Abram's wife took Hagar her maid the Egyptian, after Abram had dwelt ten years in the land of Canaan, and gave her to her husband Abram *to be* his wife. And he went in unto Hagar, and she conceived: and when she saw that she had conceived, her mistress was despised in her eyes (*Genesis 16:3-4*).

And seest among the captives a beautiful woman, and hast a *desire* unto her, that thou wouldest have her to thy wife (*Deuteronomy 21:11*).

4c. So God *created* man in his own image, in the image of God *created* he him; male and female *created* he them (*Genesis 1:27*).

This is the book of the generations of Adam. In the day that God *created* man, in the likeness of God made he him; Male and female *created* he them; and blessed them, and called their name Adam, in the day when they were *created* (*Genesis 5:1-2*).

How long wilt thou go about, O thou backsliding daughter? for the LORD hath *created* a new thing in the earth, A woman shall compass a man (*Jeremiah 31:22*).

And he arose from thence, and cometh into the coasts of Judaea by the farther side of Jordan: and the people resort unto him again; and, as he was wont, he taught them again. And the Pharisees came to him, and asked him, Is it lawful for a man to put away his wife? tempting him. And he answered and said unto them, What did Moses command you? And they said, Moses suffered to write a bill of divorcement, and to put her away. And Jesus answered and said unto them, For the hardness of your heart he wrote you this precept. But *from the beginning of the* creation **God made them male and female.** For this cause shall a man leave his father and mother, and cleave to his wife; And they twain shall be one flesh: so then they are no more twain, but one flesh. **What therefore God hath joined together, let not man put asunder.** And in the house his disciples asked him again of the same matter. And he saith unto them, Whosoever shall put away his wife, and marry another, committeth adultery against her. And if a woman shall put away her husband, and be married to another, she committeth adultery (*Mark 10:1-12*).

And the LORD shall guide thee continually, and satisfy thy soul in drought, and *make fat* thy bones: and thou shalt be like a watered garden, and like a spring of water, whose waters fail not. And they that shall be of thee shall build the old waste places: ***thou shalt raise up the foundations of many generations***; and thou shalt be called, The repairer of the breach, The restorer of paths to dwell in. If thou turn away thy foot from the sabbath, from doing thy pleasure on my holy day; and call the sabbath a delight, the holy of the LORD, honorable; and shalt honor him, not doing thine own ways, nor finding thine own pleasure, nor speaking thine own words: Then shalt thou delight thyself in the LORD; and I will cause thee to ride upon the high places of the earth, and feed thee with the heritage of Jacob thy father: for the mouth of the LORD hath spoken it (*Isaiah 58:11-14*).

All the souls that came with Jacob into Egypt, which came out of his *loins*, besides Jacob's sons' wives, all the souls were threescore and six; And the sons of Joseph, which were born him in Egypt, were two souls: all the souls of the house of Jacob, which came into Egypt, were threescore and ten (*Genesis 46:26-27*).

And all the souls that came out of *the loins* of Jacob were seventy souls: for Joseph was in Egypt already (*Exodus 1:5*).

But I have chosen Jerusalem, that my name might be there; and have chosen David to be over my people Israel. Now it was in the heart of David my father to build a house for the name of the LORD God of Israel. But the LORD said to David my father, Forasmuch as it was in thine heart to build an house for my name, thou didst well in that it was in thine heart: Notwithstanding thou shalt not build the house; but thy son which shall come forth out of thy *loins*, he shall build the house for my name (*2 Chronicles 6:6-9*).

4d.   So God *created* man in his own image, in the image of God *created* he him; male and female *created* he them (*Genesis 1:27*).

This is the book of the generations of Adam. In the day that God *created* man, in the likeness of God made he him; Male and female *created* he them; and blessed them, and called their name Adam, in the day when they were *created* (*Genesis 5:1-2*).

How long wilt thou go about, O thou backsliding daughter? for the LORD hath *created* a new thing in the earth, A woman shall compass a man (*Jeremiah 31:22*).

And he arose from thence, and cometh into the coasts of Judaea by the farther side of Jordan: and the people resort unto him again; and, as he was wont, he taught them again. And the Pharisees came to him, and asked him, Is it lawful for a man to put away his wife? tempting him. And he answered and said unto them, What did Moses command you? And they said, Moses suffered to write a bill of divorcement, and to put her away. And Jesus answered and said unto them, For the hardness of your heart he wrote you this precept. But *from the beginning of the creation* **God made them male and female.** For this cause shall a man leave his father and mother, and cleave to his wife; And they twain shall be one flesh: so then they are no more twain, but one flesh. ***What therefore God hath joined together, let not man put asunder.*** And in the house his disciples asked him again of the same matter. And he saith unto them, Whosoever shall put away his wife, and marry another, committeth adultery against her. And if a woman shall put away her husband, and be married to another, she committeth adultery (*Mark 10:1-12*).

Behold now, I have two daughters which have not known man; let me, I pray you, bring them out unto you, and *do* ye to them as is good in your eyes: only unto these men *do* nothing; for therefore came they under the shadow of my roof (*Genesis 19:8*).

And it came to pass after this, that Absalom the son of David had a fair sister, whose name was Tamar; and Amnon the son of David loved her. And Amnon was so vexed, that he fell sick for his sister Tamar; for she was a virgin; and Amnon thought it hard for him to *do* anything to her (*2 Samuel 13:1-2*).

And it came to pass, that in the morning, behold, it was Leah: and he said to Laban, What is this thou hast done unto me? did not I serve with thee for Rachel? wherefore then hast thou beguiled me? And Laban said, It must not be so done in our country, *to give* the younger before the firstborn. Fulfill her week, and we will give thee this also for the service which thou shalt serve with me yet seven other years. And Jacob did so, and fulfilled her week: and he gave him Rachel his daughter to wife also. And Laban gave to Rachel his daughter Bilhah his handmaid to be her maid. And he went in also unto Rachel, and he loved also Rachel more than Leah, and served with him yet seven other years. And when the

LORD saw that Leah was hated, he opened her womb: but Rachel was barren. And Leah conceived, and bare a son, and she called his name Reuben: for she said, Surely the LORD hath looked upon my affliction; now therefore my husband will love me. And she conceived again, and bare a son; and said, Because the LORD hath heard that I was hated, he hath therefore given me this son also: and she called his name Simeon. And she conceived again, and bare a son; and said, Now this time will my husband be joined unto me, because I have born him three sons: therefore was his name called Levi. And she conceived again, and bare a son: and she said, Now will I praise the LORD: therefore she called his name Judah; and left bearing (*Genesis 29:25-35*).

Therefore shall a man leave his father and his mother, and shall *cleave* unto his wife: and they shall be one flesh (*Genesis 2:24*).

And she conceived again, and bare a son; and said, Now this time will my husband *be joined* unto me, because I have born him three sons: therefore was his name called Levi (*Genesis 29:34*).

And Sarai Abram's wife took Hagar her maid the Egyptian, after Abram had dwelt ten years in the land of Canaan, and gave her to her husband Abram *to be* his wife. And he went in unto Hagar, and she conceived: and when she saw that she had conceived, her mistress was despised in her eyes (*Genesis 16:3-4*).

Thou shalt not *covet* thy neighbor's house, thou shalt not *covet* thy neighbor's wife, nor his manservant, nor his maidservant, nor his ox, nor his ass, nor any thing that is thy neighbor's (*Exodus 20:17*).

To keep thee from the evil woman, from the flattery of the tongue of a strange woman. *Lust* not *after* her beauty in thine heart; neither let her take thee with her eyelids. For by means of a whorish woman a man is brought to a piece of bread: and the adulteress will hunt for the precious life. Can a man take fire in his bosom, and his clothes not be burned (*Proverbs 6:24-27*)?

4e. So God *created* man in his own image, in the image of God *created* he him; male and female *created* he them (*Genesis 1:27*).

This is the book of the generations of Adam. In the day that God *created* man, in the likeness of God made he him; Male and female *created* he them; and blessed them, and called their name Adam, in the day when they were *created* (*Genesis 5:1-2*).

How long wilt thou go about, O thou backsliding daughter? for the LORD hath *created* a new thing in the earth, A woman shall compass a man (*Jeremiah 31:22*).

And he arose from thence, and cometh into the coasts of Judaea by the farther side of Jordan: and the people resort unto him again; and, as he was wont, he taught them again. And the Pharisees came to him, and asked him, Is it lawful for a man to put away his wife? tempting him. And he answered and said unto them, What did Moses command you? And they said, Moses suffered to write a bill of divorcement, and to put her away. And Jesus answered and said unto them, For the hardness of your heart he wrote you this precept. But *from the beginning of the creation God made them male and female*. For this cause shall a man leave his father and mother, and cleave to his wife; And they twain shall be one flesh: so then they are no more twain, but one flesh. ***What therefore God hath joined together, let not man put asunder***. And in the house his disciples asked him again of the same matter. And he saith unto them, Whosoever shall put away his wife, and marry another, committeth adultery against her. And if a woman shall put away her husband, and be married to another, she committeth adultery (*Mark 10:1-12*).

Behold now, I have two daughters which have not known man; let me, I pray you, bring them out unto you, and *do* ye to them as is good in your eyes: only unto these men *do* nothing; for therefore came they under the shadow of my roof (*Genesis 19:8*).

And Jacob came out of the field in the evening, and Leah went out to meet him, and said, Thou must come in unto me; for surely I have hired thee with my son's mandrakes. And he *lay* with her that night (*Genesis 29:26*).

And it came to pass after these things, that his master's wife cast her eyes upon Joseph; and she said, *Lie* with me (*Genesis 39:7*).

And she said unto her, Is it a small matter that thou hast taken my husband? and wouldest thou take away my son's mandrakes also? And Rachel said, Therefore he shall *lie* with thee to night for thy son's mandrakes. And Jacob came out of the field in the evening, and Leah went out to meet him, and said, Thou must come in unto me; for surely I have hired thee with my son's mandrakes. And he *lay* with her that night. And God hearkened unto Leah, and she conceived, and bare Jacob the fifth son (*Genesis 30:15-17*).

4f. So God *created* man in his own image, in the image of God *created* he him; male and female *created* he them (*Genesis 1:27*).

This is the book of the generations of Adam. In the day that God *created* man, in the likeness of God made he him; Male and female *created* he them; and blessed them, and called their name Adam, in the day when they were *created* (*Genesis 5:1-2*).

How long wilt thou go about, O thou backsliding daughter? for the LORD hath *created* a new thing in the earth, A woman shall compass a man (*Jeremiah 31:22*).

And he arose from thence, and cometh into the coasts of Judaea by the farther side of Jordan: and the people resort unto him again; and, as he was wont, he taught them again. And the Pharisees came to him, and asked him, Is it lawful for a man to put away his wife? tempting him. And he answered and said unto them, What did Moses command you? And they said, Moses suffered to write a bill of divorcement, and to put her away. And Jesus answered and said unto them, For the hardness of your heart he wrote you this precept. But *from the beginning of the creation **God made them male and female***. For this cause shall a man leave his father and mother, and cleave to his wife; And they twain shall be one flesh: so then they are no more twain, but one flesh. ***What therefore God hath joined together, let not man put asunder***. And in the house his disciples asked him again of the same matter. And he saith unto them, Whosoever shall put away his wife, and marry another, committeth adultery against her. And if a woman shall put away her husband, and be married to another, she committeth adultery (*Mark 10:1-12*).

Behold now, I have two daughters which have not known man; let me, I pray you, bring them out unto you, and *do* ye to them as is good in your eyes: only unto these men *do* nothing; for therefore came they under the shadow of my roof (*Genesis 19:8*).

And it came to pass after this, that Absalom the son of David had a fair sister, whose name was Tamar; and Amnon the son of David loved her. And Amnon was so vexed, that he fell sick for his sister Tamar; for she was a virgin; and Amnon thought it hard for him to *do* anything to her (*2 Samuel 13:1-2*).

And my master made me swear, saying, Thou shalt not *take* a wife to my son of the daughters of the Canaanites, in whose land I dwell: But thou shalt go unto my father's house, and to my kindred, and *take* a wife unto my son. And I said unto my master, Peradventure the woman will not follow me. And he said unto me, The LORD, before whom I walk, will send his angel with thee, and prosper thy way; and thou shalt *take* a wife for my son of my kindred, and of my father's house (*Genesis 24:37-40*).

And she conceived again, and bare a son; and said, Now this time will my husband *be joined* unto me, because I have born him three sons: therefore was his name called Levi (*Genesis 29:34*).

And Sarai Abram's wife took Hagar her maid the Egyptian, after Abram had dwelt ten years in the land of Canaan, and gave her to her husband Abram *to be* his wife. And he went in unto Hagar, and she conceived: and when she saw that she had conceived, her mistress was despised in her eyes (*Genesis 16:3-4*).

4g.   So God *created* man in his own image, in the image of God *created* he him; male and female *created* he them (*Genesis 1:27*).

This is the book of the generations of Adam. In the day that God *created* man, in the likeness of God made he him; Male and female *created* he them; and blessed them, and called their name Adam, in the day when they were *created* (*Genesis 5:1-2*).

How long wilt thou go about, O thou backsliding daughter? for the LORD hath *created* a new thing in the earth, A woman shall compass a man (*Jeremiah 31:22*).

And he arose from thence, and cometh into the coasts of Judaea by the farther side of Jordan: and the people resort unto him again; and, as he was wont, he taught them again. And the Pharisees came to him, and asked him, Is it lawful for a man to put away his wife? tempting him. And he answered and said unto them, What did Moses command you? And they said, Moses suffered to write a bill of divorcement, and to put her away. And Jesus answered and said unto them, For the hardness of your heart he wrote you this precept. But *from the beginning of the creation God made them male and female*. For this cause shall a man leave his father and mother, and cleave to his wife; And they twain shall be one flesh: so then they are no more twain, but one flesh. *What therefore God hath joined together, let not man put asunder*. And in the house his disciples asked him again of the same matter. And he saith unto them, Whosoever shall put away his wife, and marry another, committeth adultery against her. And if a woman shall put away her husband, and be married to another, she committeth adultery (*Mark 10:1-12*).

Behold now, I have two daughters which have not known man; let me, I pray you, bring them out unto you, and *do* ye to them as is good in your eyes: only unto these men *do* nothing; for therefore came they under the shadow of my roof (*Genesis 19:8*).

And it came to pass after this, that Absalom the son of David had a fair sister, whose name was Tamar; and Amnon the son of David loved her. And Amnon was so vexed, that he fell sick for his sister Tamar; for she was a virgin; and Amnon thought it hard for him to *do* anything to her (*2 Samuel 13:1-2*).

But thou shalt go unto my country, and to my kindred, and *take* a wife unto my son Isaac (*Genesis 24:4*).

And whereas thou sawest iron mixed with miry clay, they shall *mingle* themselves with the seed of men: but they shall not cleave one to another, even as iron is not mixed with clay (*Daniel 2:43*).

And it came to pass, when he had been there a long time, that Abimelech king of the Philistines looked out at a window, and saw, and, behold, Isaac was sporting with Rebekah his wife. And Abimelech called Isaac, and said, Behold, of a *surety* she is thy wife:

and how saidst thou, She is my sister? And Isaac said unto him, Because I said, Lest I die for her. And Abimelech said, What is this thou hast done unto us? one of the people might lightly have lain with thy wife, and thou shouldest have brought guiltiness upon us (*Genesis 26:8-10*).

Come, let us make our father drink wine, and we will *lie with him*, that we may preserve seed of our father (*Genesis 19:32*).

And it came to pass after these things, that his master's wife cast her eyes upon Joseph; and she said, *Lie* with me (*Genesis 39:7*).

And she said unto her, Is it a small matter that thou hast taken my husband? and wouldest thou take away my son's mandrakes also? And Rachel said, Therefore he shall *lie* with thee to night for thy son's mandrakes. And Jacob came out of the field in the evening, and Leah went out to meet him, and said, Thou must come in unto me; for surely I have hired thee with my son's mandrakes. And he lay with her that night. And God hearkened unto Leah, and she conceived, and bare Jacob the fifth son (*Genesis 30:15-17*).

And they called unto Lot, and said unto him, Where are the men which came in to thee this night? bring them out unto us, that we may *know* them. Lot went out at the door unto them, and shut the door after him, And said, I pray you, brethren, do not so wickedly. Behold now, I have two daughters which have not *know[n]* man; let me, I pray you, bring them out unto you, and do ye to them as is good in your eyes: only unto these men do nothing; for therefore came they under the shadow of my roof (*Genesis 19:5-8*).

4h.   So God *created* man in his own image, in the image of God *created* he him; male and female *created* he them (*Genesis 1:27*).

This is the book of the generations of Adam. In the day that God *created* man, in the likeness of God made he him; Male and female *created* he them; and blessed them, and called their name Adam, in the day when they were *created* (*Genesis 5:1-2*).

How long wilt thou go about, O thou backsliding daughter? for the Lord hath *created* a new thing in the earth, A woman shall compass a man (*Jeremiah 31:22*).

And he arose from thence, and cometh into the coasts of Judaea by the farther side of Jordan: and the people resort unto him again; and, as he was wont, he taught them again. And the Pharisees came to him, and asked him, Is it lawful for a man to put away his wife? tempting him. And he answered and said unto them, What did Moses command you? And they said, Moses suffered to write a bill of divorcement, and to put her away. And Jesus answered and said unto them, For the hardness of your heart he wrote you this precept. But *from the beginning of the creation **God made them male and female***. For this cause shall a man leave his father and mother, and cleave to his wife; And they twain shall be one flesh: so then they are no more twain, but one flesh. ***What therefore God hath joined together, let not man put asunder***. And in the house his disciples asked him again of the same matter. And he saith unto them, Whosoever shall put away his wife, and marry another, committeth adultery against her. And if a woman shall put away her husband, and be married to another, she committeth adultery (*Mark 10:1-12*).

And you, be ye fruitful, and multiply; bring forth abundantly in the earth, and multiply therein. And God spake unto Noah, and to his sons with him, saying, And I, behold, I establish my *covenant* with you, and with your seed after you (*Genesis 9:7-9*);

Behind the doors also and the posts hast thou set up thy remembrance: for thou hast discovered thyself to another than me, and art gone up; thou hast enlarged thy bed, and made thee a *covenant* with them; thou lovedst their bed where thou sawest it (*Isaiah 57:8*).

Then may also my *covenant* be broken with David my servant, that he should not have a son to reign upon his throne; and with the Levites the priests, my ministers (*Jeremiah 33:21*).

When a man hath taken a wife, and married her, and it come to pass that she find no favor in his eyes, because he hath found some uncleanness in her: then let him write her a bill of *divorce[ment]*, and give it in her hand, and send her out of his house. And when she is departed out of his house, she may go and be another man's wife. And if the latter husband hate her, and write her a bill of *divorce[ment]*, and giveth it in her hand, and sendeth her out of his house; or if the latter husband die, which took her to be his wife;

135

Her former husband, which sent her away, may not take her again to be his wife, after that she is defiled; for that is abomination before the Lord: and thou shalt not cause the land to sin, which the Lord thy God giveth thee for an inheritance. When a man hath taken a new wife, he shall not go out to war, neither shall he be charged with any business: but he shall be free at home one year, and shall cheer up his wife which he hath taken (*Deuteronomy 24:1-5*).

The Lord said also unto me in the days of Josiah the king, Hast thou seen that which backsliding Israel hath done? she is gone up upon every high mountain and under every green tree, and there hath played the harlot. And I said after she had done all these things, Turn thou unto me. But she returned not. And her treacherous sister Judah saw it. And I saw, when for all the causes whereby backsliding Israel committed adultery I had put her away, and given her a bill of *divorce*; yet her treacherous sister Judah feared not, but went and played the harlot also. And it came to pass through the lightness of her whoredom, that she defiled the land, and committed adultery with stones and with stocks (*Jeremiah 3:6-9*).

4i. So God *created* man in his own image, in the image of God *created* he him; male and female *created* he them (*Genesis 1:27*).

This is the book of the generations of Adam. In the day that God *created* man, in the likeness of God made he him; Male and female *created* he them; and blessed them, and called their name Adam, in the day when they were *created* (*Genesis 5:1-2*).

How long wilt thou go about, O thou backsliding daughter? for the LORD hath *created* a new thing in the earth, A woman shall compass a man (*Jeremiah 31:22*).

And he arose from thence, and cometh into the coasts of Judaea by the farther side of Jordan: and the people resort unto him again; and, as he was wont, he taught them again. And the Pharisees came to him, and asked him, Is it lawful for a man to put away his wife? tempting him. And he answered and said unto them, What did Moses command you? And they said, Moses suffered to write a bill of divorcement, and to put her away. And Jesus answered and said unto them, For the hardness of your heart he wrote you this precept. But

from the beginning of the creation **God made them male and female.**
For this cause shall a man leave his father and mother, and cleave to
his wife; And they twain shall be one flesh: so then they are no more
twain, but one flesh. **What therefore God hath joined together, let not
man put asunder.** And in the house his disciples asked him again of
the same matter. And he saith unto them, Whosoever shall put away
his wife, and marry another, committeth adultery against her. And
if a woman shall put away her husband, and be married to another,
she committeth adultery (*Mark 10:1-12*).

That the sons of God saw the daughters of men that they were fair;
and they took them wives of all which they *cho[o]se* (*Genesis 6:2*).

And in the end of years they shall *join* themselves together; for the
king's daughter of the south shall come to the king of the north
to make an agreement: but she shall not retain the power of the
arm; neither shall he stand, nor his arm: but she shall be given
up, and they that brought her, and he that begat her, and he that
strengthened her in these times. But out of a branch of her roots
shall one stand up in his estate, which shall come with an army,
and shall enter into the fortress of the king of the north, and shall
deal against them, and shall prevail (*Daniel 11:6-7*).

Woe be unto the pastors that destroy and scatter the sheep of my
pasture! saith the Lord. Therefore thus saith the Lord God of
Israel against the pastors that feed my people; Ye have scattered my
flock, and driven them away, and have not visited them: behold,
I will visit upon you the evil of your doings, saith the Lord. And
I will gather the remnant of my flock out of all countries whither
I have driven them, and will bring them again to their folds; and
they shall be fruitful and *increase*. And I will set up shepherds over
them which shall feed them: and they shall fear no more, nor be
dismayed, neither shall they be lacking, saith the Lord. Behold,
the days come, saith the Lord, that I will raise unto David a righteous Branch, and a King shall reign and prosper, and shall execute
judgment and justice in the earth. In his days Judah shall be saved,
and Israel shall dwell safely: and this is his name whereby he shall
be called, THE Lord OUR RIGHTEOUSNESS. Therefore,
behold, the days come, saith the Lord, that they shall no more
say, The Lord liveth, which brought up the children of Israel out
of the land of Egypt (*Jeremiah 23:1-7*).

And I will multiply men upon you, all the house of Israel, even all of it: and the cities shall be inhabited, and the wastes shall be builded: And I will multiply upon you man and beast; and they shall *increase* and bring fruit: and I will settle you after your old estates, and will do better unto you than at your beginnings: and ye shall know that I am the Lord (*Ezekiel 36:10-11*).

4j. So God *created* man in his own image, in the image of God *created* he him; male and female *created* he them (*Genesis 1:27*).

This is the book of the generations of Adam. In the day that God *created* man, in the likeness of God made he him; Male and female *created* he them; and blessed them, and called their name Adam, in the day when they were *created* (*Genesis 5:1-2*).

How long wilt thou go about, O thou backsliding daughter? for the Lord hath *created* a new thing in the earth, A woman shall compass a man (*Jeremiah 31:22*).

And he arose from thence, and cometh into the coasts of Judaea by the farther side of Jordan: and the people resort unto him again; and, as he was wont, he taught them again. And the Pharisees came to him, and asked him, Is it lawful for a man to put away his wife? tempting him. And he answered and said unto them, What did Moses command you? And they said, Moses suffered to write a bill of divorcement, and to put her away. And Jesus answered and said unto them, For the hardness of your heart he wrote you this precept. But ***from the beginning of the*** creation **God made them male and female**. For this cause shall a man leave his father and mother, and cleave to his wife; And they twain shall be one flesh: so then they are no more twain, but one flesh. ***What therefore God hath joined together, let not man put asunder***. And in the house his disciples asked him again of the same matter. And he saith unto them, Whosoever shall put away his wife, and marry another, committeth adultery against her. And if a woman shall put away her husband, and be married to another, she committeth adultery (*Mark 10:1-12*).

That the sons of God saw the daughters of men that they were fair; and they took them wives of all which they *cho[o]se* (*Genesis 6:2*).

And in the end of years they shall *join* themselves together; for the king's daughter of the south shall come to the king of the north to make an agreement: but she shall not retain the power of the arm; neither shall he stand, nor his arm: but she shall be given up, and they that brought her, and he that begat her, and he that strengthened her in these times. But out of a branch of her roots shall one stand up in his estate, which shall come with an army, and shall enter into the fortress of the king of the north, and shall deal against them, and shall prevail (*Daniel 11:6-7*).

And Abraham journeyed from thence toward the south country, and dwelled between Kadesh and Shur, and sojourned in Gerar. And Abraham said of Sarah his wife, She is my sister: and Abimelech king of Gerar sent, and took Sarah. But God came to Abimelech in a dream by night, and said to him, Behold, thou art but a dead man, for the woman which thou hast taken; for she is a man's wife. But Abimelech had not *come near* her: and he said, LORD, wilt thou slay also a righteous nation? Said he not unto me, She is my sister? and she, even she herself said, He is my brother: in the integrity of my heart and innocency of my hands have I done this. And God said unto him in a dream, Yea, I know that thou didst this in the integrity of thy heart; for I also withheld thee from sinning against me: therefore suffered I thee not to touch her. Now therefore restore the man his wife; for he is a prophet, and he shall pray for thee, and thou shalt live: and if thou restore her not, know thou that thou shalt surely die, thou, and all that are thine (*Genesis 20:1-7*).

And it came to pass after these things, that his master's wife cast her eyes upon Joseph; and she said, *Lie with me*. But he refused, and said unto his master's wife, Behold, my master wotteth not what is with me in the house, and he hath committed all that he hath to my hand; There is none greater in this house than I; neither hath he kept back any thing from me but thee, because thou art his wife: how then can I do this great wickedness, and sin against God? And it came to pass, as she spake to Joseph day by day, that he hearkened not unto her, to *lie by her*, or to be with her. And it came to pass about this time, that Joseph went into the house to do his business; and there was none of the men of the house there within. And she caught him by his garment, saying, *Lie with me*: and he left his garment in her hand, and fled, and got him out (*Genesis 39:7-12*).

5a.   Verily I say unto you, This generation shall not pass, till all these things be fulfilled. *Heaven* and earth shall pass away, but my words shall not pass away. But of that day and hour knoweth no man, no, not the angels of heaven, but my Father only. But as the days of Noah were, so shall also the coming of the Son of man be. For as in the days that were before the flood they were eating and drinking, marrying and giving in marriage, until the day that Noah entered into the ark, And knew not until the flood came, and took them all away; so shall also the coming of the Son of man be. (*Matthew 24:34–39*)

Thus the *heaven[s]* and the earth were finished, and all the host of them (*Genesis 2:1*).

These are the generations of the *heaven[s]* and of the earth when they were created, in the day that the LORD God made the earth and the heavens (*Genesis 2:4*).

Hear, O *heaven[s]*, and give ear, O earth: for the LORD hath spoken, I have nourished and brought up children, and they have rebelled against me (*Isaiah 1:2*).

Hath a nation changed their gods, which are yet no gods? but my people have changed their glory for that which doth not profit. Be astonished, O ye *heaven*[s], at this, and be horribly afraid, be ye very desolate, saith the Lord. 13 For my people have committed two evils; they have forsaken me the fountain of living waters, and hewed them out cisterns, broken cisterns, that can hold no water. (*Jeremiah 2:11–13*)

Male and female created he them; and blessed them, and called their *name* Adam, in the day when they were created (*Genesis 5:2*).

Again I say unto you, That if two of you shall agree on earth as touching any thing that they shall ask, it shall be done for them of my Father which is in heaven. For where two or three are gathered together in my *name*, there am I in the midst of them (*Matthew 18:19–20*).

And she shall bring forth a son, and thou shalt call his *name* JESUS: for he shall save his people from their sins. Now all this was done, that it might be fulfilled which was spoken of the Lord by the prophet, saying, Behold, a virgin shall be with child, and shall bring forth a son, and they shall call his *name* Emmanuel, which being interpreted is, God with us. Then Joseph being raised from sleep did as the angel of the Lord had bidden him, and took unto him his wife: And knew her not till she had brought forth her firstborn son: and he called his *name* JESUS (*Matthew 1:21-25*).

And when thy days be fulfilled, and thou shalt sleep with thy fathers, I will *set up* thy seed after thee, which shall proceed out of thy bowels, and I will establish his kingdom (*2 Samuel 7:12*).

Nevertheless for David's sake did the LORD his God give him a lamp in Jerusalem, to *set up* his son after him, and to establish Jerusalem (*1 Kings 15:4*).

And the LORD said unto Abram, after that Lot was separated from him, Lift up now thine eyes, and look from the place where thou art northward, and southward, and eastward, and westward: For all the land which thou seest, to thee will I give it, and to thy seed for ever. And I will *make* thy seed as the dust of the earth: so that if a man can number the dust of the earth, then shall thy seed also be numbered (*Genesis 13:14-16*).

And the angel of the LORD said unto her, Behold, thou art with child, and shalt *bear* a son, and shalt call his name Ishmael; because the LORD hath heard thy affliction (*Genesis 16:11*).

But the angel said unto him, Fear not, Zacharias: for thy prayer is heard; and thy wife Elisabeth shall *bear* thee a son, and thou shalt call his name John (*Luke 1:13*).

Unto the woman he said, I will greatly multiply thy sorrow and thy conception; in sorrow thou shalt *bring forth* children; and thy desire shall be to thy husband, and he shall rule over thee (*Genesis 3:16*).

And she shall *bring forth* a son, and thou shalt call his name JESUS: for he shall save his people from their sins. Now all this was done, that it might be fulfilled which was spoken of the Lord by the prophet, saying, Behold, a virgin shall be with child, and shall *bring forth* a son, and they shall call his name Emmanuel, which being interpreted is, God with us. Then Joseph being raised from sleep did as the angel of the Lord had bidden him, and took unto him his wife: And knew her not till she had brought forth her firstborn son: and he called his name JESUS (*Matthew 1:21-25*).

Now these are the generations of the sons of Noah, Shem, Ham, and Japheth: and unto them were sons *born* after the flood (*Genesis 10:1*).

And Abraham was an hundred years old, when his son Isaac was born unto him. And Sarah said, God hath made me to laugh, so that all that hear will laugh with me. And she said, Who would have said unto Abraham, that Sarah should have given children suck? for I have *born* him a son in his old age (*Genesis 21:5-7*).

And Jacob begat Joseph the husband of Mary, of whom was *born* Jesus, who is called Christ (*Matthew 1:16*).

And when her days to *be delivered* were fulfilled, behold, there were twins in her womb (*Genesis 25:24*).

And his daughter in law, Phinehas' wife, was with child, near to *be delivered*: and when she heard the tidings that the ark of God was taken, and that her father in law and her husband were dead, she bowed herself and travailed; for her pains came upon her (*1 Samuel 4:19*).

A woman when she is in travail hath sorrow, because her hour is come: but as soon as she is delivered of the child, she remembereth no more the anguish, for joy that a man is born into the world (*John 16:21*).

5b.   Verily I say unto you, This generation shall not pass, till all these things be fulfilled. *Heaven* and earth shall pass away, but my words shall not pass away. But of that day and hour knoweth no man, no, not the angels of heaven, but my Father only. But as the days of Noah were, so shall also the coming of the Son of man be. For as in the days that were before the flood they were eating and drinking, marrying and giving in marriage, until the day that Noah entered into the ark, And knew not until the flood came, and took them all away; so shall also the coming of the Son of man be. (*Matthew 24:34-39*)

Thus the *heaven[s]* and the earth were finished, and all the host of them (*Genesis 2:1*).

These are the generations of the *heaven[s]* and of the earth when they were created, in the day that the LORD God made the earth and the heavens (*Genesis 2:4*).

Hear, O *heaven[s]*, and give ear, O earth: for the LORD hath spoken, I have nourished and brought up children, and they have rebelled against me (*Isaiah 1:2*).

Hath a nation changed their gods, which are yet no gods? but my people have changed their glory for that which doth not profit. Be astonished, O ye *heaven*[s], at this, and be horribly afraid, be ye very desolate, saith the Lord. 13 For my people have committed two evils; they have forsaken me the fountain of living waters, and hewed them out cisterns, broken cisterns, that can hold no water (*Jeremiah 2:11-13*).

Male and female created he them; and blessed them, and called their *name* Adam, in the day when they were created (*Genesis 5:2*).

Again I say unto you, That if two of you shall agree on earth as touching any thing that they shall ask, it shall be done for them of my Father which is in heaven. For where two or three are gathered together in my *name*, there am I in the midst of them (*Matthew 18:19-20*).

And Noah begat three sons, *Shem*, Ham, and Japheth (*Genesis 6:10*).

And Adam knew his wife again; and she bare *a son*, and called his name Seth: For God, said she, hath appointed me another seed instead of Abel, whom Cain slew (*Genesis 4:25*).

And, behold, I purpose *to build* an house unto the name of the LORD my God, as the LORD spake unto David my father, saying, Thy son, whom I will set upon thy throne in thy room, he shall build an house unto my name (*1 Kings 5:5*).

Now Sarai Abram's wife bare him no children: and she had a handmaid, an Egyptian, whose name was Hagar. And Sarai said unto Abram, Behold now, the Lord hath restrained me from bearing: I pray thee, go in unto my maid; it may be that I may *obtain children* by her. And Abram hearkened to the voice of Sarai (*Genesis 16:1-2*).

And the LORD said unto Abram, after that Lot was separated from him, Lift up now thine eyes, and look from the place where thou art northward, and southward, and eastward, and westward: For all the land which thou seest, to thee will I give it, and to thy seed for ever. And I will *make* thy seed as the dust of the earth: so that if a man can number the dust of the earth, then shall thy seed also be numbered (*Genesis 13:14-16*).

And the angel of the Lord said unto her, Behold, thou art with child, and shalt *bear* a son, and shalt call his name Ishmael; because the LORD hath heard thy affliction (*Genesis 16:11*).

But the angel said unto him, Fear not, Zacharias: for thy prayer is heard; and thy wife Elisabeth shall *bear* thee a son, and thou shalt call his name John (*Luke 1:13*).

Unto the woman he said, I will greatly multiply thy sorrow and thy conception; in sorrow thou shalt *bring forth* children; and thy desire shall be to thy husband, and he shall rule over thee (*Genesis 3:16*).

And she shall *bring forth* a son, and thou shalt call his name JESUS: for he shall save his people from their sins. Now all this was done, that it might be fulfilled which was spoken of the Lord by the prophet, saying, Behold, a virgin shall be with child, and shall *bring forth* a son, and they shall call his name Emmanuel, which being interpreted is, God with us. Then Joseph being raised from sleep did as the angel of the Lord had bidden him, and took unto him his wife: And knew her not till she had brought forth her firstborn son: and he called his name JESUS (*Matthew 1:21-25*).

Now these are the generations of the sons of Noah, Shem, Ham, and Japheth: and unto them were sons *born* after the flood (*Genesis 10:1*).

And Abraham was an hundred years old, when his son Isaac was born unto him. And Sarah said, God hath made me to laugh, so that all that hear will laugh with me. And she said, Who would have said unto Abraham, that Sarah should have given children suck? for I have *born* him a son in his old age (*Genesis 21:5-7*).

And Jacob begat Joseph the husband of Mary, of whom was *born* Jesus, who is called Christ (*Matthew 1:16*).

And when her days to *be delivered* were fulfilled, behold, there were twins in her womb (*Genesis 25:24*).

And his daughter in law, Phinehas' wife, was with child, near to *be delivered*: and when she heard the tidings that the ark of God was taken, and that her father in law and her husband were dead, she bowed herself and travailed; for her pains came upon her (*1 Samuel 4:19*).

A woman when she is in travail hath sorrow, because her hour is come: but as soon as she is delivered of the child, she remembereth no more the anguish, for joy that a man is born into the world (*John 16:21*).

5c.   Verily I say unto you, This generation shall not pass, till all these things be fulfilled. *Heaven* and earth shall pass away, but my words shall not pass away. But of that day and hour knoweth no man, no, not the angels of heaven, but my Father only. But as the days of Noah were, so shall also the coming of the Son of man be. For as in the days that were before the flood they were eating and drinking, marrying and giving in marriage, until the day that Noah entered into the ark, And knew not until the flood came, and took them all away; so shall also the coming of the Son of man be. (*Matthew 24:34-39*)

Thus the *heaven[s]* and the earth were finished, and all the host of them (*Genesis 2:1*).

These are the generations of the *heaven[s]* and of the earth when they were created, in the day that the LORD God made the earth and the heavens (*Genesis 2:4*).

Hear, O *heaven[s]*, and give ear, O earth: for the LORD hath spoken, I have nourished and brought up children, and they have rebelled against me (*Isaiah 1:2*).

Hath a nation changed their gods, which are yet no gods? but my people have changed their glory for that which doth not profit. Be astonished, O ye *heaven[s]*, at this, and be horribly afraid, be ye very desolate, saith the Lord. 13 For my people have committed two evils; they have forsaken me the fountain of living waters, and hewed them out cisterns, broken cisterns, that can hold no water. (*Jeremiah 2:11-13*)

Male and female created he them; and blessed them, and called their *name* Adam, in the day when they were created (*Genesis 5:2*).

Again I say unto you, That if two of you shall agree on earth as touching any thing that they shall ask, it shall be done for them of my Father which is in heaven. For where two or three are gathered together in my *name*, there am I in the midst of them (*Matthew 18:19-20*).

And Noah begat three sons, *Shem*, Ham, and Japheth (*Genesis 6:10*).

And Adam knew his wife again; and she bare *a son*, and called his name Seth: For God, said she, hath appointed me another seed instead of Abel, whom Cain slew (*Genesis 4:25*).

And I will *make* thy seed as the dust of the earth: so that if a man can number the dust of the earth, then shall thy seed also be numbered (*Genesis 13:16*).

And it came to pass after this, that Absalom the son of David had a fair sister, whose name was Tamar; and Amnon the son of David loved her. And Amnon was so vexed, that he fell sick for his sister Tamar; for she was a virgin; and Amnon thought it hard for him to *do* any thing to her (*2 Samuel 13:1-2*).

But thou shalt go unto my country, and to my kindred, and *take* a wife unto my son Isaac (*Genesis 24:4*).

And whereas thou sawest iron mixed with miry clay, they shall *mingle* themselves with the seed of men: but they shall not cleave one to another, even as iron is not mixed with clay (*Daniel 2:43*).

And it came to pass, when he had been there a long time, that Abimelech king of the Philistines looked out at a window, and saw, and, behold, Isaac was sporting with Rebekah his wife. And Abimelech called Isaac, and said, Behold, of a *surety* she is thy wife: and how saidst thou, She is my sister? And Isaac said unto him, Because I said, Lest I die for her. And Abimelech said, What is this thou hast done unto us? one of the people might lightly have lien with thy wife, and thou shouldest have brought guiltiness upon us (*Genesis 26:8-10*).

Come, let us make our father drink wine, and we will *lie with him*, that we may preserve seed of our father (*Genesis 19:32*).

And they called unto Lot, and said unto him, Where are the men which came in to thee this night? bring them out unto us, that we may *know* them. Lot went out at the door unto them, and shut the door after him, And said, I pray you, brethren, do not so wickedly. Behold now, I have two daughters which have not *know[n]* man; let me, I pray you, bring them out unto you, and do ye to them as is good in your eyes: only unto these men do nothing; for therefore came they under the shadow of my roof (*Genesis 19:5-8*).

5d.   Verily I say unto you, This generation shall not pass, till all these things be fulfilled. *Heaven* and earth shall pass away, but my words shall not pass away. But of that day and hour knoweth no man, no, not the angels of heaven, but my Father only. But as the days of Noah were, so shall also the coming of the Son of man be. For as in the days that were before the flood they were eating and drinking, marrying and giving in marriage, until the day that Noah entered into the ark, And knew not until the flood came, and took them all away; so shall also the coming of the Son of man be. (*Matthew 24:34-39*)

Thus the *heaven[s]* and the earth were finished, and all the host of them (*Genesis 2:1*).

These are the generations of the *heaven[s]* and of the earth when they were created, in the day that the LORD God made the earth and the heavens (*Genesis 2:4*).

Hear, O *heaven[s]*, and give ear, O earth: for the LORD hath spoken, I have nourished and brought up children, and they have rebelled against me (*Isaiah 1:2*).

Hath a nation changed their gods, which are yet no gods? but my people have changed their glory for that which doth not profit. Be astonished, O ye *heaven*[s], at this, and be horribly afraid, be ye very desolate, saith the Lord. 13 For my people have committed two evils; they have forsaken me the fountain of living waters, and hewed them out cisterns, broken cisterns, that can hold no water (*Jeremiah 2:11-13*).

Then said the Jews, Forty and six years was this temple in building, and wilt thou *rear* it up in three days (*John 2:20*)?

But the angel said unto him, Fear not, Zacharias: for thy prayer is heard; and thy wife Elisabeth shall *bear* thee a son, and thou shalt call his name John (*Luke 1:13*).

And she shall *bring forth* a son, and thou shalt call his name JESUS: for he shall save his people from their sins (*Matthew 1:21*).

Now these are the generations of the sons of Noah, Shem, Ham, and Japheth: and unto them were sons *born* after the flood (*Genesis 10:1*).

And when her days to *be delivered* were fulfilled, behold, there were twins in her womb (*Genesis 25:24*).

And his daughter in law, Phinehas' wife, was with child, near to *be delivered*: and when she heard the tidings that the ark of God was taken, and that her father in law and her husband were dead, she bowed herself and travailed; for her pains came upon her (*1 Samuel 4:19*).

A woman when she is in travail hath sorrow, because her hour is come: but as soon as she is delivered of the child, she remembereth no more the anguish, for joy that a man is born into the world (*John 16:21*).

6a.   There were giants *in the earth* in those days; and also after that, when the sons of God came in unto the daughters of men, and they bare children to them, the same became mighty men which were of old, men of renown (*Genesis 6:4*).

And Cush begat Nimrod: he began to be a mighty one *in the earth* (*Genesis 10:8*).

And God sent me before you to preserve you a posterity *in the earth*, and to save your lives by a great deliverance (*Genesis 45:7*).

Now therefore thus shalt thou say unto my servant David, Thus saith the LORD of hosts, I took thee from the sheepcote, even from following the sheep, that thou shouldest be ruler over my people Israel: And I have been with thee whithersoever thou hast walked, and have cut off all thine enemies from before thee, and have made thee a name like the name of the great men that are *in the earth*... And it shall come to pass, when thy days be expired that thou must go to be with thy fathers, that I will raise up thy seed after thee, which shall be of thy sons; and I will establish his kingdom... But I will settle him in mine house and in my kingdom for ever: and his throne shall be established for evermore (*1 Chronicles 17:7-8, 11, 14*).

Behold, this is the joy of his way, and *out of the earth* shall others grow. Behold, God will not cast away a perfect man, neither will he help the evil doers (*Job 8:19-20*).

Hear, O heavens, and give ear, O *earth*: for the LORD hath spoken, I have nourished and brought up children, and they have rebelled against me (*Isaiah 1:2*).

And when a stranger shall sojourn with thee, and will keep the passover to the LORD, let all his males be circumcised, and then let him come near and keep it; and he shall be as one that is born in the land: for no uncircumcised person shall eat thereof. One law shall be to him that is *homeborn*, and unto the stranger that sojourneth among you. Thus did all the children of

Israel; as the LORD commanded Moses and Aaron, so did they. And it came to pass the selfsame day, that the LORD did bring the children of Israel out of the land of Egypt by their armies (*Exodus 12:48-51*).

And the angel of the LORD said unto her, Behold, thou art with child, and shalt *bear* a son, and shalt call his name Ishmael; because the LORD hath heard thy affliction (*Genesis 16:11*).

But the angel said unto him, Fear not, Zacharias: for thy prayer is heard; and thy wife Elisabeth shall *bear* thee a son, and thou shalt call his name John (*Luke 1:13*).

Unto the woman he said, I will greatly multiply thy sorrow and thy conception; in sorrow thou shalt *bring forth* children; and thy desire shall be to thy husband, and he shall rule over thee (*Genesis 3:16*).

And she shall *bring forth* a son, and thou shalt call his name JESUS: for he shall save his people from their sins. Now all this was done, that it might be fulfilled which was spoken of the Lord by the prophet, saying, Behold, a virgin shall be with child, and shall *bring forth* a son, and they shall call his name Emmanuel, which being interpreted is, God with us. Then Joseph being raised from sleep did as the angel of the Lord had bidden him, and took unto him his wife: And knew her not till she had brought forth her firstborn son: and he called his name JESUS (*Matthew 1:21-25*).

Now these are the generations of the sons of Noah, Shem, Ham, and Japheth: and unto them were sons *born* after the flood (*Genesis 10:1*).

And Abraham was an hundred years old, when his son Isaac was born unto him. And Sarah said, God hath made me to laugh, so that all that hear will laugh with me. And she said, Who would have said unto Abraham, that Sarah should have given children suck? for I have *born* him a son in his old age (*Genesis 21:5-7*).

And Jacob begat Joseph the husband of Mary, of whom was *born* Jesus, who is called Christ (*Matthew 1:16*).

And when her days to *be delivered* were fulfilled, behold, there were twins in her womb (*Genesis 25:24*).

And his daughter in law, Phinehas' wife, was with child, near to *be delivered*: and when she heard the tidings that the ark of God was taken, and that her father in law and her husband were dead, she bowed herself and travailed; for her pains came upon her (*1 Samuel 4:19*).

A woman when she is in travail hath sorrow, because her hour is come: but as soon as she is delivered of the child, she remembereth no more the anguish, for joy that a man is born into the world (*John 16:21*).

6b. There were giants *in the earth* in those days; and also after that, when the sons of God came in unto the daughters of men, and they bare children to them, the same became mighty men which were of old, men of renown (*Genesis 6:4*).

And Cush begat Nimrod: he began to be a mighty one *in the earth* (*Genesis 10:8*).

And God sent me before you to preserve you a posterity *in the earth*, and to save your lives by a great deliverance (*Genesis 45:7*).

Now therefore thus shalt thou say unto my servant David, Thus saith the LORD of hosts, I took thee from the sheepcote, even from following the sheep, that thou shouldest be ruler over my people Israel: And I have been with thee whithersoever thou hast walked, and have cut off all thine enemies from before thee, and have made thee a name like the name of the great men that are *in the earth*... And it shall come to pass, when thy days be expired that thou must go to be with thy fathers, that I will raise up thy seed after thee, which shall be of thy sons; and I will establish his kingdom... But I will settle him in mine house and in my kingdom for ever: and his throne shall be established for evermore (*1 Chronicles 17:7-8, 11, 14*).

Behold, this is the joy of his way, and *out of the earth* shall others grow. Behold, God will not cast away a perfect man, neither will he help the evil doers (*Job 8:19-20*).

Hear, O heavens, and give ear, O *earth*: for the LORD hath spoken, I have nourished and brought up children, and they have rebelled against me (*Isaiah 1:2*).

Say ye unto your brethren, Ammi; and to your sisters, Ruhamah. Plead with your mother, plead: for she is not my wife, neither am I her husband: let her therefore put away her whoredoms out of her sight, and her adulteries from between her breasts; Lest I strip her naked, and set her as in the day that she was born, and make her as a wilderness, and set her like a dry *land*, and slay her with thirst. And I will not have mercy upon her children; for they be the children of whoredoms. For their mother hath played the harlot: she that conceived them hath done shamefully: for she said, I will go after my lovers, that give me my bread and my water, my wool and my flax, mine oil and my drink (*Hosea 2:1-5*).

And I will make thee exceeding fruitful, and I will make *nations* of thee, and kings shall come out of thee (*Genesis 17:6*).

And in thy seed shall all the *nations* of the earth be blessed; because thou hast obeyed my voice (*Genesis 22:18*).

And Isaac entreated the LORD for his wife, because she was barren: and the LORD was entreated of him, and Rebekah his wife conceived. And the children struggled together within her; and she said, If it be so, why am I thus? And she went to inquire of the LORD. And the LORD said unto her, Two *nations* are in thy womb, and two manner of people shall be separated from thy bowels; and the one people shall be stronger than the other people; and the elder shall serve the younger. And when her days to be delivered were fulfilled, behold, there were twins in her womb (*Genesis 25:21-24*).

And I will bless her, and give thee a son also of her: yea, I will bless her, and she shall be *a mother* of nations; kings of people shall be of her (*Genesis 17:16*).

As for me, behold, my covenant is with thee, and thou shalt be a *father* of many nations (*Genesis 17:4*).

And think not to say within yourselves, We have Abraham to our *father*: for I say unto you, that God is able of these stones to raise up children unto Abraham (*Matthew 3:9*).

Have we not all one *father*? hath not one God created us? why do we deal treacherously every man against his brother, by profaning the covenant of our fathers (*Malachi 2:10*)?

And Adam knew his wife again; and she bare *a son*, and called his name Seth: For God, said she, hath appointed me another seed instead of Abel, whom Cain slew (*Genesis 4:25*).

And the LORD said unto Abram, after that Lot was separated from him, Lift up now thine eyes, and look from the place where thou art northward, and southward, and eastward, and westward: For all the land which thou seest, to thee will I give it, and to thy seed for ever. And I will *make* thy seed as the dust of the earth: so that if a man can number the dust of the earth, then shall thy seed also be numbered (*Genesis 13:14-16*).

And the angel of the LORD said unto her, Behold, thou art with child, and shalt *bear* a son, and shalt call his name Ishmael; because the LORD hath heard thy affliction (*Genesis 16:11*).

But the angel said unto him, Fear not, Zacharias: for thy prayer is heard; and thy wife Elisabeth shall *bear* thee a son, and thou shalt call his name John (*Luke 1:13*).

Unto the woman he said, I will greatly multiply thy sorrow and thy conception; in sorrow thou shalt *bring forth* children; and thy desire shall be to thy husband, and he shall rule over thee (*Genesis 3:16*).

And she shall *bring forth* a son, and thou shalt call his name JESUS: for he shall save his people from their sins. Now all this was done, that it might be fulfilled which was spoken of the Lord by the prophet, saying, Behold, a virgin shall be with child, and shall *bring forth* a son, and they shall call his name Emmanuel, which being interpreted is, God with us. Then Joseph being raised from sleep did as the angel of the Lord had bidden him, and took unto him his wife: And knew her not till she had brought forth her firstborn son: and he called his name JESUS (*Matthew 1:21-25*).

Now these are the generations of the sons of Noah, Shem, Ham, and Japheth: and unto them were sons *born* after the flood (*Genesis 10:1*).

And Abraham was an hundred years old, when his son Isaac was born unto him. And Sarah said, God hath made me to laugh, so that all that hear will laugh with me. And she said, Who would have said unto Abraham, that Sarah should have given children suck? for I have *born* him a son in his old age (*Genesis 21:5-7*).

And Jacob begat Joseph the husband of Mary, of whom was *born* Jesus, who is called Christ (*Matthew 1:16*).

And when her days to *be delivered* were fulfilled, behold, there were twins in her womb (*Genesis 25:24*).

And his daughter in law, Phinehas' wife, was with child, near to *be delivered*: and when she heard the tidings that the ark of God was taken, and that her father in law and her husband were dead, she bowed herself and travailed; for her pains came upon her (*1 Samuel 4:19*).

A woman when she is in travail hath sorrow, because her hour is come: but as soon as she is delivered of the child, she remembereth no more the anguish, for joy that a man is born into the world (*John 16:21*).

6c. There were giants *in the earth* in those days; and also after that, when the sons of God came in unto the daughters of men, and they bare children to them, the same became mighty men which were of old, men of renown (*Genesis 6:4*).

And Cush begat Nimrod: he began to be a mighty one *in the earth* (*Genesis 10:8*).

And God sent me before you to preserve you a posterity *in the earth*, and to save your lives by a great deliverance (*Genesis 45:7*).

Now therefore thus shalt thou say unto my servant David, Thus saith the LORD of hosts, I took thee from the sheepcote, even from following the sheep, that thou shouldest be ruler over my people Israel: And I have been with thee whithersoever thou hast walked, and have cut off all thine enemies from before thee, and have made thee a name like the name of the great men that are *in the earth* ... And it shall come to pass, when thy days be expired that thou must go to be with thy fathers, that I will raise up thy seed after thee, which shall be of thy sons; and I will establish his kingdom... But I will settle him in mine house and in my kingdom for ever: and his throne shall be established for evermore (*1 Chronicles 17:7-8, 11, 14*).

Behold, this is the joy of his way, and *out of the earth* shall others grow. Behold, God will not cast away a perfect man, neither will he help the evil doers (*Job 8:19-20*).

Hear, O heavens, and give ear, O *earth*: for the LORD hath spoken, I have nourished and brought up children, and they have rebelled against me (*Isaiah 1:2*).

Now the LORD had said unto Abram, Get thee out of thy country, and from thy *kindred*, and from thy father's house, unto a land that I will show thee: And I will make of thee a great nation, and I will bless thee, and make thy name great; and thou shalt be a blessing (*Genesis 12:1-2*).

And the angel of the LORD said unto her, Behold, thou art with child, and shalt *bear* a son, and shalt call his name Ishmael; because the LORD hath heard thy affliction (*Genesis 16:11*).

But the angel said unto him, Fear not, Zacharias: for thy prayer is heard; and thy wife Elisabeth shall *bear* thee a son, and thou shalt call his name John (*Luke 1:13*).

Unto the woman he said, I will greatly multiply thy sorrow and thy conception; in sorrow thou shalt *bring forth* children; and thy desire shall be to thy husband, and he shall rule over thee (*Genesis 3:16*).

And she shall *bring forth* a son, and thou shalt call his name JESUS: for he shall save his people from their sins. Now all this was done, that it might be fulfilled which was spoken of the Lord by the prophet, saying, Behold, a virgin shall be with child, and shall *bring forth* a son, and they shall call his name Emmanuel, which being interpreted is, God with us. Then Joseph being raised from sleep did as the angel of the Lord had bidden him, and took unto him his wife: And knew her not till she had brought forth her firstborn son: and he called his name JESUS (*Matthew 1:21-25*).

Now these are the generations of the sons of Noah, Shem, Ham, and Japheth: and unto them were sons *born* after the flood (*Genesis 10:1*).

And Abraham was an hundred years old, when his son Isaac was born unto him. And Sarah said, God hath made me to laugh, so that all that hear will laugh with me. And she said, Who would have said unto Abraham, that Sarah should have given children suck? for I have *born* him a son in his old age (*Genesis 21:5-7*).

And Jacob begat Joseph the husband of Mary, of whom was *born* Jesus, who is called Christ (*Matthew 1:16*).

And when her days to *be delivered* were fulfilled, behold, there were twins in her womb (*Genesis 25:24*).

And his daughter in law, Phinehas' wife, was with child, near to *be delivered*: and when she heard the tidings that the ark of God was taken, and that her father in law and her husband were dead, she bowed herself and travailed; for her pains came upon her (*1 Samuel 4:19*).

A woman when she is in travail hath sorrow, because her hour is come: but as soon as she is delivered of the child, she remembereth no more the anguish, for joy that a man is born into the world (*John 16:21*).

7. Is it not yet a very little while, and Lebanon shall be turned into a fruitful field, and the fruitful field shall be esteemed as a forest? And in that day shall the deaf hear the words of the book, and the eyes of the blind hall see out of obscurity, and out of darkness. The meek also shall increase their joy in the LORD, and the poor among men shall rejoice in the Holy One of Israel. For the terrible one is *brought to nought*, and the scorner is consumed, and all that watch for iniquity are cut off: That make a man an offender for a word, and lay a snare for him that reproveth in the gate, and turn aside the just for a *thing of nought*. Therefore thus saith the LORD, who

redeemed Abraham, concerning the house of Jacob, Jacob shall not now be ashamed, neither shall his face now wax pale. But when he seeth his children, the work of mine hands, in the midst of him, they shall sanctify my name, and sanctify the Holy One of Jacob, and shall fear the God of Israel (*Isaiah 29:17-23*).

And Solomon made affinity with Pharaoh king of Egypt, and took Pharaoh's daughter, and brought her into the city of David, until he had made *an end* of building his own house, and the house of the LORD, and the wall of Jerusalem round about (*1 Kings 3:1*).

For the children of Ammon and Moab stood up against the inhabitants of mount Seir, utterly to slay and destroy them: and when they had made *an end* of the inhabitants of Seir, every one helped to destroy another. And when Judah came toward the watch tower in the wilderness, they looked unto the multitude, and, behold, they were dead bodies fallen to the earth, and none escaped (*2 Chronicles 20:23-24*).

And he said, What hast thou done? the voice of thy brother's *blood* crieth unto me from the ground (*Genesis 4:10*).

And they journeyed from Bethel; and there was but a little way to come to Ephrath: and Rachel travailed, and she had hard labour. And it came to pass, when she was in hard labor, that the midwife said unto her, Fear not; thou shalt have this son also. And it came to pass, *as her soul was in departing, (for she died)* that she called his name Ben-oni: but his father called him Benjamin. And Rachel died, and was buried in the way to Ephrath, which is Bethlehem (*Genesis 35:16-19*).

The LORD hath opened his armory, and hath brought forth the weapons of his indignation: for this is the work of the LORD God of hosts in the land of the Chaldeans. Come against her from the utmost border, open her storehouses: cast her up as heaps, and destroy her utterly: *let nothing of her be left* (*Jeremiah 50:25-26*).

8a.   And Caleb stilled the people before Moses, and said, Let us go up at once, and possess it; for we are well able to overcome it. But the men that went up with him said, We be not able to go up against the people; for they are stronger than we. And they brought up an

157

evil report of the land which they had searched unto the children of Israel, saying, The land, through which we have gone to search it, is a land that eateth up the inhabitants thereof; and all the people that we saw in it are men of a great stature. And there we saw the *giants*, the sons of Anak, which come of the *giants*: and we were in our own sight as grasshoppers, and so we were in their sight (*Numbers 13:30-33*).

For the LORD will have mercy on Jacob, and will yet choose Israel, and set them in their own land: and the strangers shall be joined with them, and they shall cleave to the house of Jacob. And the people shall take them, and bring them to their place: and the house of Israel shall possess them in the land of the LORD for servants and handmaids: and they shall take them captives, whose captives they were; and they shall rule over their oppressors. And it shall come to pass in the day that the LORD shall give thee rest from thy sorrow, and from thy fear, and from the hard bondage wherein thou wast made to serve, That thou shalt take up this proverb against the king of Babylon, and say, How hath the oppressor ceased! the golden city ceased! The LORD hath broken the staff of the wicked, and the scepter of the rulers. He who smote the people in wrath with a continual stroke, he that ruled the nations in anger, is persecuted, and none hindereth. The whole earth is at rest, and is quiet: they break forth into singing. Yea, the fir trees rejoice at thee, and the cedars of Lebanon, saying, Since thou art laid down, no *feller* is come up against us. (*Isaiah 14:1-8*)

8b.   And Caleb stilled the people before Moses, and said, Let us go up at once, and possess it; for we are well able to overcome it. But the men that went up with him said, We be not able to go up against the people; for they are stronger than we. And they brought up an evil report of the land which they had searched unto the children of Israel, saying, The land, through which we have gone to search it, is a land that eateth up the inhabitants thereof; and all the people that we saw in it are men of a great stature. And there we saw the *giants*, the sons of Anak, which come of the *giants*: and we were in our own sight as grasshoppers, and so we were in their sight (*Numbers 13:30-33*).

And Abraham said, Because I thought, Surely the fear of God is not in this place; and they will slay me for my wife's sake. And yet indeed she is my sister; she is the *daughter* of my father, but not the *daughter* of my mother; and she became my wife (*Genesis 20:11-12*).

And Leah said, God hath endued me with a good dowry; now will my husband dwell with me, because I have born him six sons: and she called his name Zebulun. And afterwards she bare a *daughter*, and called her name Dinah (*Genesis 30:20-21*).

And David said to Abishai, and to all his servants, Behold, my son, which came *forth of* my bowels, seeketh my life: how much more now may this Benjamite do it? let him alone, and let him curse; for the LORD hath bidden him (*2 Samuel 16:11*).

As he came *forth of* his mother's womb, naked shall he return to go as he came, and shall take nothing of his labour, which he may carry away in his hand (*Ecclesiastes 5:15*).

The sorrows of a travailing woman shall come upon him: he is an unwise son; for he should not stay long in the place of the breaking *forth of* children (*Hosea 13:13*).

And Isaac entreated the LORD for his wife, because she was barren: and the LORD was entreated of him, and Rebekah his wife conceived. And the children struggled together *within* her; and she said, If it be so, why am I thus? And she went to inquire of the LORD. And the LORD said unto her, Two nations are in thy womb, and two manner of people shall be separated from thy bowels; and the one people shall be stronger than the other people; and the elder shall serve the younger. And when her days to be delivered were fulfilled, behold, there were twins in her womb (*Genesis 25:21-24*).

Now Sarai Abram's wife bare him no children: and she had a handmaid, an Egyptian, whose name was Hagar. And Sarai said unto Abram, Behold now, the LORD hath restrained me from bearing: I pray thee, go in unto my maid; it may be that I may *obtain children* by her. And Abram hearkened to the voice of Sarai. And Sarai Abram's wife took Hagar her maid the Egyptian, after Abram had dwelt ten years in the land of Canaan, and gave her to her husband Abram to be his wife (*Genesis 16:1-3*).

And the LORD said unto Abram, after that Lot was separated from him, Lift up now thine eyes, and look from the place where thou art northward, and southward, and eastward, and westward: For all the land which thou seest, to thee will I give it, and to thy seed for ever. And I will *make* thy seed as the dust of the earth: so that if a man can number the dust of the earth, then shall thy seed also be numbered (*Genesis 13:14-16*).

And when thy days be fulfilled, and thou shalt sleep with thy fathers, I will *set up* thy seed after thee, which shall proceed out of thy bowels, and I will establish his kingdom (*2 Samuel 7:12*).

Nevertheless for David's sake did the LORD his God give him a lamp in Jerusalem, to *set up* his son after him, and to establish Jerusalem (*1 Kings 15:4*).

And the LORD said unto Abram, after that Lot was separated from him, Lift up now thine eyes, and look from the place where thou art northward, and southward, and eastward, and westward: For all the land which thou seest, to thee will I give it, and to thy seed for ever. And I will *make* thy seed as the dust of the earth: so that if a man can number the dust of the earth, then shall thy seed also be numbered (*Genesis 13:14-16*).

And the angel of the LORD said unto her, Behold, thou art with child, and shalt *bear* a son, and shalt call his name Ishmael; because the LORD hath heard thy affliction (*Genesis 16:11*).

But the angel said unto him, Fear not, Zacharias: for thy prayer is heard; and thy wife Elisabeth shall *bear* thee a son, and thou shalt call his name John (*Luke 1:13*).

Unto the woman he said, I will greatly multiply thy sorrow and thy conception; in sorrow thou shalt *bring forth* children; and thy desire shall be to thy husband, and he shall rule over thee (*Genesis 3:16*).

And she shall *bring forth* a son, and thou shalt call his name JESUS: for he shall save his people from their sins. Now all this was done, that it might be fulfilled which was spoken of the Lord by the prophet, saying, Behold, a virgin shall be with child, and shall *bring forth* a son, and they shall call his name Emmanuel, which being interpreted is, God with us. Then Joseph being raised from sleep did as the angel of the Lord had bidden him, and took unto him his wife: And knew her not till she had brought forth her firstborn son: and he called his name JESUS (*Matthew 1:21-25*).

And Joseph brought them out from between his knees, and he bowed himself with his face to the earth. And Joseph took them both, Ephraim in his right hand toward Israel's left hand, and Manasseh in his left hand toward Israel's right hand, and brought them near unto him. And Israel stretched out his right hand, and laid it upon Ephraim's head, who was the younger, and his left hand upon Manasseh's head, guiding his hands wittingly; for Manasseh was the firstborn. And he blessed Joseph, and said, God, before whom my fathers Abraham and Isaac did walk, the God which fed me all my life long unto this day, The Angel which redeemed me from all evil, bless the lads; and let my name be named on them, and the name of my fathers Abraham and Isaac; and let them *grow* into a multitude in the midst of the earth (*Genesis 48:12-16*).

As thou knowest not what is the way of the spirit, nor how the bones do *grow* in the womb of her that is with child: even so thou knowest not the works of God who maketh all (*Ecclesiastes 11:5*).

But David took not the number of them from twenty years old and under: because the LORD had said he would *increase* Israel like to the stars of the heavens (*1 Chronicles 27:23*).

And the angel of the LORD said unto her, Behold, thou art with child, and shalt *bear* a son, and shalt call his name Ishmael; because the LORD hath heard thy affliction (*Genesis 16:11*).

But the angel said unto him, Fear not, Zacharias: for thy prayer is heard; and thy wife Elisabeth shall *bear* thee a son, and thou shalt call his name John (*Luke 1:13*).

Unto the woman he said, I will greatly multiply thy sorrow and thy conception; in sorrow thou shalt *bring forth* children; and thy desire shall be to thy husband, and he shall rule over thee (*Genesis 3:16*).

And she shall *bring forth* a son, and thou shalt call his name JESUS: for he shall save his people from their sins. Now all this was done,

that it might be fulfilled which was spoken of the Lord by the prophet, saying, Behold, a virgin shall be with child, and shall *bring forth* a son, and they shall call his name Emmanuel, which being interpreted is, God with us. Then Joseph being raised from sleep did as the angel of the Lord had bidden him, and took unto him his wife: And knew her not till she had brought forth her firstborn son: and he called his name JESUS (*Matthew 1:21-25*).

Now these are the generations of the sons of Noah, Shem, Ham, and Japheth: and unto them were sons *born* after the flood (*Genesis 10:1*).

And Abraham was an hundred years old, when his son Isaac was born unto him. And Sarah said, God hath made me to laugh, so that all that hear will laugh with me. And she said, Who would have said unto Abraham, that Sarah should have given children suck? for I have *born* him a son in his old age (*Genesis 21:5-7*).

And when her days to *be delivered* were fulfilled, behold, there were twins in her womb (*Genesis 25:24*).

And his daughter in law, Phinehas' wife, was with child, near to *be delivered*: and when she heard the tidings that the ark of God was taken, and that her father in law and her husband were dead, she bowed herself and travailed; for her pains came upon her (*1 Samuel 4:19*).

A woman when she is in travail hath sorrow, because her hour is come: but as soon as she is delivered of the child, she remembereth no more the anguish, for joy that a man is born into the world (*John 16:21*).

9. And he gave Joshua the son of Nun a charge, and said, Be strong and of a good courage: for thou shalt bring the children of Israel into the land which I sware unto them: and I will be with thee. And it came to pass, when Moses had made an end of writing the words of this law in a book, until they *were finished*, That Moses commanded the Levites, which bare the ark of the covenant of the LORD, saying, Take this book of the law, and put it in the side of the ark of the covenant of the LORD your God, that it may be there for a witness against thee (*Deuteronomy 31:23-26*).

Knowest thou the time when the wild goats of the rock bring forth? or canst thou mark when the hinds do calve? Canst thou number the months that they *fulfill*? or knowest thou the time when they bring forth? They bow themselves, they bring forth their young ones, they cast out their sorrows (*Job 39:1-3*).

And when her days to be delivered were *fulfill[ed]*, behold, there were twins in her womb (*Genesis 25:24*).

And it came to pass, that in the morning, behold, it was Leah: and he said to Laban, What is this thou hast done unto me? did not I serve with thee for Rachel? wherefore then hast thou beguiled me? And Laban said, It must not be so done in our country, to give the younger before the firstborn. *Fulfill* her week, and we will give thee this also for the service which thou shalt serve with me yet seven other years. And Jacob did so, and *fulfill[ed]* her week: and he gave him Rachel his daughter to wife also. And Laban gave to Rachel his daughter Bilhah his handmaid to be her maid. And he went in also unto Rachel, and he loved also Rachel more than Leah, and served with him yet seven other years (*Genesis 29:25-30*).

When he is about *to fill* his belly, God shall cast the fury of his wrath upon him, and shall rain it upon him while he is eating (*Job 20:23*).

If the clouds *be full of* rain, they empty themselves upon the earth: and if the tree fall toward the south, or toward the north, in the place where the tree falleth, there it shall be. He that observeth the wind shall not sow; and he that regardeth the clouds shall not reap. As thou knowest not what is the way of the spirit, nor how the bones do grow in the womb of her that is with child: even so thou knowest not the works of God who maketh all. In the morning sow thy seed, and in the evening withhold not thine hand: for thou knowest not whether shall prosper, either this or that, or whether they both shall be alike good (*Ecclesiastes 11:3-6*).

From men which are thy hand, O Lord, from men of the world, which have their portion in this life, and whose belly thou fillest with thy hid treasure: they are *full of* children, and leave the rest of their substance to their babes (*Psalm 17:14*).

As thou knowest not what is the way of the spirit, nor how the bones do grow in the womb of *her that is with child*: even so thou knowest not the works of God who maketh all (*Ecclesiastes 11:5*).

Now the birth of Jesus Christ was on this wise: When as his mother Mary was espoused to Joseph, before they came together, *she was found with child* of the Holy Ghost (*Matthew 1:18*).

10a.   And the LORD spake unto Moses and unto Aaron, saying, Every man of the children of Israel shall pitch by his own standard, with the ensign of their father's house: far off about the tabernacle of the congregation shall they pitch. And on the east side toward the rising of the sun shall they of the standard of the camp of Judah pitch throughout their armies: and Nahshon the son of Amminadab shall be captain of the children of Judah. And his *host*, and those that were numbered of them, were threescore and fourteen thousand and six hundred (*Numbers 2:1-4*).

And when Saul saw David go forth against the Philistine, he said unto Abner, the captain of the *host*, Abner, whose son is this youth? And Abner said, As thy soul liveth, O king, I cannot tell. And the king said, Inquire thou whose son the stripling is. (*1 Samuel 17:55-56*)

Fear took hold upon them there, and *pain*, as of a woman in travail (*Psalm 48:6*).

And the angel of the LORD said unto her, Behold, thou art with child, and shalt *bear* a son, and shalt call his name Ishmael; because the LORD hath heard thy affliction (*Genesis 16:11*).

But the angel said unto him, Fear not, Zacharias: for thy prayer is heard; and thy wife Elisabeth shall *bear* thee a son, and thou shalt call his name John (*Luke 1:13*).

Unto the woman he said, I will greatly multiply thy sorrow and thy conception; in sorrow thou shalt *bring forth* children; and thy desire shall be to thy husband, and he shall rule over thee (*Genesis 3:16*).

And she shall *bring forth* a son, and thou shalt call his name JESUS: for he shall save his people from their sins. Now all this was done,

that it might be fulfilled which was spoken of the Lord by the prophet, saying, Behold, a virgin shall be with child, and shall *bring forth* a son, and they shall call his name Emmanuel, which being interpreted is, God with us. Then Joseph being raised from sleep did as the angel of the Lord had bidden him, and took unto him his wife: And knew her not till she had brought forth her firstborn son: and he called his name JESUS (*Matthew 1:21-25*).

Now these are the generations of the sons of Noah, Shem, Ham, and Japheth: and unto them were sons *born* after the flood (*Genesis 10:1*).

And Abraham was an hundred years old, when his son Isaac was born unto him. And Sarah said, God hath made me to laugh, so that all that hear will laugh with me. And she said, Who would have said unto Abraham, that Sarah should have given children suck? for I have *born* him a son in his old age (*Genesis 21:5-7*).

And when her days to *be delivered* were fulfilled, behold, there were twins in her womb (*Genesis 25:24*).

And his daughter in law, Phinehas' wife, was with child, near to *be delivered*: and when she heard the tidings that the ark of God was taken, and that her father in law and her husband were dead, she bowed herself and travailed; for her pains came upon her (*1 Samuel 4:19*).

A woman when she is in travail hath sorrow, because her hour is come: but as soon as she is delivered of the child, she remembereth no more the anguish, for joy that a man is born into the world (*John 16:21*).

11a. <u>These are the *generations* of the heavens and of the earth</u> when they were created, in the day that the LORD God made the earth and the heavens, And every plant of the field before it was in the earth, and every herb of the field before it grew: for the LORD God had not caused it to rain upon the earth, and there was not a man to till the ground. But there went up a mist from the earth, and watered the whole face of the ground. And the LORD God formed man of the dust of the ground, and breathed into his nostrils the breath of life; and man became a living soul (*Genesis 2:4-7*).

This is the book of the *generations* of Adam. In the day that God created man, in the likeness of God made he him; Male and female created he them; and blessed them, and called their name Adam, in the day when they were created. And Adam lived an hundred and thirty years, and begat a son in his own likeness, after his image; and called his name Seth: And the days of Adam after he had begotten Seth were eight hundred years: and he begat sons and daughters: And all the days that Adam lived were nine hundred and thirty years: and he died (*Genesis 5:1-5*).

These are the *generations* of Noah: Noah was a just man and perfect in his generations, and Noah walked with God. And Noah begat three sons, Shem, Ham, and Japheth (*Genesis 6:9, 10*).

Now these are the *generations* of the sons of Noah, Shem, Ham, and Japheth: and unto them were sons born after the flood. The sons of Japheth; Gomer, and Magog, and Madai, and Javan, and Tubal, and Meshech, and Tiras...... And the sons of Ham; Cush, and Mizraim, and Phut, and Canaan (*Genesis 10:1-6*).

These are the *generations* of Shem: Shem was an hundred years old, and begat Arphaxad two years after the flood (*Genesis 11:10*):

Now these are the *generations* of Terah: Terah begat Abram, Nahor, and Haran; and Haran begat Lot (*Genesis 11:27*).

Now these are the *generations* of Ishmael, Abraham's son, whom Hagar the Egyptian, Sarah's handmaid, bare unto Abraham: And these are the names of the sons of Ishmael, by their names, according to their generations: the firstborn of Ishmael, Nebajoth; and Kedar, and Adbeel, and Mibsam (*Genesis 25:12, 13*),

And these are the *generations* of Isaac, Abraham's son: Abraham begat Isaac: And Isaac was forty years old when he took Rebekah to wife, the daughter of Bethuel the Syrian of Padan-aram, the sister to Laban the Syrian. And Isaac entreated the LORD for his wife, because she was barren: and the LORD was entreated of him, and Rebekah his wife conceived. And the children struggled together within her; and she said, If it be so, why am I thus? And she went to inquire of the LORD. And the LORD said unto her, Two nations are in thy womb, and two manner of people shall be separated from thy bowels; and the one people shall be stronger than the other people; and the elder shall serve the younger. And when her days to be delivered were fulfilled, behold, there were twins in her womb. And the first came out red, all over like a hairy garment; and they called his name Esau. And after that came his brother out, and his hand took hold on Esau's heel; and his name was called Jacob: and Isaac was threescore years old when she bare them (*Genesis 25:19-26*).

Now these are the *generations* of Esau, who is Edom. Esau took his wives of the daughters of Canaan; Adah the daughter of Elon the Hittite, and Aholibamah the daughter of Anah the daughter of Zibeon the Hivite; And Bashemath Ishmael's daughter, sister of Nebajoth. And Adah bare to Esau Eliphaz; and Bashemath bare Reuel; And Aholibamah bare Jeush, and Jaalam, and Korah: these are the sons of Esau, which were born unto him in the land of Canaan (*Genesis 36:1-5*).

And these are the *generations* of Esau the father of the Edomites in mount Seir: These are the names of Esau's sons; Eliphaz the son of Adah the wife of Esau, Reuel the son of Bashemath the wife of Esau. (*Genesis 36:9*).

These are the *generations* of Jacob. Joseph, being seventeen years old, was feeding the flock with his brethren; and the lad was with the sons of Bilhah, and with the sons of Zilpah, his father's wives: and Joseph brought unto his father their evil report. Now Israel loved Joseph more than all his children, because he was the son of his old age: and he made him a coat of many colors (*Genesis 37:2,3*).

Now these are the *generations* of Pharez: Pharez begat Hezron (*Ruth 4:18*),

And Jacob begat Joseph the husband of Mary, of whom was born Jesus, who is called Christ. So all the *generations* from Abraham to David are fourteen generations; and from David until the carrying away into Babylon are fourteen generations; and from the carrying away into Babylon unto Christ are fourteen generations (*Matthew 1:16-17*).

And the angel of the LORD said unto her, Behold, thou art with child, and shalt *bear* a son, and shalt call his name Ishmael; because the LORD hath heard thy affliction (*Genesis 16:11*).

But the angel said unto him, Fear not, Zacharias: for thy prayer is heard; and thy wife Elisabeth shall *bear* thee a son, and thou shalt call his name John (*Luke 1:13*).

Unto the woman he said, I will greatly multiply thy sorrow and thy conception; in sorrow thou shalt *bring forth* children; and thy desire shall be to thy husband, and he shall rule over thee (*Genesis 3:16*).

And she shall *bring forth* a son, and thou shalt call his name JESUS: for he shall save his people from their sins. Now all this was done, that it might be fulfilled which was spoken of the Lord by the prophet, saying, Behold, a virgin shall be with child, and shall *bring forth* a son, and they shall call his name Emmanuel, which being interpreted is, God with us. Then Joseph being raised from sleep did as the angel of the Lord had bidden him, and took unto him his wife: And knew her not till she had brought forth her firstborn son: and he called his name JESUS (*Matthew 1:21-25*).

Now these are the generations of the sons of Noah, Shem, Ham, and Japheth: and unto them were sons *born* after the flood (*Genesis 10:1*).

And Abraham was an hundred years old, when his son Isaac was born unto him. And Sarah said, God hath made me to laugh, so that all that hear will laugh with me. And she said, Who would have said unto Abraham, that Sarah should have given children suck? for I have *born* him a son in his old age (*Genesis 21:5-7*).

And Jacob begat Joseph the husband of Mary, of whom was *born* Jesus, who is called Christ (*Matthew 1:16*).

And when her days to *be delivered* were fulfilled, behold, there were twins in her womb (*Genesis 25:24*).

And his daughter in law, Phinehas' wife, was with child, near to *be delivered*: and when she heard the tidings that the ark of God was taken, and that her father in law and her husband were dead,

she bowed herself and travailed; for her pains came upon her (*1 Samuel 4:19*).

A woman when she is in travail hath sorrow, because her hour is come: but as soon as she is delivered of the child, she remembereth no more the anguish, for joy that a man is born into the world (*John 16:21*).

Fear took hold upon them there, and *pain*, as of *a woman in travail* (*Psalm 48:6*).

11b. <u>These are the *generations* of the heavens and of the earth</u> when they were created, in the day that the LORD God made the earth and the heavens, And every plant of the field before it was in the earth, and every herb of the field before it grew: for the LORD God had not caused it to rain upon the earth, and there was not a man to till the ground. But there went up a mist from the earth, and watered the whole face of the ground. And the LORD God formed man of the dust of the ground, and breathed into his nostrils the breath of life; and man became a living soul (*Genesis 2:4-7*).

This is the book of the *generations* of Adam. In the day that God created man, in the likeness of God made he him; Male and female created he them; and blessed them, and called their name Adam, in the day when they were created. And Adam lived an hundred and thirty years, and begat a son in his own likeness, after his image; and called his name Seth: And the days of Adam after he had begotten Seth were eight hundred years: and he begat sons and daughters: And all the days that Adam lived were nine hundred and thirty years: and he died (*Genesis 5:1-5*).

<u>These are the *generations* of Noah</u>: Noah was a just man and perfect in his generations, and Noah walked with God. And Noah begat three sons, Shem, Ham, and Japheth (*Genesis 6:9, 10*).

Now <u>these are the *generations* of the sons of Noah, Shem, Ham, and Japheth</u>: and unto them were sons born after the flood. The sons of Japheth; Gomer, and Magog, and Madai, and Javan, and Tubal, and Meshech, and Tiras...... And the sons of Ham; Cush, and Mizraim, and Phut, and Canaan (*Genesis 10:1-6*).

These are the *generations* of Shem: Shem was an hundred years old, and begat Arphaxad two years after the flood (*Genesis 11:10*):

Now these are the *generations* of Terah: Terah begat Abram, Nahor, and Haran; and Haran begat Lot (*Genesis 11:27*).

Now these are the *generations* of Ishmael, Abraham's son, whom Hagar the Egyptian, Sarah's handmaid, bare unto Abraham: And these are the names of the sons of Ishmael, by their names, according to their generations: the firstborn of Ishmael, Nebajoth; and Kedar, and Adbeel, and Mibsam (*Genesis 25:12, 13*),

And these are the *generations* of Isaac, Abraham's son: Abraham begat Isaac: And Isaac was forty years old when he took Rebekah to wife, the daughter of Bethuel the Syrian of Padan-aram, the sister to Laban the Syrian. And Isaac entreated the LORD for his wife, because she was barren: and the LORD was entreated of him, and Rebekah his wife conceived. And the children struggled together within her; and she said, If it be so, why am I thus? And she went to inquire of the LORD. And the LORD said unto her, Two nations are in thy womb, and two manner of people shall be separated from thy bowels; and the one people shall be stronger than the other people; and the elder shall serve the younger. And when her days to be delivered were fulfilled, behold, there were twins in her womb. And the first came out red, all over like a hairy garment; and they called his name Esau. And after that came his brother out, and his hand took hold on Esau's heel; and his name was called Jacob: and Isaac was threescore years old when she bare them (*Genesis 25:19-26*).

Now these are the *generations* of Esau, who is Edom. Esau took his wives of the daughters of Canaan; Adah the daughter of Elon the Hittite, and Aholibamah the daughter of Anah the daughter of Zibeon the Hivite; And Bashemath Ishmael's daughter, sister of Nebajoth. And Adah bare to Esau Eliphaz; and Bashemath bare Reuel; And Aholibamah bare Jeush, and Jaalam, and Korah: these are the sons of Esau, which were born unto him in the land of Canaan (*Genesis 36:1-5*).

And these are the *generations* of Esau the father of the Edomites in mount Seir: These are the names of Esau's sons; Eliphaz the son of Adah the wife of Esau, Reuel the son of Bashemath the wife of Esau. (*Genesis 36:9*).

These are the *generations* of Jacob. Joseph, being seventeen years old, was feeding the flock with his brethren; and the lad was with the sons of Bilhah, and with the sons of Zilpah, his father's wives: and Joseph brought unto his father their evil report. Now Israel loved Joseph more than all his children, because he was the son of his old age: and he made him a coat of many colors (*Genesis 37:2,3*).

Now these are the *generations* of Pharez: Pharez begat Hezron (*Ruth 4:18*),

And Jacob begat Joseph the husband of Mary, of whom was born Jesus, who is called Christ. So all the *generations* from Abraham to David are fourteen generations; and from David until the carrying away into Babylon are fourteen generations; and from the carrying away into Babylon unto Christ are fourteen generations (*Matthew 1:16-17*).

And thou shalt take two onyx stones, and grave on them the names of the children of Israel: Six of their names on one stone, and the other six names of the rest on the other stone, according to their *birth* (*Exodus 28:9-10*).

Shall I bring to the *birth*, and not cause to bring forth? saith the LORD: shall I cause to bring forth, and shut the womb? saith thy God (*Isaiah 66:9*).

And when her days to be delivered were fulfilled, behold, there were twins in her *womb* (*Genesis 25:24*).

The sorrows of a travailing woman shall come upon him: he is an unwise son; for he should not stay long in the place of the *breaking forth* of children (*Hosea 13:13*).

And it came to pass, as he drew back his hand, that, behold, his brother came out: and she said, How hast thou *broken [breaking] forth*? this breach be upon thee: therefore his name was called Pharez (*Genesis 38:29*).

And Abram said, Behold, to me thou hast given no seed: and, lo, one born in my house is mine heir. And, behold, the word of the LORD came unto him, saying, This shall not be thine heir; but he that shall come *forth* out of thine own bowels shall be thine heir. And he brought him forth abroad, and said, Look now toward heaven, and tell the stars, if thou be able to number them: and he said unto him, So shall thy seed be (*Genesis 15:3-5*).

And the angel of the LORD said unto her, Behold, thou art with child, and shalt *bear* a son, and shalt call his name Ishmael; because the LORD hath heard thy affliction (*Genesis 16:11*).

But the angel said unto him, Fear not, Zacharias: for thy prayer is heard; and thy wife Elisabeth shall *bear* thee a son, and thou shalt call his name John (*Luke 1:13*).

Unto the woman he said, I will greatly multiply thy sorrow and thy conception; in sorrow thou shalt *bring forth* children; and thy desire shall be to thy husband, and he shall rule over thee (*Genesis 3:16*).

And she shall *bring forth* a son, and thou shalt call his name JESUS: for he shall save his people from their sins. Now all this was done, that it might be fulfilled which was spoken of the Lord by the prophet, saying, Behold, a virgin shall be with child, and shall *bring forth* a son, and they shall call his name Emmanuel, which being interpreted is, God with us. Then Joseph being raised from sleep did as the angel of the Lord had bidden him, and took unto him his wife: And knew her not till she had brought forth her firstborn son: and he called his name JESUS (*Matthew 1:21-25*).

Now these are the generations of the sons of Noah, Shem, Ham, and Japheth: and unto them were sons *born* after the flood (*Genesis 10:1*).

And Abraham was an hundred years old, when his son Isaac was born unto him. And Sarah said, God hath made me to laugh, so that all that hear will laugh with me. And she said, Who would have said unto Abraham, that Sarah should have given children suck? for I have *born* him a son in his old age (*Genesis 21:5-7*).

And Jacob begat Joseph the husband of Mary, of whom was *born* Jesus, who is called Christ (*Matthew 1:16*).

And when her days to *be delivered* were fulfilled, behold, there were twins in her womb (*Genesis 25:24*).

And his daughter in law, Phinehas' wife, was with child, near to *be delivered*: and when she heard the tidings that the ark of God was taken, and that her father in law and her husband were dead, she bowed herself and travailed; for her pains came upon her (*1 Samuel 4:19*).

A woman when she is in travail hath sorrow, because her hour is come: but as soon as she is delivered of the child, she remembereth no more the anguish, for joy that a man is born into the world (*John 16:21*).

Fear took hold upon them there, and *pain*, as of *a woman in travail* (*Psalm 48:6*).

12.   And to Seth, to him also there *was* born a son; and he called his name Enos: then began men to call upon the name of the LORD (*Genesis 4:26*).

And they smote all the souls that were therein with the edge of the sword, utterly destroying them: there was not any left *to breathe*: and he burnt Hazor with fire (*Joshua 11:11*).

And when her days *to be* delivered were fulfilled, behold, there were twins in her womb (*Genesis 25:24*).

And the angel of the LORD said unto her, Behold, thou art with child, and shalt *bear* a son, and shalt call his name Ishmael; because the LORD hath heard thy affliction (*Genesis 16:11*).

But the angel said unto him, Fear not, Zacharias: for thy prayer is heard; and thy wife Elisabeth shall *bear* thee a son, and thou shalt call his name John (*Luke 1:13*).

Unto the woman he said, I will greatly multiply thy sorrow and thy conception; in sorrow thou shalt *bring forth* children; and thy desire shall be to thy husband, and he shall rule over thee (*Genesis 3:16*).

And she shall *bring forth* a son, and thou shalt call his name JESUS: for he shall save his people from their sins. Now all this was done, that it might be fulfilled which was spoken of the Lord by the prophet, saying, Behold, a virgin shall be with child, and shall *bring forth* a son, and they shall call his name Emmanuel, which being interpreted is, God with us. Then Joseph being raised from sleep did as the angel of the Lord had bidden him, and took unto him his wife: And knew her not till she had brought forth her firstborn son: and he called his name JESUS (*Matthew 1:21-25*).

Now these are the generations of the sons of Noah, Shem, Ham, and Japheth: and unto them were sons *born* after the flood (*Genesis 10:1*).

And Abraham was an hundred years old, when his son Isaac was born unto him. And Sarah said, God hath made me to laugh, so that all that hear will laugh with me. And she said, Who would have said unto Abraham, that Sarah should have given children suck? for I have *born* him a son in his old age (*Genesis 21:5-7*).

And Jacob begat Joseph the husband of Mary, of whom was *born* Jesus, who is called Christ (*Matthew 1:16*).

And when her days to *be delivered* were fulfilled, behold, there were twins in her womb (*Genesis 25:24*).

And his daughter in law, Phinehas' wife, was with child, near to *be delivered*: and when she heard the tidings that the ark of God was taken, and that her father in law and her husband were dead, she bowed herself and travailed; for her pains came upon her (*1 Samuel 4:19*).

A woman when she is in travail hath sorrow, because her hour is come: but as soon as she is delivered of the child, she remembereth no more the anguish, for joy that a man is born into the world (*John 16:21*).

13a.   I beheld the earth, and, lo, it was *without form*, and void; and the heavens, and they had no light. I beheld the mountains, and, lo, they trembled, and all the hills moved lightly. I beheld, and, lo, there was no man, and all the birds of the heavens were fled. I beheld, and, lo, the fruitful place was a wilderness, and all the cities thereof were broken down at the presence of the LORD, and by his fierce anger. For thus hath the LORD said, The whole land shall be desolate; yet will I not make a full end. For this shall the earth mourn, and the heavens above be black: because I have spoken it, I have purposed it, and will not repent, neither will I turn back from it. The whole city shall flee for the noise of the horsemen and bowmen; they shall go into thickets, and climb up upon the rocks: every city shall be forsaken, and not a man dwell therein. And when thou art spoiled, what wilt thou do? Though thou clothest thyself with crimson, though thou deckest thee with ornaments of gold, though thou rentest thy face with painting, in vain shalt thou make thyself fair; thy lovers will despise thee, they will seek thy life. *For I have heard a voice as of a woman in travail,* and the anguish as of her that bringeth forth her first child, the voice of the daughter of Zion, that bewaileth herself, that spreadeth her hands, saying, Woe is me now! for my soul is wearied because of murderers (*Jeremiah 4:23–31*).

Look unto Abraham your father, and unto Sarah that bare you: for I called him alone, and blessed him, and increased him. For the LORD shall comfort Zion: he will comfort all her waste places; and he will make her wilderness like Eden, and her *desert* like the garden of the LORD; joy and gladness shall be found therein, thanksgiving, and the voice of melody (*Isaiah 51:2–3*).

But if ye will not hear these words, I swear by myself, saith the LORD, that this house shall become a *desolation*. For thus saith the LORD unto the king's house of Judah; Thou art Gilead unto me, and the head of Lebanon: yet surely I will make thee a wilderness, and cities which are not inhabited. And I will prepare destroyers against thee, every one with his weapons: and they shall cut down thy choice cedars, and cast them into the fire (*Jeremiah 22:5–7*).

Let death seize upon them, and let them go down quick into hell: for wickedness is in their dwellings, and among them (*Psalm 55:15*).

13b. I beheld the earth, and, lo, it was *without form*, and void; and the heavens, and they had no light. I beheld the mountains, and, lo, they trembled, and all the hills moved lightly. I beheld, and, lo, there was no man, and all the birds of the heavens were fled. I beheld, and, lo, the fruitful place was a wilderness, and all the cities thereof were broken down at the presence of the LORD, and by his fierce anger. For thus hath the LORD said, The whole land shall be desolate; yet will I not make a full end. For this shall the earth mourn, and the heavens above be black: because I have spoken it, I have purposed it, and will not repent, neither will I turn back from it. The whole city shall flee for the noise of the horsemen and bowmen; they shall go into thickets, and climb up upon the rocks: every city shall be forsaken, and not a man dwell therein. And when thou art spoiled, what wilt thou do? Though thou clothest thyself with crimson, though thou deckest thee with ornaments of gold, though thou rentest thy face with painting, in vain shalt thou make thyself fair; thy lovers will despise thee, they will seek thy life. For *I have heard a voice as of a woman in travail, and the anguish as of her that bringeth forth her first child*, the voice of the daughter of Zion, that bewaileth herself, that spreadeth her hands, saying, Woe is me now! for my soul is wearied because of murderers (*Jeremiah 4:23-31*).

Look unto Abraham your father, and unto Sarah that bare you: for I called him alone, and blessed him, and increased him. For the LORD shall comfort Zion: he will comfort all her waste places; and he will make her wilderness like Eden, and her *desert* like the garden of the LORD; joy and gladness shall be found therein, thanksgiving, and the voice of melody (*Isaiah 51:2-3*).

And when a stranger shall sojourn with thee, and will keep the passover to the LORD, let all his males be circumcised, and then let him come near and keep it; and he shall be as one that is born in the land: for no uncircumcised person shall eat thereof. One law shall be to him that is *homeborn*, and unto the stranger that sojourneth among you. Thus did all the children of Israel; as the LORD commanded Moses and Aaron, so did they. And it came to pass the selfsame day, that the LORD did bring the children of Israel out of the land of Egypt by their armies (*Exodus 12:48-51*).

And the angel of the LORD said unto her, Behold, thou art with child, and shalt *bear* a son, and shalt call his name Ishmael; because the LORD hath heard thy affliction (*Genesis 16:11*).

Unto the woman he said, I will greatly multiply thy sorrow and thy conception; in sorrow thou shalt *bring forth* children; and thy desire shall be to thy husband, and he shall rule over thee (*Genesis 3:16*).

And she shall *bring forth* a son, and thou shalt call his name JESUS: for he shall save his people from their sins. Now all this was done, that it might be fulfilled which was spoken of the Lord by the prophet, saying, Behold, a virgin shall be with child, and shall *bring forth* a son, and they shall call his name Emmanuel, which being interpreted is, God with us. Then Joseph being raised from sleep did as the angel of the Lord had bidden him, and took unto him his wife: And knew her not till she had brought forth her firstborn son: and he called his name JESUS (*Matthew 1:21-25*).

Now these are the generations of the sons of Noah, Shem, Ham, and Japheth: and unto them were sons *born* after the flood (*Genesis 10:1*).

And Abraham was an hundred years old, when his son Isaac was born unto him. And Sarah said, God hath made me to laugh, so that all that hear will laugh with me. And she said, Who would have said unto Abraham, that Sarah should have given children suck? for I have *born* him a son in his old age (*Genesis 21:5-7*).

And Jacob begat Joseph the husband of Mary, of whom was *born* Jesus, who is called Christ (*Matthew 1:16*).

And when her days to *be delivered* were fulfilled, behold, there were twins in her womb (*Genesis 25:24*).

And his daughter in law, Phinehas' wife, was with child, near to *be delivered*: and when she heard the tidings that the ark of God was taken, and that her father in law and her husband were dead, she bowed herself and travailed; for her pains came upon her (*1 Samuel 4:19*).

A woman when she is in travail hath sorrow, because her hour is come: but as soon as she is delivered of the child, she remembereth no more the anguish, for joy that a man is born into the world (*John 16:21*).

Fear took hold upon them there, and *pain*, as of *a woman in travail* (*Psalm 48:6*).

13c. I beheld the earth, and, lo, it was *without form*, and void; and the heavens, and they had no light. I beheld the mountains, and, lo, they trembled, and all the hills moved lightly. I beheld, and, lo, there was no man, and all the birds of the heavens were fled. I beheld, and, lo, the fruitful place was a wilderness, and all the cities thereof were broken down at the presence of the LORD, and by his fierce anger. For thus hath the LORD said, The whole land shall be desolate; yet will I not make a full end. For this shall the earth mourn, and the heavens above be black: because I have spoken it, I have purposed it, and will not repent, neither will I turn back from it. The whole city shall flee for the noise of the horsemen and bowmen; they shall go into thickets, and climb up upon the rocks: every city shall be forsaken, and not a man dwell therein. And when thou art spoiled, what wilt thou do? Though thou clothest thyself with crimson, though thou deckest thee with ornaments of gold, though thou rentest thy face with painting, in vain shalt thou make thyself fair; thy lovers will despise thee, they will seek thy life. For *I have heard a voice as of a woman in travail, and the anguish as of her that bringeth forth her first child*, the voice of the daughter of Zion, that bewaileth herself, that spreadeth her hands, saying, Woe is me now! for my soul is wearied because of murderers (*Jeremiah 4:23-31*).

Is it not yet a very little while, and Lebanon shall be turned into a fruitful field, and the fruitful field shall be esteemed as a forest? And in that day shall the deaf hear the words of the book, and the eyes of the blind hall see out of obscurity, and out of darkness. The meek also shall increase their joy in the LORD, and the poor among men shall rejoice in the Holy One of Israel. For the terrible one is *brought to naught*, and the scorner is consumed, and all that watch for iniquity are cut off: That make a man an offender for a word, and lay a snare for him that reproveth in the gate, and turn aside the just for a *thing of naught*. Therefore thus saith the LORD, who redeemed Abraham, concerning the house of Jacob, Jacob shall not now be ashamed, neither shall his face now wax pale. But when he seeth his children, the work of mine hands, in the midst of him, they shall sanctify my name, and sanctify the Holy One of Jacob, and shall fear the God of Israel (*Isaiah 29:17-23*).

And Solomon made affinity with Pharaoh king of Egypt, and took Pharaoh's daughter, and brought her into the city of David, until he had made *an end* of building his own house, and the house of the LORD, and the wall of Jerusalem round about (*1 Kings 3:1*).

For the children of Ammon and Moab stood up against the inhabitants of mount Seir, utterly to slay and destroy them: and when they had made *an end* of the inhabitants of Seir, every one helped to destroy another. And when Judah came toward the watch tower in the wilderness, they looked unto the multitude, and, behold, they were dead bodies fallen to the earth, and none escaped (*2 Chronicles 20:23-24*).

And he said, What hast thou done? the voice of thy brother's *blood* crieth unto me from the ground (*Genesis 4:10*).

And they journeyed from Bethel; and there was but a little way to come to Ephrath: and Rachel travailed, and she had hard labour. And it came to pass, when she was in hard labor, that the midwife said unto her, Fear not; thou shalt have this son also. And it came to pass, *as her soul was in departing, (for she died)* that she called his name Ben-oni: but his father called him Benjamin. And Rachel died, and was buried in the way to Ephrath, which is Bethlehem (*Genesis 35:16-19*).

The LORD hath opened his armory, and hath brought forth the weapons of his indignation: for this is the work of the LORD God of hosts in the land of the Chaldeans. Come against her from the utmost border, open her storehouses: cast her up as heaps, and destroy her utterly: *let nothing of her be left* (*Jeremiah 50:25-26*).

14.   She is empty, and *void*, and waste: and the heart melteth, and the knees smite together, and much pain is in all loins, and the faces of them all gather blackness (*Nahum 2:10*).

Hear ye this word which I take up against you, even a lamentation, O house of Israel. The virgin of Israel is fallen; she shall no more rise: she is forsaken upon her land; there is none to raise her up. For thus saith the LORD God; The city that went out by a thousand shall leave an hundred, and that which went forth by an hundred shall leave ten, to the house of Israel. For thus saith the LORD unto the house of Israel, Seek ye me, and ye shall live: But seek not Bethel, nor enter into Gilgal, and pass not to Beer-sheba: for Gilgal shall surely go into captivity, and Bethel shall *come to naught*. Seek the LORD, and ye shall live; lest he break out like fire in the house of Joseph, and devour it, and there be none to quench it in Bethel (*Amos 5:1-6*).

And they smote all the souls that were therein with the edge of the sword, utterly destroying them: there was not any left *to breathe*: and he burnt Hazor with fire (*Joshua 11:11*).

And when her days *to be* delivered were fulfilled, behold, there were twins in her womb (*Genesis 25:24*).

And the angel of the LORD said unto her, Behold, thou art with child, and shalt *bear* a son, and shalt call his name Ishmael; because the LORD hath heard thy affliction (*Genesis 16:11*).

But the angel said unto him, Fear not, Zacharias: for thy prayer is heard; and thy wife Elisabeth shall *bear* thee a son, and thou shalt call his name John (*Luke 1:13*).

Unto the woman he said, I will greatly multiply thy sorrow and thy conception; in sorrow thou shalt *bring forth* children; and thy desire shall be to thy husband, and he shall rule over thee (*Genesis 3:16*).

And she shall *bring forth* a son, and thou shalt call his name JESUS: for he shall save his people from their sins. Now all this was done, that it might be fulfilled which was spoken of the Lord by the prophet, saying, Behold, a virgin shall be with child, and shall *bring forth* a son, and they shall call his name Emmanuel, which being interpreted is, God with us. Then Joseph being raised from sleep did as the angel of the Lord had bidden him, and took unto him his wife: And knew her not till she had brought forth her firstborn son: and he called his name JESUS (*Matthew 1:21-25*).

Now these are the generations of the sons of Noah, Shem, Ham, and Japheth: and unto them were sons *born* after the flood (*Genesis 10:1*).

And Abraham was an hundred years old, when his son Isaac was born unto him. And Sarah said, God hath made me to laugh, so that all that hear will laugh with me. And she said, Who would have said unto Abraham, that Sarah should have given children suck? for I have *born* him a son in his old age (*Genesis 21:5-7*).

And Jacob begat Joseph the husband of Mary, of whom was *born* Jesus, who is called Christ (*Matthew 1:16*).

And when her days to *be delivered* were fulfilled, behold, there were twins in her womb (*Genesis 25:24*).

And his daughter in law, Phinehas' wife, was with child, near to *be delivered*: and when she heard the tidings that the ark of God was taken, and that her father in law and her husband were dead, she bowed herself and travailed; for her pains came upon her (*1 Samuel 4:19*).

A woman when she is in travail hath sorrow, because her hour is come: but as soon as she is delivered of the child, she remembereth no more the anguish, for joy that a man is born into the world (*John 16:21*).

Fear took hold upon them there, and *pain*, as of *a woman in travail* (*Psalm 48:6*).

15a.   And the sons of Nadab; Seled, and Appaim: but Seled died *without* children (*1 Chronicles 2:30*).

And the women said unto Naomi, Blessed be the LORD, which hath not left thee this day *without* a kinsman, that his name may be famous in Israel (*Ruth 4:14*).

And it shall come to pass, that as the LORD rejoiced over you to do you good, and to multiply you; so the LORD will rejoice over you to destroy you, and to bring you *to naught*; and ye shall be plucked from off the land whither thou goest to possess it (*Deuteronomy 28:63*).

And when a stranger shall sojourn with thee, and will keep the passover to the LORD, let all his males be circumcised, and then let him come near and keep it; and he shall be as one that is born in the land: for no uncircumcised person shall eat thereof. One law shall be to him that is *homeborn*, and unto the stranger that sojourneth among you. Thus did all the children of Israel; as the Lord commanded Moses and Aaron, so did they. And it came to pass the selfsame day, *that* the LORD did bring the children of Israel out of the land of Egypt by their armies. (*Exodus 12:48-51*).

And the angel of the LORD said unto her, Behold, thou art with child, and shalt *bear* a son, and shalt call his name Ishmael; because the LORD hath heard thy affliction (*Genesis 16:11*).

But the angel said unto him, Fear not, Zacharias: for thy prayer is heard; and thy wife Elisabeth shall *bear* thee a son, and thou shalt call his name John (*Luke 1:13*).

Unto the woman he said, I will greatly multiply thy sorrow and thy conception; in sorrow thou shalt *bring forth* children; and thy desire shall be to thy husband, and he shall rule over thee (*Genesis 3:16*).

And she shall *bring forth* a son, and thou shalt call his name JESUS: for he shall save his people from their sins. Now all this was done, that it might be fulfilled which was spoken of the Lord by the prophet, saying, Behold, a virgin shall be with child, and shall *bring forth* a son, and they shall call his name Emmanuel, which being interpreted is, God with us. Then Joseph being raised from sleep did as the angel of the Lord had bidden him, and took unto him his wife: And knew her not till she had brought forth her firstborn son: and he called his name JESUS (*Matthew 1:21-25*).

Now these are the generations of the sons of Noah, Shem, Ham, and Japheth: and unto them were sons *born* after the flood (*Genesis 10:1*).

And Abraham was an hundred years old, when his son Isaac was born unto him. And Sarah said, God hath made me to laugh, so that all that hear will laugh with me. And she said, Who would have said unto Abraham, that Sarah should have given children suck? for I have *born* him a son in his old age (*Genesis 21:5-7*).

And Jacob begat Joseph the husband of Mary, of whom was *born* Jesus, who is called Christ (*Matthew 1:16*).

And when her days to *be delivered* were fulfilled, behold, there were twins in her womb (*Genesis 25:24*).

And his daughter in law, Phinehas' wife, was with child, near to *be delivered*: and when she heard the tidings that the ark of God was taken, and that her father in law and her husband were dead, she bowed herself and travailed; for her pains came upon her (*1 Samuel 4:19*).

A woman when she is in travail hath sorrow, because her hour is come: but as soon as she is delivered of the child, she remembereth no more the anguish, for joy that a man is born into the world (*John 16:21*).

Fear took hold upon them there, and *pain*, as of *a woman in travail* (*Psalm 48:6*).

15b.   And the sons of Nadab; Seled, and Appaim: but Seled died *without* children (*1 Chronicles 2:30*).

And the women said unto Naomi, Blessed be the LORD, which hath not left thee this day *without* a kinsman, that his name may be famous in Israel (*Ruth 4:14*).

Man that is born of a woman is of few days, and full of trouble. He cometh forth like a flower, and is cut down: he fleeth also as a shadow, and continueth not. And dost thou open thine eyes upon such an one, and bringest me into judgment with thee? Who can bring a clean thing out of an unclean? not one. Seeing his days are determined, the number of his months are with thee, thou hast appointed his bounds that he cannot pass; Turn from him, that he may rest, till he shall accomplish, as an hireling, his day. For there is hope of a tree, if it be cut down, that it will sprout again, and that the tender branch thereof will not *cease*. Though the root thereof wax old in the earth, and the stock thereof die in the ground; Yet through the scent of water it will bud, and bring forth boughs like a plant. But man dieth, and wasteth away: yea, man giveth up the ghost, and where is he? As the waters fail from the sea, and the flood decayeth and drieth up: So man lieth down, and riseth not: till the heavens be no more, they shall not awake, nor be raised out of their sleep. O that thou wouldest hide me in the grave, that thou wouldest keep me secret, until thy wrath be past, that thou wouldest appoint me a set time, and remember me! If a man die, shall he live again? All the days of my appointed time will I wait, till my change come. (*Job 14:1-14*)

Thus saith the LORD, which giveth the sun for a light by day, and the ordinances of the moon and of the stars for a light by night, which divideth the sea when the waves thereof roar; The LORD of hosts is his name: If those ordinances depart from before me, saith the LORD, then the seed of Israel also shall *cease* from being a nation before me forever. Thus saith the LORD; If heaven above can be measured, and the foundations of the earth searched out beneath, I will also cast off all the seed of Israel for all that they have done, saith the LORD (*Jeremiah 31:35-37*).

And Joseph returned into Egypt, he, and his brethren, and all that went up with him to bury his father, after he had buried his father. And when Joseph's brethren saw that their father was *dead*, they said, Joseph will peradventure hate us, and will certainly requite us all the evil which we did unto him (*Genesis 50:14-15*).

15c.   I beheld the earth, and, lo, it was *without* form, and void; and the heavens, and they had no light. I beheld the mountains, and, lo, they trembled, and all the hills moved lightly. I beheld, and, lo, there was no man, and all the birds of the heavens were fled. I beheld, and, lo, the fruitful place was a wilderness, and all the cities thereof were broken down at the presence of the LORD, and by his fierce anger. For thus hath the LORD said, The whole land shall be desolate; yet will I not make a full end. For this shall the earth mourn, and the heavens above be black: because I have spoken it, I have purposed it, and will not repent, neither will I turn back from it. The whole city shall flee for the noise of the horsemen and bowmen; they shall go into thickets, and climb up upon the rocks: every city shall be forsaken, and not a man dwell therein. And when thou art spoiled, what wilt thou do? Though thou clothest thyself with crimson, though thou deckest thee with ornaments of gold, though thou rentest thy face with painting, in vain shalt thou make thyself fair; thy lovers will despise thee, they will seek thy life. For *I have heard a voice as of a woman in travail, and the anguish as of her that bringeth forth her first child*, the voice of the daughter of Zion, that bewaileth herself, that spreadeth her hands, saying, Woe is me now! for my soul is wearied because of murderers (*Jeremiah 4:23-31*).

Is it not yet a very little while, and Lebanon shall be turned into a fruitful field, and the fruitful field shall be esteemed as a forest? And in that day shall the deaf hear the words of the book, and the eyes of the blind hall see out of obscurity, and out of darkness. The meek also shall increase their joy in the LORD, and the poor among men shall rejoice in the Holy One of Israel. For the terrible one is *brought to naught*, and the scorner is consumed, and all that watch for iniquity are cut off: That make a man an offender for a word, and lay a snare for him that reproveth in the gate, and turn aside the just for a *thing of naught*. Therefore thus saith the LORD, who redeemed Abraham, concerning the house of Jacob, Jacob shall not now be ashamed, neither shall his face now wax pale. But when he seeth his children, the work of mine hands, in the midst of him, they shall sanctify my name, and sanctify the Holy One of Jacob, and shall fear the God of Israel (*Isaiah 29:17-23*).

And Solomon made affinity with Pharaoh king of Egypt, and took Pharaoh's daughter, and brought her into the city of David, until he had made *an end* of building his own house, and the house of the LORD, and the wall of Jerusalem round about (*1 Kings 3:1*).

For the children of Ammon and Moab stood up against the inhabitants of mount Seir, utterly to slay and destroy them: and when they had made *an end* of the inhabitants of Seir, every one helped to destroy another. And when Judah came toward the watch tower in the wilderness, they looked unto the multitude, and, behold, they were dead bodies fallen to the earth, and none escaped (*2 Chronicles 20:23-24*).

And he said, What hast thou done? the voice of thy brother's *blood* crieth unto me from the ground (*Genesis 4:10*).

15d.   I beheld the earth, and, lo, it was *without* form, and void; and the heavens, and they had no light. I beheld the mountains, and, lo, they trembled, and all the hills moved lightly. I beheld, and, lo, there was no man, and all the birds of the heavens were fled. I beheld, and, lo, the fruitful place was a wilderness, and all the cities thereof were broken down at the presence of the LORD, and by his fierce anger. For thus hath the LORD said, The whole land shall be desolate; yet will I not make a full end. For this shall the earth mourn, and the heavens above be black: because I have spoken it, I have purposed it, and will not repent, neither will I turn back from it. The whole city shall flee for the noise of the horsemen and bowmen; they shall go into thickets, and climb up upon the rocks: every city shall be forsaken, and not a man dwell therein. And when thou art spoiled, what wilt thou do? Though thou clothest thyself with crimson, though thou deckest thee with ornaments of gold, though thou rentest thy face with painting, in vain shalt thou make thyself fair; thy lovers will despise thee, they will seek thy life. For *I have heard a voice as of a woman in travail, and the anguish as of her that bringeth forth her first child*, the voice of the daughter of Zion, that bewaileth herself, that spreadeth her hands, saying, Woe is me now! for my soul is wearied because of murderers (*Jeremiah 4:23-31*).

Hearken to me, ye that follow after righteousness, ye that seek the LORD: look unto the rock whence ye are hewn, and to the hole of the pit whence ye are digged. Look unto Abraham your father, and unto Sarah that bare you: for I called him alone, and blessed him, and increased him. For the LORD shall comfort Zion: he will comfort all her waste places; and he will make her wilderness like Eden, and her *desert* like the garden of the LORD; joy and gladness shall be found therein, thanksgiving, and the voice of melody (*Isaiah 51:1-3*).

Let death seize upon them, and let them go down quick into hell: for wickedness is in their dwellings, and among them (*Psalm 55:15*).

15e. And the sons of Nadab; Seled, and Appaim: but Seled died *without* children (*1 Chronicles 2:30*).

And the women said unto Naomi, Blessed be the LORD, which hath not left thee this day *without* a kinsman, that his name may be famous in Israel (*Ruth 4:14*).

And it shall come to pass, that as the LORD rejoiced over you to do you good, and to multiply you; so the LORD will rejoice over you to destroy you, and to bring you *to naught*; and ye shall be plucked from off the land whither thou goest to possess it (*Deuteronomy 28:63*).

And they journeyed from Bethel; and there was but a little way to come to Ephrath: and Rachel travailed, and she had hard labor. And it came to pass, when she was in hard labor, that the midwife said unto her, Fear not; thou shalt have this *son* also. And it came to pass, as her soul was in departing, (for she died) that she called his name *Ben-oni*: but his father called him *Benjamin*. And Rachel died, and was buried in the way to Ephrath, which is Bethlehem (*Genesis 35:16-19*).

15f.   And Ham, the father of Canaan, saw the nakedness of his father, and told his two brethren *without*. And Shem and Japheth took a garment, and laid it upon both their shoulders, and went backward, and covered the nakedness of their father; and their faces were backward, and they saw not their father's nakedness (*Genesis 9:22,23*).

And it shall come to pass, that as the LORD rejoiced over you to do you good, and to multiply you; so the LORD will rejoice over you to destroy you, and to bring you *to naught*; and ye shall be plucked from off the land whither thou goest to possess it (*Deuteronomy 28:63*).

And they journeyed from Bethel; and there was but a little way to come to Ephrath: and Rachel travailed, and she had hard labor. And it came to pass, when she was in hard labor, that the midwife said unto her, Fear not; thou shalt have this son also. And it came to pass, as her soul was in departing, (for she died) that she called his name Ben-oni: but his father called him Benjamin. And Rachel died, and was buried in the way to Ephrath, which is Bethlehem. And Jacob set a pillar upon her grave: that is the pillar of Rachel's grave unto this day (*Genesis 35:16-20*).

16.   And he said unto her, What *form* is he of? And she said, An old man cometh up; and he is covered with a mantle. And Saul perceived that it was Samuel, and he stooped with his face to the ground, and bowed himself (*1 Samuel 28:14*).

Thus saith the LORD that made thee, and *form[ed]* thee from the womb, which will help thee; Fear not, O Jacob, my servant; and thou, Jeshurun, whom I have chosen (*Isaiah 44:2*).

And now, saith the LORD that *form[ed]* me from the womb to be his servant, to bring Jacob again to him, Though Israel be not gathered, yet shall I be glorious in the eyes of the LORD, and my God shall be my strength (*Isaiah 49:5*).

Before I *form[ed]* thee in the belly I knew thee; and before thou camest forth out of the womb I sanctified thee, and I ordained thee a prophet unto the nations (*Jeremiah 1:5*).

So Boaz took Ruth, and she was his wife: and when he went in unto her, the LORD gave her *conception*, and she bare a son (*Ruth 4:13*).

And the angel of the LORD appeared unto the woman, and said unto her, Behold now, thou art barren, and bearest not: but thou shalt *conceive*, and bear a son (*Judges 13:3*).

And the angel of the LORD said unto her, Behold, thou art with child, and shalt *bear* a son, and shalt call his name Ishmael; because the LORD hath heard thy affliction (*Genesis 16:11*).

But the angel said unto him, Fear not, Zacharias: for thy prayer is heard; and thy wife Elisabeth shall *bear* thee a son, and thou shalt call his name John (*Luke 1:13*).

Unto the woman he said, I will greatly multiply thy sorrow and thy conception; in sorrow thou shalt *bring forth* children; and thy desire shall be to thy husband, and he shall rule over thee (*Genesis 3:16*).

Now these are the generations of the sons of Noah, Shem, Ham, and Japheth: and unto them were sons *born* after the flood (*Genesis 10:1*).

And Abraham was an hundred years old, when his son Isaac was born unto him. And Sarah said, God hath made me to laugh, so that all that hear will laugh with me. And she said, Who would have said unto Abraham, that Sarah should have given children suck? for I have *born* him a son in his old age (*Genesis 21:5-7*).

And Jacob begat Joseph the husband of Mary, of whom was *born* Jesus, who is called Christ (*Matthew 1:16*).

And when her days to *be delivered* were fulfilled, behold, there were twins in her womb (*Genesis 25:24*).

And his daughter in law, Phinehas' wife, was with child, near to *be delivered*: and when she heard the tidings that the ark of God was taken, and that her father in law and her husband were dead, she bowed herself and travailed; for her pains came upon her (*1 Samuel 4:19*).

A woman when she is in travail hath sorrow, because her hour is come: but as soon as she is delivered of the child, she remembereth no more the anguish, for joy that a man is born into the world (*John 16:21*).

17a. I sent Moses also and Aaron, and I plagued Egypt, according to that which I did among them: and afterward I brought you out. And I brought your fathers out of Egypt: and ye came unto the sea; and the Egyptians pursued after your fathers with chariots and horsemen unto the Red sea. And when they cried unto the LORD, he put *darkness* between you and the Egyptians, and brought the sea upon them, and covered them; and your eyes have seen what I have done in Egypt: and ye dwelt in the wilderness a long season. And I brought you into the land of the Amorites, which dwelt on the other side Jordan; and they fought with you: and I gave them into your hand, that ye might possess their land; and I destroyed them from before you (*Joshua 24:5-8*).

After this opened Job his mouth, and cursed his day. And Job spake, and said, Let the day perish wherein I was born, and the night in which it was said, There is a man child conceived. Let that day be *darkness*; let not God regard it from above, neither let the light shine upon it. Let *darkness* and the shadow of death stain it; let a cloud dwell upon it; let the blackness of the day terrify it. As for that night, let *darkness* seize upon it; let it not be joined unto the days of the year, let it not come into the number of the months. Lo, let that night be solitary, let no joyful voice come therein. Let them curse it that curse the day, who are ready to raise up their mourning. Let the stars of the twilight thereof be dark; let it look for light, but have none; neither let it see the dawning of the day:

Because it shut not up the doors of my mother's womb, nor hid sorrow from mine eyes. Why died I not from the womb? why did I not give up the ghost when I came out of the belly (*Job 3:1-11*)?

And it came to pass, as her soul was in departing, (for she died) that she called his name Ben-oni: but his father called him Benjamin. And Rachel died, and was buried in the way to Ephrath, which is Bethlehem. And Jacob set a pillar upon her grave: that is the pillar of Rachel's grave unto this day (*Genesis 35:18-20*).

And the LORD spake unto Moses after the *death* of the two sons of Aaron, when they offered before the LORD, and died (*Leviticus 16:1*).

And Isaac brought her into his mother Sarah's tent, and took Rebekah, and she became his wife; and he loved her: and Isaac was comforted after his mother's *death* (*Genesis 24:67*).

To every thing there is a season, and a time to every purpose under the heaven: A time to be born, and a time *to die*; a time to plant, and a time to pluck up that which is planted; A time to kill, and a time to heal; a time to break down, and a time to build up (*Ecclesiastes 3:1-3*).

And Isaac entreated the LORD for his wife, because she was barren: and the LORD was entreated of him, and Rebekah his wife conceived. And the children struggled together within her; and she said, If it be so, why am I thus? And she went to inquire of the LORD. And the LORD said unto her, Two nations are in thy womb, and two manner of people shall be separated from thy bowels; and the one people shall be stronger than the other people; and the elder shall serve the younger. And when her days to be delivered were fulfilled, behold, there were twins in her womb. And the *first* came out red, all over like a hairy garment; and they called his name Esau (*Genesis 25:21-25*).

And Adam knew his wife again; and she bare *a son*, and called his name Seth: For God, said she, hath appointed me another seed instead of Abel, whom Cain slew. And to Seth, to him also there was born *a son*; and he called his name Enos: then began men to call upon the name of the LORD (*Genesis 4:25-26*).

And I will *make* thy seed as the dust of the earth: so that if a man can number the dust of the earth, then shall thy seed also be numbered (*Genesis 13:16*).

To every thing there is a season, and a time to every purpose under the heaven: A time to be born, and a time to die; a time to plant, and a time to pluck up that which is planted; A time to kill, and a time to heal; a time to break down, and a time *to build up* (*Ecclesiastes 3:1–3*).

And the angel of the LORD said unto her, Behold, thou art with child, and shalt *bear* a son, and shalt call his name Ishmael; because the LORD hath heard thy affliction (*Genesis 16:11*).

But the angel said unto him, Fear not, Zacharias: for thy prayer is heard; and thy wife Elisabeth shall *bear* thee a son, and thou shalt call his name John (*Luke 1:13*).

Unto the woman he said, I will greatly multiply thy sorrow and thy conception; in sorrow thou shalt *bring forth* children; and thy desire shall be to thy husband, and he shall rule over thee (*Genesis 3:16*).

And she shall *bring forth* a son, and thou shalt call his name JESUS: for he shall save his people from their sins. Now all this was done, that it might be fulfilled which was spoken of the Lord by the prophet, saying, Behold, a virgin shall be with child, and shall *bring forth* a son, and they shall call his name Emmanuel, which being interpreted is, God with us. Then Joseph being raised from sleep did as the angel of the Lord had bidden him, and took unto him his wife: And knew her not till she had brought forth her firstborn son: and he called his name JESUS (*Matthew 1:21-25*).

Now these are the generations of the sons of Noah, Shem, Ham, and Japheth: and unto them were sons *born* after the flood (*Genesis 10:1*).

And Abraham was an hundred years old, when his son Isaac was born unto him. And Sarah said, God hath made me to laugh, so that all that hear will laugh with me. And she said, Who would have said unto Abraham, that Sarah should have given children suck? for I have *born* him a son in his old age (*Genesis 21:5-7*).

And Jacob begat Joseph the husband of Mary, of whom was *born* Jesus, who is called Christ (*Matthew 1:16*).

And when her days to *be delivered* were fulfilled, behold, there were twins in her womb (*Genesis 25:24*).

And his daughter in law, Phinehas' wife, was with child, near to *be delivered*: and when she heard the tidings that the ark of God was taken, and that her father in law and her husband were dead, she bowed herself and travailed; for her pains came upon her (*1 Samuel 4:19*).

A woman when she is in travail hath sorrow, because her hour is come: but as soon as she is delivered of the child, she remembereth no more the anguish, for joy that a man is born into the world (*John 16:21*).

17b. I sent Moses also and Aaron, and I plagued Egypt, according to that which I did among them: and afterward I brought you out. And I brought your fathers out of Egypt: and ye came unto the sea; and the Egyptians pursued after your fathers with chariots and horsemen unto the Red sea. And when they cried unto the LORD, he put *darkness* between you and the Egyptians, and brought the sea upon them, and covered them; and your eyes have seen what I have done in Egypt: and ye dwelt in the wilderness a long season. And I brought you into the land of the Amorites, which dwelt on the other side Jordan; and they fought with you: and I gave them into your hand, that ye might possess their land; and I destroyed them from before you (*Joshua 24:5-8*).

After this opened Job his mouth, and cursed his day. And Job spake, and said, Let the day perish wherein I was born, and the night in which it was said, There is a man child conceived. Let that day be *darkness*; let not God regard it from above, neither let the light shine upon it. Let *darkness* and the shadow of death stain it; let a cloud dwell upon it; let the blackness of the day terrify it. As for that night, let *darkness* seize upon it; let it not be joined unto the days of the year, let it not come into the number of the months. Lo, let that night be solitary, let no joyful voice come therein. Let them curse it that curse the day, who are ready to raise up their mourning. Let the stars of the twilight thereof be dark; let it look for light, but have none; neither let it see the dawning of the day: Because it shut not up the doors of my mother's womb, nor hid sorrow from mine eyes. Why died I not from the womb? why did I not give up the ghost when I came out of the belly (*Job 3:1-11*)?

But the LORD thy God shall deliver them unto thee, and shall destroy them with a mighty *destruction*, until they be destroyed. And he shall deliver their kings into thine hand, and thou shalt destroy their name from under heaven: there shall no man be able to stand before thee, until thou have destroyed them (*Deuteronomy 7:23-24*).

And the LORD spake unto Moses after the *death* of the two sons of Aaron, when they offered before the LORD, and died (*Leviticus 16:1*).

And Isaac brought her into his mother Sarah's tent, and took Rebekah, and she became his wife; and he loved her: and Isaac was comforted after his mother's *death* (*Genesis 24:67*).

And he said, My son shall not go down with you; for his brother is dead, and he is left alone: if mischief befall him by the way in the which ye go, then shall ye bring down my gray hairs with *sorrow* to the grave (*Genesis 42:38*).

Because it shut not up the doors of my mother's womb, nor hid *sorrow* from mine eyes. Why died I not from the womb? why did I not give up the ghost when I came out of the belly? Why did the knees prevent me? or why the breasts that I should suck? For now should I have lain still and been quiet, I should have slept: then had I been at rest, With kings and counselors of the earth, which built desolate places for themselves; Or with princes that had gold, who filled their houses with silver: Or *as an hidden untimely birth I had not been; as infants which never saw light* (*Job 3:10-16*).

Fear took hold upon them there, and *pain*, as of a woman in travail (*Psalm 48:6*).

And the angel of the LORD said unto her, Behold, thou art with child, and shalt *bear* a son, and shalt call his name Ishmael; because the LORD hath heard thy affliction (*Genesis 16:11*).

But the angel said unto him, Fear not, Zacharias: for thy prayer is heard; and thy wife Elisabeth shall *bear* thee a son, and thou shalt call his name John (*Luke 1:13*).

Unto the woman he said, I will greatly multiply thy sorrow and thy conception; in sorrow thou shalt *bring forth* children; and thy desire shall be to thy husband, and he shall rule over thee (*Genesis 3:16*).

And she shall *bring forth* a son, and thou shalt call his name JESUS: for he shall save his people from their sins. Now all this was done, that it might be fulfilled which was spoken of the Lord by the prophet, saying, Behold, a virgin shall be with child, and shall *bring forth* a son, and they shall call his name Emmanuel, which being interpreted is, God with us. Then Joseph being raised from sleep did as the angel of the Lord had bidden him, and took unto him his wife: And knew her not till she had brought forth her firstborn son: and he called his name JESUS (*Matthew 1:21-25*).

And it came to pass in the time of her *travail*, that, behold, twins were in her womb (*Genesis 38:27*).

Now these are the generations of the sons of Noah, Shem, Ham, and Japheth: and unto them were sons *born* after the flood (*Genesis 10:1*).

And Abraham was an hundred years old, when his son Isaac was born unto him. And Sarah said, God hath made me to laugh, so that all that hear will laugh with me. And she said, Who would have said unto Abraham, that Sarah should have given children suck? for I have *born* him a son in his old age (*Genesis 21:5-7*).

And Jacob begat Joseph the husband of Mary, of whom was *born* Jesus, who is called Christ (*Matthew 1:16*).

And when her days to *be delivered* were fulfilled, behold, there were twins in her womb (*Genesis 25:24*).

And his daughter in law, Phinehas' wife, was with child, near to *be delivered*: and when she heard the tidings that the ark of God was taken, and that her father in law and her husband were dead,

she bowed herself and travailed; for her pains came upon her (*1 Samuel 4:19*).

A woman when she is in travail hath sorrow, because her hour is come: but as soon as she is delivered of the child, she remembereth no more the anguish, for joy that a man is born into the world (*John 16:21*).

Fear took hold upon them there, and *pain*, as of *a woman in travail* (*Psalm 48:6*).

17c. And thou shalt grope at noonday, as the blind gropeth in *darkness*, and thou shalt not prosper in thy ways: and thou shalt be only oppressed and spoiled evermore, and no man shall save thee. Thou shalt betroth a wife, and another man shall lie with her: thou shalt build an house, and thou shalt not dwell therein: thou shalt plant a vineyard, and shalt not gather the grapes thereof (*Deuteronomy 28:29-30*).

I sent Moses also and Aaron, and I plagued Egypt, according to that which I did among them: and afterward I brought you out. And I brought your fathers out of Egypt: and ye came unto the sea; and the Egyptians pursued after your fathers with chariots and horsemen unto the Red sea. And when they cried unto the Lord, he put *darkness* between you and the Egyptians, and brought the sea upon them, and covered them; and your eyes have seen what I have done in Egypt: and ye dwelt in the wilderness a long season. And I brought you into the land of the Amorites, which dwelt on the other side Jordan; and they fought with you: and I gave them into your hand, that ye might possess their land; and I destroyed them from before you (*Joshua 24:5-8*).

After this opened Job his mouth, and cursed his day. And Job spake, and said, Let the day perish wherein I was born, and the night in which it was said, There is a man child conceived. Let that day be *darkness*; let not God regard it from above, neither let the light shine upon it. Let *darkness* and the shadow of death stain it; let a cloud dwell upon it; let the blackness of the day terrify it. As for that night, let *darkness* seize upon it; let it not be joined unto the days of the year, let it not come into the number of the months. Lo, let that night be solitary, let no joyful voice come therein. Let them curse it that curse the day, who are ready to raise up their mourning. Let the stars of the twilight thereof be dark; let it look for light, but have none; neither let it see the dawning of the day: Because it shut not up the doors of my mother's womb, nor hid sorrow from mine eyes. Why died I not from the womb? why did I not give up the ghost when I came out of the belly (*Job 3:1-11*)?

Wherefore is light given to him that is in *misery*, and life unto the bitter in soul; Which long for death, but it cometh not; and dig for it more than for hid treasures (Job 3:20-21);

And the LORD spake unto Moses after the *death* of the two sons of Aaron, when they offered before the LORD, and died (*Leviticus 16:1*).

And Isaac brought her into his mother Sarah's tent, and took Rebekah, and she became his wife; and he loved her: and Isaac was comforted after his mother's *death* (*Genesis 24:67*).

But the LORD thy God shall deliver them unto thee, and shall destroy them with a mighty *destruction*, until they be destroyed. And he shall deliver their kings into thine hand, and thou shalt destroy their name from under heaven: there shall no man be able to stand before thee, until thou have destroyed them (*Deuteronomy 7:23-24*).

And they journeyed from Bethel; and there was but a little way to come to Ephrath: and Rachel travailed, and she had hard *labor*. And it came to pass, when she was in hard *labor*, that the midwife said unto her, Fear not; thou shalt have this son also. And it came to pass, as her soul was in departing, (for she died) that she called his name Ben-oni: but his father called him Benjamin. And Rachel died, and was buried in the way to Ephrath, which is Bethlehem (*Genesis 35:16-19*).

And it came to pass in the time of her *travail*, that, behold, twins were in her womb (*Genesis 38:27*).

And the angel of the LORD said unto her, Behold, thou art with child, and shalt *bear* a son, and shalt call his name Ishmael; because the LORD hath heard thy affliction (*Genesis 16:11*).

But the angel said unto him, Fear not, Zacharias: for thy prayer is heard; and thy wife Elisabeth shall *bear* thee a son, and thou shalt call his name John (*Luke 1:13*).

Unto the woman he said, I will greatly multiply thy sorrow and thy conception; in sorrow thou shalt *bring forth* children; and thy desire shall be to thy husband, and he shall rule over thee (*Genesis 3:16*).

And she shall *bring forth* a son, and thou shalt call his name JESUS: for he shall save his people from their sins. Now all this was done, that it might be fulfilled which was spoken of the Lord by the prophet, saying, Behold, a virgin shall be with child, and shall *bring forth* a son, and they shall call his name Emmanuel, which being interpreted is, God with us. Then Joseph being raised from sleep did as the angel of the Lord had bidden him, and took unto him his wife: And knew her not till she had brought forth her firstborn son: and he called his name JESUS (*Matthew 1:21-25*).

And when her days to *be delivered* were fulfilled, behold, there were twins in her womb (*Genesis 25:24*).

And his daughter in law, Phinehas' wife, was with child, near to *be delivered*: and when she heard the tidings that the ark of God was taken, and that her father in law and her husband were dead, she bowed herself and travailed; for her pains came upon her (*1 Samuel 4:19*).

A woman when she is in travail hath sorrow, because her hour is come: but as soon as she is delivered of the child, she remembereth no more the anguish, for joy that a man is born into the world (*John 16:21*).

Fear took hold upon them there, and *pain*, as of *a woman in travail* (*Psalm 48:6*).

18a. And he said, Hagar, Sarai's maid, whence camest thou? and whither wilt thou go? And she said, I flee from the *face* of my mistress Sarai (*Genesis 16:8*).

And he built there an altar, and called the place El-beth-el: because there God appeared unto him, when he fled from the *face* of his brother (*Genesis 35:7*).

Now when Pharaoh heard this thing, he sought to slay Moses. But Moses fled from the *face* of Pharaoh, and dwelt in the land of Midian: and he sat down by a well (*Exodus 2:15*).

And Abner sent messengers to David on his behalf, saying, Whose is the land? saying also, Make thy league with me, and, behold, my hand shall be with thee, to bring about all Israel unto thee. And he said, Well; I will make a league with thee: but one thing I require of thee, that is, Thou shalt not see my *face*, except thou first bring Michal Saul's daughter, when thou comest to see my face. And David sent messengers to Ish-bosheth Saul's son, saying, Deliver me my wife Michal, which I espoused to me for an hundred foreskins of the Philistines (*2 Samuel 3:12-14*).

And he said unto her, What *form* is he of? And she said, An old man cometh up; and he is covered with a mantle. And Saul perceived that it was Samuel, and he stooped with his face to the ground, and bowed himself (*1 Samuel 28:14*).

Thus saith the LORD that made thee, and *form[ed]* thee from the womb, which will help thee; Fear not, O Jacob, my servant; and thou, Jeshurun, whom I have chosen (*Isaiah 44:2*).

And now, saith the LORD that *form[ed]* me from the womb to be his servant, to bring Jacob again to him, Though Israel be not gathered, yet shall I be glorious in the eyes of the LORD, and my God shall be my strength (*Isaiah 49:5*).

Before I *form[ed]* thee in the belly I knew thee; and before thou camest forth out of the womb I sanctified thee, and I ordained thee a prophet unto the nations (*Jeremiah 1:5*).

So Boaz took Ruth, and she was his wife: and when he went in unto her, the LORD gave her *conception*, and she bare a son (*Ruth 4:13*).

And the angel of the LORD appeared unto the woman, and said unto her, Behold now, thou art barren, and bearest not: but thou shalt *conceive*, and bear a son (*Judges 13:3*).

And the angel of the LORD said unto her, Behold, thou art with child, and shalt *bear* a son, and shalt call his name Ishmael; because the LORD hath heard thy affliction (*Genesis 16:11*).

But the angel said unto him, Fear not, Zacharias: for thy prayer is heard; and thy wife Elisabeth shall *bear* thee a son, and thou shalt call his name John (*Luke 1:13*).

Unto the woman he said, I will greatly multiply thy sorrow and thy conception; in sorrow thou shalt *bring forth* children; and thy desire shall be to thy husband, and he shall rule over thee (*Genesis 3:16*).

Now these are the generations of the sons of Noah, Shem, Ham, and Japheth: and unto them were sons *born* after the flood (*Genesis 10:1*).

And Abraham was an hundred years old, when his son Isaac was born unto him. And Sarah said, God hath made me to laugh, so that all that hear will laugh with me. And she said, Who would have said unto Abraham, that Sarah should have given children suck? for I have *born* him a son in his old age (*Genesis 21:5-7*).

And Jacob begat Joseph the husband of Mary, of whom was *born* Jesus, who is called Christ (*Matthew 1:16*).

And when her days to *be delivered* were fulfilled, behold, there were twins in her womb (*Genesis 25:24*).

And his daughter in law, Phinehas' wife, was with child, near to *be delivered*: and when she heard the tidings that the ark of God was taken, and that her father in law and her husband were dead, she bowed herself and travailed; for her pains came upon her (*1 Samuel 4:19*).

A woman when she is in travail hath sorrow, because her hour is come: but as soon as she is delivered of the child, she remembereth no more the anguish, for joy that a man is born into the world (*John 16:21*).

18c.   And he said, Hagar, Sarai's maid, whence camest thou? and whither wilt thou go? And she said, I flee from the *face* of my mistress Sarai (*Genesis 16:8*).

And he built there an altar, and called the place El-beth-el: because there God appeared unto him, when he fled from the *face* of his brother (*Genesis 35:7*).

Now when Pharaoh heard this thing, he sought to slay Moses. But Moses fled from the *face* of Pharaoh, and dwelt in the land of Midian: and he sat down by a well (*Exodus 2:15*).

And Abner sent messengers to David on his behalf, saying, Whose is the land? saying also, Make thy league with me, and, behold, my hand shall be with thee, to bring about all Israel unto thee. And he said, Well; I will make a league with thee: but one thing I require of thee, that is, Thou shalt not see my *face*, except thou first bring Michal Saul's daughter, when thou comest to see my face. And David sent messengers to Ish-bosheth Saul's son, saying, Deliver me my wife Michal, which I espoused to me for an hundred foreskins of the Philistines (*2 Samuel 3:12-14*).

Surely your turning of things *upside down* shall be esteemed as the potter's clay: for shall the work say of him that made it, He made me not? or shall the thing framed say of him that framed it, He had no understanding? Is it not yet a very little while, and Lebanon shall be turned into a fruitful field, and the fruitful field shall be esteemed as a forest (*Isaiah 29:16-18*)?

19a.   Even by the God of thy father, who shall help thee; and by the Almighty, who shall bless thee with blessings of heaven above, blessings of the *deep* that lieth under, blessings of the breasts, and of the womb (*Genesis 49:25*).

Hath the rain a father? or who hath begotten the drops of dew? Out of whose womb came the ice? and the hoary frost of heaven, who hath gendered it? The waters are hid as with a stone, and the face of the *deep* is frozen (*Job 38:28-30*).

And the angel of the LORD said unto her, I will *multiply* thy seed exceedingly, that it shall not be numbered for multitude (*Genesis 16:10*).

If the clouds *be full of* rain, they empty themselves upon the earth: and if the tree fall toward the south, or toward the north, in the place where the tree falleth, there it shall be. He that observeth the wind shall not sow; and he that regardeth the clouds shall not reap. As thou knowest not what is the way of the spirit, nor how the bones do grow in the womb of her that is with child: even so thou knowest not the works of God who maketh all. In the morning sow thy seed, and in the evening withhold not thine hand: for thou knowest not whether shall prosper, either this or that, or whether they both shall be alike good (*Ecclesiastes 11:3-6*).

And the sucking child shall play on the hole of the asp, and the weaned child shall put his hand on the cockatrice' den. They shall not hurt nor destroy in all my holy mountain: for the earth shall *be full of* the knowledge of the LORD, as the waters cover the sea. And in that day there shall be a root of Jesse, which shall stand for an ensign of the people; to it shall the Gentiles seek: and his rest shall be glorious (*Isaiah 11:8-10*).

From men which are thy hand, O LORD, from men of the world, which have their portion in this life, and whose belly thou fillest with thy hid treasure: they are *full* of children, and leave the rest of their substance to their babes (*Psalm 17:14*).

As thou knowest not what is the way of the spirit, nor how the bones do grow in the womb of *her that is with child*: even so thou knowest not the works of God who maketh all (*Ecclesiastes 11:5*).

Now the birth of Jesus Christ was on this wise: When as his mother Mary was espoused to Joseph, before they came together, *she was found with child* of the Holy Ghost (*Matthew 1:18*).

19b. Even by the God of thy father, who shall help thee; and by the Almighty, who shall bless thee with blessings of heaven above, blessings of the *deep* that lieth under, blessings of the breasts, and of the womb (*Genesis 49:25*).

Hath the rain a father? or who hath begotten the drops of dew? Out of whose womb came the ice? and the hoary frost of heaven, who hath gendered it? The waters are hid as with a stone, and the face of the *deep* is frozen (*Job 38:28-30*).

And when a stranger shall sojourn with thee, and will keep the passover to the LORD, let all his males be circumcised, and then let him come near and keep it; and he shall be as one that is born in the land: for no uncircumcised person shall eat thereof. One law shall be to him that is *homeborn*, and unto the stranger that sojourneth among you. Thus did all the children of Israel; as the LORD commanded Moses and Aaron, so did they. And it came to pass the selfsame day, that the LORD did bring the children of Israel out of the land of Egypt by their armies (*Exodus 12:48-51*).

And the angel of the LORD said unto her, Behold, thou art with child, and shalt *bear* a son, and shalt call his name Ishmael; because the LORD hath heard thy affliction (*Genesis 16:11*).

Unto the woman he said, I will greatly multiply thy sorrow and thy conception; in sorrow thou shalt *bring forth* children; and thy desire shall be to thy husband, and he shall rule over thee (*Genesis 3:16*).

And she shall *bring forth* a son, and thou shalt call his name JESUS: for he shall save his people from their sins. Now all this was done, that it might be fulfilled which was spoken of the Lord by the prophet, saying, Behold, a virgin shall be with child, and shall *bring forth* a son, and they shall call his name Emmanuel, which being interpreted is, God with us. Then Joseph being raised from sleep did as the angel of the Lord had bidden him, and took unto him his wife: And knew her not till she had brought forth her firstborn son: and he called his name JESUS (*Matthew 1:21-25*).

Now these are the generations of the sons of Noah, Shem, Ham, and Japheth: and unto them were sons *born* after the flood (*Genesis 10:1*).

And Abraham was an hundred years old, when his son Isaac was born unto him. And Sarah said, God hath made me to laugh, so that all that hear will laugh with me. And she said, Who would have said unto Abraham, that Sarah should have given children suck? for I have *born* him a son in his old age (*Genesis 21:5-7*).

And Jacob begat Joseph the husband of Mary, of whom was *born* Jesus, who is called Christ (*Matthew 1:16*).

And when her days to *be delivered* were fulfilled, behold, there were twins in her womb (*Genesis 25:24*).

And his daughter in law, Phinehas' wife, was with child, near to *be delivered*: and when she heard the tidings that the ark of God was taken, and that her father in law and her husband were dead, she bowed herself and travailed; for her pains came upon her (*1 Samuel 4:19*).

A woman when she is in travail hath sorrow, because her hour is come: but as soon as she is delivered of the child, she remembereth no more the anguish, for joy that a man is born into the world (*John 16:21*).

Fear took hold upon them there, and *pain*, as of *a woman in travail* (*Psalm 48:6*).

20.   And the LORD said, My *spirit* shall not always strive with man, for that he also is flesh: yet his days shall be an hundred and twenty years (*Genesis 6:3*).

All the while my breath is in me, and the *spirit* of God is in my nostrils (*Job 27:3*).

Thou hidest thy face, they are troubled: thou takest away their breath, they die, and return to their dust. Thou sendest forth thy *spirit*, they are created: and thou renewest the face of the earth (*Psalm 104:29-30*).

For I will pour water upon him that is thirsty, and floods upon the dry ground: I will pour my *spirit* upon thy seed, and my blessing upon thine offspring (*Isaiah 44:3*).

And the LORD God formed man of the dust of the ground, and breathed into his nostrils the breath of *life*; and man became a living soul (*Genesis 2:7*).

And they smote all the souls that were therein with the edge of the sword, utterly destroying them: there was not any left *to breathe*: and he burnt Hazor with fire (*Joshua 11:11*).

And the LORD God formed man of the dust of the ground, and breathed into his nostrils the breath of life; and man became a living *soul* (*Genesis 2:7*).

21a. And all flesh died that *moved* upon the earth, both of fowl, and of cattle, and of beast, and of every creeping thing that creepeth upon the earth, and every man: All in whose nostrils was the breath of life, of all that was in the dry land, died (*Genesis 7:21-22*).

My beloved put in his hand by the hole of the door, and my bowels were *moved* for him. I rose up to open to my beloved; and my hands dropped with myrrh, and my fingers with sweet smelling myrrh, upon the handles of the lock (*Song 5:4-5*).

And all the people returned to the camp to Joshua at Makkedah in peace: none *moved* his tongue against any of the children of Israel (*Joshua 10:21*).

Now Hannah, she spake in her heart; only her lips *moved*, but her voice was not heard: therefore Eli thought she had been drunken (*1 Samuel 1:13*).

And the angel of the LORD said unto her, I will *multiply* thy seed exceedingly, that it shall not be numbered for multitude (*Genesis 16:10*).

From men which are thy hand, O LORD, from men of the world, which have their portion in this life, and whose belly thou fillest with thy hid treasure: they are *full of* children, and leave the rest of their substance to their babes (*Psalm 17:14*).

As thou knowest not what is the way of the spirit, nor how the bones do grow in the womb of *her that is with child*: even so thou knowest not the works of God who maketh all (*Ecclesiastes 11:5*).

Now the birth of Jesus Christ was on this wise: When as his mother Mary was espoused to Joseph, before they came together, *she was found with child* of the Holy Ghost (*Matthew 1:18*).

21b. And all flesh died that *moved* upon the earth, both of fowl, and of cattle, and of beast, and of every creeping thing that creepeth upon the earth, and every man: All in whose nostrils was the breath of life, of all that was in the dry land, died (*Genesis 7:21-22*).

My beloved put in his hand by the hole of the door, and my bowels were *moved* for him. I rose up to open to my beloved; and my hands dropped with myrrh, and my fingers with sweet smelling myrrh, upon the handles of the lock (*Song 5:4-5*).

And all the people returned to the camp to Joshua at Makkedah in peace: none *moved* his tongue against any of the children of Israel (*Joshua 10:21*).

Now Hannah, she spake in her heart; only her lips *moved*, but her voice was not heard: therefore Eli thought she had been drunken (*1 Samuel 1:13*).

As for me, behold, my covenant is with thee, and thou shalt be a father of *many* nations. Neither shall thy name any more be called Abram, but thy name shall be Abraham; for a father of many nations have I made thee (*Genesis 17:4-5*).

And Adam knew Eve his wife; and she *conceived*, and bare Cain, and said, I have gotten a man from the LORD. And she *again* bare his brother Abel. And Abel was a keeper of sheep, but Cain was a tiller of the ground (*Genesis 4:1-2*).

And she conceived, and bare a son; and said, God hath taken away my reproach: And she called his name Joseph; and said, The LORD shall *add* to me another son (*Genesis 30:23-24*).

22a. For I will pour water upon him that is thirsty, and floods upon the dry ground: I will pour my spirit *upon* thy seed, and my blessing upon thine offspring (*Isaiah 44:3*).

And, behold, the word of the LORD came unto him, saying, This shall not be thine heir; but he that shall come forth *out of* thine own bowels shall be thine heir (*Genesis 15:4*).

And the LORD said unto her, Two nations are in thy *womb*, and two manner of people shall be separated from thy bowels; and the one people shall be stronger than the other people; and the elder shall serve the younger. And when her days to be delivered were fulfilled, behold, there were twins in her *womb*. And the first came out red, all over like a hairy garment; and they called his name Esau. And after that came his brother out, and his hand took hold on Esau's heel; and his name was called Jacob: and Isaac was threescore years old when she bare them (*Genesis 25:23-26*).

22b. For I will pour water upon him that is thirsty, and floods upon the dry ground: I will pour my spirit *upon* thy seed, and my blessing upon thine offspring (*Isaiah 44:3*).

And David said to Abishai, and to all his servants, Behold, my son, which came *forth of* my bowels, seeketh my life: how much more now may this Benjamite do it? let him alone, and let him curse; for the LORD hath bidden him (*2 Samuel 16:11*).

As he came *forth of* his mother's womb, naked shall he return to go as he came, and shall take nothing of his labour, which he may carry away in his hand (*Ecclesiastes 5:15*).

And Abram said, Behold, to me thou hast given no seed: and, lo, one born in my house is mine heir. And, behold, the word of the LORD came unto him, saying, This shall not be thine heir; but he that shall come *forth* out *of* thine own bowels shall be thine heir. And he brought him forth abroad, and said, Look now toward heaven, and tell the stars, if thou be able to number them: and he said unto him, So shall thy seed be (*Genesis 15:3-5*).

And the days of Adam after he had *begotten* Seth were eight hundred years: and he begat sons and daughters (*Genesis 5:4*).

For God so loved the world, that he gave his only *begotten* Son, that who-soever believeth in him should not perish, but have everlasting life. For God sent not his Son into the world to condemn the world; but that the world through him might be saved. He that believeth on him is not condemned: but he that believeth not is condemned already, because he hath not believed in the name of the only *begotten* Son of God (*John 3:16*).

Unto the woman he said, I will greatly multiply thy sorrow and thy con-ception; in sorrow thou shalt *bring forth* children; and thy desire shall be to thy husband, and he shall rule over thee (*Genesis 3:16*).

And she shall *bring forth* a son, and thou shalt call his name JESUS: for he shall save his people from their sins. Now all this was done, that it might be fulfilled which was spoken of the Lord by the prophet, saying, Behold, a virgin shall be with child, and shall *bring forth* a son, and they shall call his name Emmanuel, which being interpreted is, God with us. Then Joseph being raised from sleep did as the angel of the Lord had bidden him, and took unto him his wife: And knew her not till she had brought forth her firstborn son: and he called his name JESUS (*Matthew 1:21-25*).

A woman when she is in travail hath sorrow, because her hour is come: but as soon as she is delivered of the child, she remembereth no more the anguish, for joy that a man is born into the world (*John 16:21*).

Fear took hold upon them there, and *pain*, as of *a woman in travail* (*Psalm 48:6*).

Now these are the generations of the sons of Noah, Shem, Ham, and Japheth: and unto them were sons *born* after the flood (*Genesis 10:1*).

And Abraham was an hundred years old, when his son Isaac was born unto him. And Sarah said, God hath made me to laugh, so that all that hear will laugh with me. And she said, Who would have said unto Abraham, that Sarah should have given children suck? for I have *born* him a son in his old age (*Genesis 21:5-7*).

And Jacob begat Joseph the husband of Mary, of whom was *born* Jesus, who is called Christ (*Matthew 1:16*).

And when her days to *be delivered* were fulfilled, behold, there were twins in her womb (*Genesis 25:24*).

And his daughter in law, Phinehas' wife, was with child, near to *be delivered*: and when she heard the tidings that the ark of God was taken, and that her father in law and her husband were dead, she bowed herself and travailed; for her pains came upon her (*1 Samuel 4:19*).

A woman when she is in travail hath sorrow, because her hour is come: but as soon as she is delivered of the child, she remembereth no more the anguish, for joy that a man is born into the world (*John 16:21*).

22c. For I will pour water upon him that is thirsty, and floods upon the dry ground: I will pour my spirit *upon* thy seed, and my blessing upon thine offspring (*Isaiah 44:3*).

And the LORD God caused a deep sleep to fall *upon* Adam and he slept: and he took one of his ribs, and closed up the flesh instead thereof (*Genesis 2:21*).

Thou shalt not bow down thyself to them, nor serve them: for I the LORD thy God am a jealous God, visiting the iniquity of the fathers *upon* the children unto the third and fourth generation of them that hate me (*Exodus 20:5*).

And it came to pass, as he drew back his hand, that, behold his brother came out: and she said, How hast thou broken forth? this breach be *upon* thee: therefore his name was called Pharez. And afterward came out his brother, that had the scarlet thread *upon* his hand: and his name was called Zarah (*Genesis 38:29-30*).

And David said to Abishai, and to all his servants, Behold, my son, which came *forth of* my bowels, seeketh my life: how much more now may this Benjamite do it? let him alone, and let him curse; for the LORD hath bidden him (*2 Samuel 16:11*).

As he came *forth of* his mother's womb, naked shall he return to go as he came, and shall take nothing of his labour, which he may carry away in his hand (*Ecclesiastes 5:15*).

And thou shalt take two onyx stones, and grave on them the names of the children of Israel: Six of their names on one stone, and the other six names of the rest on the other stone, according to their *birth* (*Exodus 28:9-10*).

Shall I bring to the *birth*, and not cause to bring forth? saith the LORD: shall I cause to bring forth, and shut the womb? saith thy God (*Isaiah 66:9*).

Shall I *bring to the birth*, and not cause to bring forth? saith the Lord: shall I cause to bring forth, and shut the womb? saith thy God (*Isaiah 66:9*).

22d. For I will pour water upon him that is thirsty, and floods upon the dry ground: I will pour my spirit *upon* thy seed, and my blessing upon thine offspring (*Isaiah 44:3*).

But there went up a mist from the earth, and watered *the whole* face of the ground (*Genesis 2:6*).

And the angel of the LORD said unto her, Behold, thou art with child, and shalt *bear* a son, and shalt call his name Ishmael; because the LORD hath heard thy affliction (*Genesis 16:11*).

And God said, Sarah thy wife shall *bear* thee a son indeed; and thou shalt call his name Isaac: and I will establish my covenant with him for an everlasting covenant and with his seed after him (*Genesis 17:19*).

But the angel said unto him, Fear not, Zacharias: for thy prayer is heard; and thy wife Elisabeth shall *bear* thee a son, and thou shalt call his name John (*Luke 1:13*).

Unto the woman he said, I will greatly multiply thy sorrow and thy conception; in sorrow thou shalt *bring forth* children; and thy desire shall be to thy husband, and he shall rule over thee (*Genesis 3:16*).

And she shall *bring forth* a son, and thou shalt call his name JESUS: for he shall save his people from their sins. Now all this was done, that it might be fulfilled which was spoken of the Lord by the prophet, saying, Behold, a virgin shall be with child, and shall *bring forth* a son, and they shall call his name Emmanuel, which being interpreted is, God with us. Then Joseph being raised from sleep did as the angel of the Lord had bidden him, and took unto him his wife: And knew her not till she had brought forth her firstborn son: and he called his name JESUS (*Matthew 1:21-25*).

And when her days to *be delivered* were fulfilled, behold, there were twins in her womb (*Genesis 25:24*).

And his daughter in law, Phinehas' wife, was with child, near to *be delivered*: and when she heard the tidings that the ark of God was taken, and that her father in law and her husband were dead, she bowed herself and travailed; for her pains came upon her (*1 Samuel 4:19*).

A woman when she is in travail hath sorrow, because her hour is come: but as soon as she is delivered of the child, she remembereth no more the anguish, for joy that a man is born into the world (*John 16:21*).

23a.   How goodly are thy tents, O Jacob, and thy tabernacles, O Israel! As the valleys are they spread forth, as gardens by the river's side, as the trees of lign aloes which the LORD hath planted, and as cedar trees beside the waters. He shall pour the water out of his buckets, and *his seed shall be in many waters*, and his king shall be higher than Agag, and his kingdom shall be exalted. God brought him forth out of Egypt; he hath as it were the strength of a unicorn: he shall eat up the nations his enemies, and shall break their bones, and pierce them through with his arrows. He couched, he lay down as a lion, and as a great lion: who shall stir him up? Blessed is he that blesseth thee, and cursed is he that curseth thee (*Numbers 24:5-9*).

Drink *waters* out of thine own cistern, and running *waters* out of thine own well. Let thy fountains be dispersed abroad, and rivers of waters in the streets. Let them be only thine own, and not strangers' with thee. Let thy fountain be blessed: and rejoice with the wife of thy youth. Let her be as the loving hind and pleasant roe; let her breasts satisfy thee at all times; and be thou ravished always with her love. And why wilt thou, my son, be ravished with a strange woman, and embrace the bosom of a stranger (*Proverbs 5:15-20*)?

The burden of Tyre. Howl, ye ships of Tarshish; for it is laid waste, so that there is no house, no entering in: from the land of Chittim it is revealed to them. Be still, ye inhabitants of the isle; thou whom the merchants of Zidon, that pass over the sea, have replenished. And by great *waters* the seed of Sihor, the harvest of the river, is her revenue; and she is a mart of nations. Be thou ashamed, O Zidon: for the sea hath spoken, even the strength of the sea, saying, I travail not, nor bring forth children, neither do I nourish up young men, nor bring up virgins (*Isaiah 23:1-4*).

Hear ye this, O house of Jacob, which are called by the name of Israel, and are come forth out of the *waters* of Judah, which swear by the name of the LORD, and make mention of the God of Israel, but not in truth, nor in righteousness (*Isaiah 48:1*).

A drought is upon her *waters*; and they shall be dried up: for it is the land of graven images, and they are mad upon their idols (*Jeremiah 50:38*).

Thy mother is like a vine in thy blood, planted by the *waters*: she was fruitful and full of branches by reason of many *waters*. And she had strong rods for the scepters of them that bare rule, and her stature was exalted among the thick branches, and she appeared in her height with the multitude of her branches (*Ezekiel 19:10-11*).

And it came to pass in the eleventh year, in the third month, in the first day of the month, that the word of the LORD came unto me, saying, Son of man, speak unto Pharaoh king of Egypt, and to his multitude; Whom art thou like in thy greatness? Behold, the Assyrian was a cedar in Lebanon with fair branches, and with a shadowing shroud, and of a high stature; and his top was among the thick boughs. The *waters* made him great, the deep set him up on high with her rivers running round about his plants, and sent out her little rivers unto all the trees of the field. Therefore his height was exalted above all the trees of the field, and his boughs were multiplied, and his branches became long because of the multitude of *waters*, when he shot forth. All the fowls of heaven made their nests in his boughs, and under his branches did all the beasts of the field bring forth their young, and under his shadow dwelt all great nations. Thus was he fair in his greatness, in the length of his branches: for his root was by great *waters* (*Ezekiel 31:1-7*).

And he made his camels to kneel down without the city by a well of water at the time of the evening, even the time that women go out to draw *water*. And he said, O LORD God of my master Abraham, I pray thee, send me good speed this day, and show kindness unto my master Abraham. Behold, I stand here by the well of water; and the daughters of the men of the city come out to draw water (*Genesis 24:11-13*).

Behold, I stand by the well of water; and it shall come to pass, that when the virgin cometh forth to draw *water*, and I say to her, Give me, I pray thee, a little water of thy pitcher to drink; And she say to me, Both drink thou, and I will also draw for thy camels: let the same be the woman whom the LORD hath appointed out for my master's son. And before I had done speaking in mine heart, behold, Rebekah came forth with her pitcher on her shoulder; and she went down unto the well, and drew water: and I said unto her, Let me drink, I pray thee (*Genesis 24:43-45*).

A garden enclosed is my sister, my spouse; a *spring* shut up, a *fountain* sealed. Thy plants are an orchard of pomegranates, with pleasant fruits; camphire, with spikenard, Spikenard and saffron; calamus and cinnamon, with all trees of frankincense; myrrh and aloes, with all the chief spices: A *fountain* of gardens, a well of living waters, and streams from Lebanon (*Song 4:12-15*).

And it shall come to pass in that day, that the mountains shall drop down new wine, and the hills shall flow with milk, and all the rivers of Judah shall flow with waters, and a *fountain* shall come forth of the house of the LORD, and shall water the valley of Shittim (*Joel 3:18*).

And now thy two sons, Ephraim and Manasseh, which were born unto thee in the land of Egypt before I came unto thee into Egypt, are mine; as Reuben and Simeon, they shall be mine. And thy *issue*, which thou begettest after them, shall be thine, and shall be called after the name of their brethren in their inheritance (*Genesis 48:5-6*).

Again the word of the Lord came unto me, saying, Son of man, cause Jerusalem to know her abominations, And say, Thus saith the Lord God unto Jerusalem; Thy birth and thy *nativity* is of the land of Canaan; thy father was an Amorite, and thy mother an Hittite. And as for thy *nativity*, in the day thou wast born thy navel was not cut, neither wast thou washed in water to supple thee; thou wast not salted at all, nor swaddled at all (*Ezekiel16:1-4*).

And it came to pass in those days, that there went out a decree from Caesar Augustus, that all the world should be taxed. (And this taxing was first made when Cyrenius was governor of Syria.) And all went to be taxed, every one into his own city. And Joseph also went up from Galilee, out of the city of Nazareth, into Judaea, unto the city of David, which is called Bethlehem; (because he was of the house and *lineage* of David:) To be taxed with Mary his espoused wife, being great with child. And so it was, that, while they were there, the days were accomplished that she should be delivered. And she brought forth her firstborn son, and wrapped him in swaddling clothes, and laid him in a manger; because there was no room for them in the inn (*Luke 2:1-7*).

Thou shalt know also that thy seed shall be great, and thine *offspring* as the grass of the earth (*Job 5:25*).

Hear this word that the Lord hath spoken against you, O children of Israel, against the whole *family* which I brought up from the land of Egypt, saying, You only have I known of all the families of the earth: therefore I will punish you for all your iniquities. (*Amos 3:1-2*)

And the days of Adam after he had *begotten* Seth were eight hundred years: and he begat sons and daughters (*Genesis 5:4*).

For God so loved the world, that he gave his only *begotten* Son, that whosoever believeth in him should not perish, but have everlasting life. For God sent not his Son into the world to condemn the world; but that the world through him might be saved. He that believeth on him is not condemned: but he that believeth not is condemned already, because he hath not believed in the name of the only *begotten* Son of God (*John 3:16-18*).

Unto the woman he said, I will greatly multiply thy sorrow and thy conception; in sorrow thou shalt *bring forth* children; and thy desire shall be to thy husband, and he shall rule over thee (*Genesis 3:16*).

And she shall *bring forth* a son, and thou shalt call his name JESUS: for he shall save his people from their sins. Now all this was done, that it might be fulfilled which was spoken of the Lord by the prophet, saying, Behold, a virgin shall be with child, and shall *bring forth* a son, and they shall call his name Emmanuel, which being interpreted is, God with us. Then Joseph being raised from sleep did as the angel of the Lord had bidden him, and took unto him his wife: And knew her not till she had brought forth her firstborn son: and he called his name JESUS (*Matthew 1:21-25*).

A woman when she is in *travail* hath sorrow, because her hour is come: but as soon as she is delivered of the child, she remembereth no more the anguish, for joy that a man is born into the world (*John 16:21*).

Now these are the generations of the sons of Noah, Shem, Ham, and Japheth: and unto them were sons *born* after the flood (*Genesis 10:1*).

And Abraham was an hundred years old, when his son Isaac was born unto him. And Sarah said, God hath made me to laugh, so that all that hear will laugh with me. And she said, Who would have said unto Abraham, that Sarah should have given children suck? for I have *born* him a son in his old age (*Genesis 21:5-7*).

And Jacob begat Joseph the husband of Mary, of whom was *born* Jesus, who is called Christ (*Matthew 1:16*).

And when her days to *be delivered* were fulfilled, behold, there were twins in her womb (*Genesis 25:24*).

And his daughter in law, Phinehas' wife, was with child, near to *be delivered*: and when she heard the tidings that the ark of God was taken, and that her father in law and her husband were dead, she bowed herself and travailed; for her pains came upon her (*1 Samuel 4:19*).

A woman when she is in travail hath sorrow, because her hour is come: but as soon as she is delivered of the child, she remembereth no more the anguish, for joy that a man is born into the world (*John 16:21*).

23b.   He shall pour the water out of his buckets, and *his seed shall be in many waters*, and his king shall be higher than Agag, and his kingdom shall be exalted (*Numbers 24:7*).

Thy mother is like a vine in thy blood, planted by the *waters*: she was fruitful and full of branches by reason of many *waters*. And she had strong rods for the scepters of them that bare rule, and her stature was exalted among the thick branches, and she appeared in her height with the multitude of her branches (*Ezekiel 19:10-11*).

And it came to pass in the eleventh year, in the third month, in the first day of the month, that the word of the LORD came unto me, saying, Son of man, speak unto Pharaoh king of Egypt, and to his multitude; Whom art thou like in thy greatness? Behold, the Assyrian was a cedar in Lebanon with fair branches, and with a shadowing shroud, and of a high stature; and his top was among the thick boughs. The *waters* made him great, the deep set him up on high with her rivers running round about his plants, and sent out her little rivers unto all the trees of the field. Therefore his height was exalted above all the trees of the field, and his boughs were multiplied, and his branches became long because of the multitude of *waters*, when he shot forth. All the fowls of heaven made their nests in his boughs, and under his branches did all the beasts of the field bring forth their young, and under his shadow dwelt all great nations. Thus was he fair in his greatness, in the length of his branches: for his root was by great *waters*. The cedars in the garden of God could not hide him: the fir trees were not like his boughs, and the chestnut trees were not like his branches; nor any tree in the garden of God was like unto him in his beauty. I have made him fair by the multitude of his branches: so that all the trees of Eden, that were in the garden of God, envied him (*Ezekiel 31:1-9*).

Hear ye this, O house of Jacob, which are called by the name of Israel, and are come forth out of the *waters* of Judah, which swear by the name of the LORD, and make mention of the God of Israel, but not in truth, nor in righteousness (*Isaiah 48:1*).

And he made his camels to kneel down without the city by a well of water at the time of the evening, even the time that women go out to draw *water*. And he said, O LORD God of my master Abraham, I pray thee, send me good speed this day, and show kindness unto my master Abraham. Behold, I stand here by the well of water; and the daughters of the men of the city come out to draw water (*Genesis 24:11-13*).

Behold, I stand by the well of water; and it shall come to pass, that when the virgin cometh forth to draw *water*, and I say to her, Give me, I pray thee, a little water of thy pitcher to drink; And she say to me, Both drink thou, and I will also draw for thy camels: let the same be the woman whom the LORD hath appointed out for my master's son. And before I had done speaking in mine heart, behold, Rebekah came forth with her pitcher on her shoulder; and she went down unto the well, and drew water: and I said unto her, Let me drink, I pray thee (*Genesis 24:43-45*).

And the angel of the LORD said unto her, Behold, thou art with child, and shalt *bear* a son, and shalt call his name Ishmael; because the LORD hath heard thy affliction (*Genesis 16:11*).

But the angel said unto him, Fear not, Zacharias: for thy prayer is heard; and thy wife Elisabeth shall *bear* thee a son, and thou shalt call his name John (*Luke 1:13*).

And God said, Sarah thy wife shall *bear* thee a son indeed; and thou shalt call his name Isaac: and I will establish my covenant with him for an everlasting covenant, and with his seed after him (*Genesis 17:19*).

And Adam knew his wife again; and she bare a son, and called his name Seth: For God, said she, hath appointed me another seed instead of Abel, whom Cain slew. And to Seth, to him also there was *born* a son; and he called his name Enos: then began men to call upon the name of the LORD (*Genesis 4:25-26*).

And when her days to *be delivered* were fulfilled, behold, there were twins in her womb (*Genesis 25:24*).

And his daughter in law, Phinehas' wife, was with child, near to *be delivered*: and when she heard the tidings that the ark of God was taken, and that her father in law and her husband were dead, she bowed herself and travailed; for her pains came upon her (*1 Samuel 4:19*).

A woman when she is in travail hath sorrow, because her hour is come: but as soon as she is delivered of the child, she remembereth no more the anguish, for joy that a man is born into the world *(John 16:21)*.

23c. He shall pour the water out of his buckets, and *his seed shall be in many waters*, and his king shall be higher than Agag, and his kingdom shall be exalted *(Numbers 24:7)*.

Thy mother is like a vine in thy blood, planted by the *waters*: she was fruitful and full of branches by reason of many *waters*. And she had strong rods for the scepters of them that bare rule, and her stature was exalted among the thick branches, and she appeared in her height with the multitude of her branches *(Ezekiel 19:10-11)*.

And it came to pass in the eleventh year, in the third month, in the first day of the month, that the word of the LORD came unto me, saying, Son of man, speak unto Pharaoh king of Egypt, and to his multitude; Whom art thou like in thy greatness? Behold, the Assyrian was a cedar in Lebanon with fair branches, and with a shadowing shroud, and of a high stature; and his top was among the thick boughs. The *waters* made him great, the deep set him up on high with her rivers running round about his plants, and sent out her little rivers unto all the trees of the field. Therefore his height was exalted above all the trees of the field, and his boughs were multiplied, and his branches became long because of the multitude of *waters*, when he shot forth. All the fowls of heaven made their nests in his boughs, and under his branches did all the beasts of the field bring forth their young, and under his shadow dwelt all great nations. Thus was he fair in his greatness, in the length of his branches: for his root was by great *waters*. The cedars in the garden of God could not hide him: the fir trees were not like his boughs, and the chestnut trees were not like his branches; nor any tree in the garden of God was like unto him in his beauty. I have made him fair by the multitude of his branches: so that all the trees of Eden, that were in the garden of God, envied him *(Ezekiel 31:1-9)*.

Hear ye this, O house of Jacob, which are called by the name of Israel, and are come forth out of the *waters* of Judah, which swear by the name of the LORD, and make mention of the God of Israel, but not in truth, nor in righteousness *(Isaiah 48:1)*.

And he made his camels to kneel down without the city by a well of water at the time of the evening, even the time that women go out to draw *water*. And he said, O LORD God of my master Abraham, I pray thee, send me good speed this day, and show kindness unto my master Abraham. Behold, I stand here by the well of water; and the daughters of the men of the city come out to draw water (*Genesis 24:11-13*).

Behold, I stand by the well of water; and it shall come to pass, that when the virgin cometh forth to draw *water*, and I say to her, Give me, I pray thee, a little water of thy pitcher to drink; And she say to me, Both drink thou, and I will also draw for thy camels: let the same be the woman whom the LORD hath appointed out for my master's son. And before I had done speaking in mine heart, behold, Rebekah came forth with her pitcher on her shoulder; and she went down unto the well, and drew water: and I said unto her, Let me drink, I pray thee (*Genesis 24:43-45*).

And the LORD shall guide thee continually, and satisfy thy soul in drought, and make fat thy bones: and thou shalt be like a watered garden, and like a spring of *water*, whose waters fail not. And they that shall be of thee shall build the old waste places: thou shalt raise up the foundations of many generations; and thou shalt be called, The repairer of the breach, The restorer of paths to dwell in (*Isaiah 58:11-12*).

Who hath heard such a thing? who hath seen such things? Shall the earth be made to bring forth in one day? or shall a nation be born at once? for as soon as Zion travailed, she brought forth her children. Shall I bring to the birth, and not *cause to bring forth*? saith the LORD : shall I *cause to bring forth*, and shut the womb? saith thy God. Rejoice ye with Jerusalem, and be glad with her, all ye that love her: rejoice for joy with her, all ye that mourn for her: That ye may suck, and be satisfied with the breasts of her consolations; that ye may milk out, and be delighted with the abundance of her glory (*Isaiah 66:8-11*).

Unto the woman he said, I will greatly multiply thy sorrow and thy con- ception; in sorrow thou shalt *bring forth* children; and thy desire shall be to thy husband, and he shall rule over thee (*Genesis 3:16*).

And Adam knew his wife again; and she bare a son, and called his name Seth: For God, said she, hath appointed me another seed instead of Abel, whom Cain slew. And to Seth, to him also there was *born* a son; and he called his name Enos: then began men to call upon the name of the LORD (*Genesis 4:25-26*).

And when her days to *be delivered* were fulfilled, behold, there were twins in her womb (*Genesis 25:24*).

And his daughter in law, Phinehas' wife, was with child, near to *be delivered*: and when she heard the tidings that the ark of God was taken, and that her father in law and her husband were dead, she bowed herself and travailed; for her pains came upon her (*1 Samuel 4:19*).

A woman when she is in travail hath sorrow, because her hour is come: but as soon as she is delivered of the child, she remembereth no more the anguish, for joy that a man is born into the world (*John 16:21*).

Fear took hold upon them there, and *pain*, as of *a woman in travail* (*Psalm 48:6*).

23d. He shall pour the water out of his buckets, and *his seed shall be in many waters*, and his king shall be higher than Agag, and his kingdom shall be exalted (*Numbers 24:7*).

Thy mother is like a vine in thy blood, planted by the *waters*: she was fruitful and full of branches by reason of many *waters*. And she had strong rods for the scepters of them that bare rule, and her stature was exalted among the thick branches, and she appeared in her height with the multitude of her branches (*Ezekiel 19:10-11*).

And it came to pass in the eleventh year, in the third month, in the first day of the month, that the word of the LORD came unto me, saying, Son of man, speak unto Pharaoh king of Egypt, and to his multitude; Whom art thou like in thy greatness? Behold, the Assyrian was a cedar in Lebanon with fair branches, and with a shadowing shroud, and of a high stature; and his top was among the thick boughs. The *waters* made him great, the deep set him up on high with her rivers running round about his plants, and sent out her little rivers unto all the trees of the field. Therefore his height was exalted above all the trees of the field, and his boughs were multiplied, and his branches became long because of the multitude of *waters*, when he shot forth. All the fowls of heaven made their nests in his boughs, and under his branches did all the beasts of the field bring forth their young, and under his shadow dwelt all great nations. Thus was he fair in his greatness, in the length of his branches: for his root was by great *waters*. The cedars in the garden of God could not hide him: the fir trees were not like his boughs, and the chestnut trees were not like his branches; nor any tree in the garden of God was like unto him in his beauty. I have made him fair by the multitude of his branches: so that all the trees of Eden, that were in the garden of God, envied him (*Ezekiel 31:1-9*).

Hear ye this, O house of Jacob, which are called by the name of Israel, and are come forth out of the *waters* of Judah, which swear by the name of the LORD, and make mention of the God of Israel, but not in truth, nor in righteousness (*Isaiah 48:1*).

And he made his camels to kneel down without the city by a well of water at the time of the evening, even the time that women go out to draw *water*. And he said, O LORD God of my master Abraham, I pray thee, send me good speed this day, and show kindness unto my master Abraham. Behold, I stand here by the well of water; and the daughters of the men of the city come out to draw water (*Genesis 24:11-13*).

Behold, I stand by the well of water; and it shall come to pass, that when the virgin cometh forth to draw *water*, and I say to her, Give me, I pray thee, a little water of thy pitcher to drink; And she say to me, Both drink thou, and I will also draw for thy camels: let the same be the woman whom the LORD hath appointed out for my master's son. And before I had done speaking in mine heart, behold, Rebekah came forth with her pitcher on her shoulder; and she went down unto the well, and drew water: and I said unto her, Let me drink, I pray thee (*Genesis 24:43-45*).

And the LORD shall guide thee continually, and satisfy thy soul in drought, and make fat thy bones: and thou shalt be like a watered garden, and like a spring of *water*, whose waters fail not. And they that shall be of thee shall build the old waste places: thou shalt raise up the foundations of many generations; and thou shalt be called, The repairer of the breach, The restorer of paths to dwell in (*Isaiah 58:11-12*).

And the angel of the LORD said unto her, Behold, thou art with child, and shalt *bear* a son, and shalt call his name Ishmael; because the LORD hath heard thy affliction (*Genesis 16:11*).

But the angel said unto him, Fear not, Zacharias: for thy prayer is heard; and thy wife Elisabeth shall *bear* thee a son, and thou shalt call his name John (*Luke 1:13*).

And God said, Sarah thy wife shall *bear* thee a son indeed; and thou shalt call his name Isaac: and I will establish my covenant with him for an everlasting covenant, and with his seed after him (*Genesis 17:19*).

After these things the word of the LORD came unto Abram in a vision, saying, Fear not, Abram: I am thy shield, and thy exceeding great reward. And Abram said, Lord GOD, what wilt thou give me, seeing I go childless, and the steward of my house is this Eliezer of Damascus? And Abram said, Behold, to me thou hast given no *seed*: and, lo, one born in my house is mine heir. And, behold, the word of the LORD came unto him, saying, This shall not be thine heir; but he that shall come forth out of thine own bowels shall be thine heir. And he brought him forth abroad, and said, Look now toward heaven, and tell the stars, if thou be able to number them: and he said unto him, So shall thy *seed* be (*Genesis 15:1-5*).

And when Rachel saw that she bare Jacob no children, Rachel envied her sister; and said unto Jacob, Give me children, or else I die. And Jacob's anger was kindled against Rachel: and he said, Am I in God's stead, who hath withheld from thee the *fruit* of the womb? And she said, Behold my maid Bilhah, go in unto her; and she shall bear upon my knees that I may also have children by her. And she gave him Bilhah her handmaid to wife: and Jacob went in unto her. And Bilhah conceived, and bare Jacob a son (*Genesis 30:1-5*).

For these two years hath the famine been in the land: and yet there are five years, in the which there shall neither be earing nor harvest. And God sent me before you to preserve you a *posterity* in the earth, and to save your lives by a great deliverance. So now it was not you that sent me hither, but God: and he hath made me a father to Pharaoh, and lord of all his house, and a ruler throughout all the land of Egypt (*Genesis 45:6-8*).

And he said, Hagar, Sarai's maid, whence camest thou? and whither wilt thou go? And she said, I flee from the face of my mistress Sarai. And the angel of the LORD said unto her, Return to thy mistress, and submit thyself under her hands. And the angel of the LORD said unto her, I will multiply thy seed exceedingly, that it shall not be numbered for multitude. And the angel of the LORD said unto her, Behold, *thou art with child*, and shalt bear a son, and shalt call his name Ishmael; because the LORD hath heard thy affliction (*Genesis 16:8-11*).

Thy seed also had been as the sand, and the *offspring* of thy bowels like the gravel thereof; his name should not have been cut off nor destroyed from before me (*Isaiah 48:19*).

And the angel of the LORD said unto her, Behold, thou art with child, and shalt *bear* a son, and shalt call his name Ishmael; because the LORD hath heard thy affliction (*Genesis 16:11*).

But the angel said unto him, Fear not, Zacharias: for thy prayer is heard; and thy wife Elisabeth shall *bear* thee a son, and thou shalt call his name John (*Luke 1:13*).

Unto the woman he said, I will greatly multiply thy sorrow and thy conception; in sorrow thou shalt *bring forth* children; and thy desire shall be to thy husband, and he shall rule over thee (*Genesis 3:16*).

And she shall *bring forth* a son, and thou shalt call his name JESUS: for he shall save his people from their sins. Now all this was done, that it might be fulfilled which was spoken of the Lord by the prophet, saying, Behold, a virgin shall be with child, and shall *bring forth* a son, and they shall call his name Emmanuel, which being interpreted is, God with us. Then Joseph being raised from sleep did as the angel of the Lord had bidden him, and took unto him his wife: And knew her not till she had brought forth her firstborn son: and he called his name JESUS (*Matthew 1:21-25*).

And Jacob begat Joseph the husband of Mary, of whom was *born* Jesus, who is called Christ (*Matthew 1:16*).

And when her days to *be delivered* were fulfilled, behold, there were twins in her womb (*Genesis 25:24*).

And his daughter in law, Phinehas' wife, was with child, near to *be delivered*: and when she heard the tidings that the ark of God was taken, and that her father in law and her husband were dead, she bowed herself and travailed; for her pains came upon her (*1 Samuel 4:19*).

A woman when she is in travail hath sorrow, because her hour is come: but as soon as she is delivered of the child, she remembereth no more the anguish, for joy that a man is born into the world (*John 16:21*).

Fear took hold upon them there, and *pain*, as of *a woman in travail* (*Psalm 48:6*).

24.   And he *said*, I will certainly return unto thee according to the time of life; and, lo, Sarah thy wife shall have a son. And Sarah heard it in the tent door, which was behind him. Now Abraham and Sarah were old and well stricken in age; and it ceased to be with Sarah after the manner of women. Therefore Sarah laughed within herself, saying, After I am waxed old shall I have pleasure, my lord being old also? And the LORD *said* unto Abraham, Wherefore did Sarah laugh, saying, Shall I of a surety bear a child, which am old? Is any thing too hard for the LORD? At the time *appoint[ed]* I will return unto thee, according to the time of life, and Sarah shall have a son. Then Sarah denied, saying, I laughed not; for she was afraid. And he *said*, Nay; but thou didst laugh. And the men rose up from thence, and looked toward Sodom: and Abraham went with them to bring them on the way. And the Lord *said*, Shall I hide from Abraham that thing which I do; Seeing that Abraham shall surely become a great and mighty nation, and all the nations of the earth shall be blessed in him (*Genesis 18:10-18*)?

For I know him, that he will *command* his children and his household after him, and they shall keep the way of the LORD, to do justice and judgment; that the LORD may bring upon Abraham that which he hath spoken of him (*Genesis 18:19*).

Man that is born of a woman is of few days, and full of trouble… If a man die, shall he live again? all the days of my *appoint[ed]* time will I wait, till my change come (*Job 14:1, 14*).

Male and *female* created he them; and blessed them, and called their name Adam, in the day when they were created (*Genesis 5:2*).

Unto the *woman* he said, I will greatly multiply thy sorrow and thy conception; in sorrow thou shalt bring forth children; and thy desire shall be to thy husband, and he shall rule over thee (*Genesis 3:16*).

And Adam knew Eve his *wife*; and she conceived, and bare Cain, and said, I have gotten a man from the LORD. And she again bare his brother Abel. And Abel was a keeper of sheep, but Cain was a tiller of the ground (*Genesis 4:1-2*).

25. *Let there be* none to extend mercy unto him: neither *let there be* any to favor his fatherless children. Let his posterity be cut off; and in the generation following let their name be blotted out (*Psalm 109:12-13*).

And they smote all the souls that were therein with the edge of the sword, utterly destroying them: there was not any left *to breathe*: and he burnt Hazor with fire (*Joshua 11:11*).

And when her days *to be* delivered were fulfilled, behold, there were twins in her womb. And the first came out red, all over like a hairy garment; and they called his name Esau (*Genesis 25:24-25*).

Seeing that Abraham shall surely *become* a great and mighty nation, and all the nations of the earth shall be blessed in him (*Genesis 18:18*)?

Then will we give our daughters unto you, and we will take your daughters to us, and we will dwell with you, and we will *become* one people (*Genesis 34:16*).

And his father refused, and said, I know it, my son, I know it: he also shall become a people, and he also shall be great: but truly his younger brother shall be greater than he, and his seed shall *become* a multitude of nations (*Genesis 48:19*).

And Adam knew Eve his wife; and she conceived, and bare Cain, and said, I *have* gotten a man from the LORD (*Genesis 4:1*).

And he said, I will certainly return unto thee according to the time of life; and, lo, Sarah thy wife shall *have* a son. And Sarah heard it in the tent door, which was behind him (*Genesis 18:10*).

And God blessed them, saying, *Be* fruitful, and multiply, and fill the waters in the seas, and let fowl multiply in the earth (*Genesis 1:22*).

And when her days to *be* delivered were fulfilled, behold, there were twins in her womb. And the first came out red, all over like a hairy garment; and they called his name Esau (*Genesis 25:24-25*).

And the angel of the LORD said unto her, Behold, thou art with child, and shalt *bear* a son, and shalt call his name Ishmael; because the LORD hath heard thy affliction (*Genesis 16:11*).

But the angel said unto him, Fear not, Zacharias: for thy prayer is heard; and thy wife Elisabeth shall *bear* thee a son, and thou shalt call his name John (*Luke 1:13*).

Unto the woman he said, I will greatly multiply thy sorrow and thy conception; in sorrow thou shalt *bring forth* children; and thy desire shall be to thy husband, and he shall rule over thee (*Genesis 3:16*).

Now these are the generations of the sons of Noah, Shem, Ham, and Japheth: and unto them were sons *born* after the flood (*Genesis 10:1*).

And Abraham was an hundred years old, when his son Isaac was born unto him. And Sarah said, God hath made me to laugh, so that all that hear will laugh with me. And she said, Who would have said unto Abraham, that Sarah should have given children suck? for I have *born* him a son in his old age (*Genesis 21:5-7*).

And when her days to *be delivered* were fulfilled, behold, there were twins in her womb (*Genesis 25:24*).

And his daughter in law, Phinehas' wife, was with child, near to *be delivered*: and when she heard the tidings that the ark of God was taken, and that her father in law and her husband were dead, she bowed herself and travailed; for her pains came upon her (*1 Samuel 4:19*).

A woman when she is in travail hath sorrow, because her hour is come: but as soon as she is delivered of the child, she remembereth no more the anguish, for joy that a man is born into the world (*John 16:21*).

Fear took hold upon them there, and *pain*, as of *a woman in travail* (*Psalm 48:6*).

26. And to Seth, to him also *there was* born a son; and he called his name Enos: then began men to call upon the name of the LORD (*Genesis 4:26*).

And they smote all the souls that were therein with the edge of the sword, utterly destroying them: there was not any left *to breathe*: and he burnt Hazor with fire (*Joshua 11:11*).

And God blessed them, saying, *Be* fruitful, and multiply, and fill the waters in the seas, and let fowl multiply in the earth (*Genesis 1:22*).

And when her days to *be* delivered were fulfilled, behold, there were twins in her womb. And the first came out red, all over like a hairy garment; and they called his name Esau (*Genesis 25:24-25*).

Seeing that Abraham shall surely *become* a great and mighty nation, and all the nations of the earth shall be blessed in him (*Genesis 18:18*)?

Then will we give our daughters unto you, and we will take your daughters to us, and we will dwell with you, and we will *become* one people (*Genesis 34:16*).

And his father refused, and said, I know it, my son, I know it: he also shall become a people, and he also shall be great: but truly his younger brother shall be greater than he, and his seed shall *become* a multitude of nations (*Genesis 48:19*).

And Adam knew Eve his wife; and she conceived, and bare Cain, and said, I *have* gotten a man from the LORD (*Genesis 4:1*).

And he said, I will certainly return unto thee according to the time of life; and, lo, Sarah thy wife shall *have* a son. And Sarah heard it in the tent door, which was behind him (*Genesis 18:10*).

And the angel of the LORD said unto her, Behold, thou art with child, and shalt *bear* a son, and shalt call his name Ishmael; because the LORD hath heard thy affliction (*Genesis 16:11*).

But the angel said unto him, Fear not, Zacharias: for thy prayer is heard; and thy wife Elisabeth shall *bear* thee a son, and thou shalt call his name John (*Luke 1:13*).

Unto the woman he said, I will greatly multiply thy sorrow and thy conception; in sorrow thou shalt *bring forth* children; and thy desire shall be to thy husband, and he shall rule over thee (*Genesis 3:16*).

Now these are the generations of the sons of Noah, Shem, Ham, and Japheth: and unto them were sons *born* after the flood (*Genesis 10:1*).

And Abraham was an hundred years old, when his son Isaac was born unto him. And Sarah said, God hath made me to laugh, so that all that hear will laugh with me. And she said, Who would have said unto Abraham, that Sarah should have given children suck? for I have *born* him a son in his old age (*Genesis 21:5-7*).

And when her days to *be delivered* were fulfilled, behold, there were twins in her womb (*Genesis 25:24*).

And his daughter in law, Phinehas' wife, was with child, near to *be delivered*: and when she heard the tidings that the ark of God was taken, and that her father in law and her husband were dead,

she bowed herself and travailed; for her pains came upon her (*1 Samuel 4:19*).

A woman when she is in travail hath sorrow, because her hour is come: but as soon as she is delivered of the child, she remembereth no more the anguish, for joy that a man is born into the world (*John 16:21*).

Fear took hold upon them there, and *pain*, as of *a woman in travail* (*Psalm 48:6*).

27. Or as a hidden untimely birth I had not been; as infants which never saw *light* (*Job 3:16*).

As a snail which melteth, let every one of them pass away: like the untimely birth of a woman, that they *may not see the sun* (*Psalm 58:8*).

And it came to pass in the evening, that he took Leah his daughter, and brought her to him; and he went in unto her. And Laban gave unto his daughter Leah Zilpah his maid for a handmaid. And it came to pass, that in the *morning*, behold, it was Leah: and he said to Laban, What is this thou hast done unto me? did not I serve with thee for Rachel? wherefore then hast thou beguiled me (*Genesis 29:23-25*)?

Tarry this night, and it shall be in the *morning*, that if he will perform unto thee the part of a kinsman, well; let him do the kinsman's part: but if he will not do the part of a kinsman to thee, then will I do the part of a kinsman to thee, as the Lord liveth: lie down until the morning. And she lay at his feet until the morning: and she rose up before one could know another. And he said, Let it not be known that a woman came into the floor (*Ruth 3:13-14*).

In the *morning* sow thy seed, and in the evening withhold not thine hand: for thou knowest not whether shall prosper, either this or that, or whether they both shall be alike good (*Ecclesiastes 11:6*).

And Samson's wife wept before him, and said, Thou dost but hate me, and lovest me not: thou hast put forth a riddle unto the children of my people, and hast not told it me. And he said unto her, Behold, I have not told it my father nor my mother, and shall I tell it thee? And she wept before him the seven days, while their feast lasted: and it came to pass on the seventh day, that he told her, because she lay sore upon him: and she told the riddle to the children of her people. And the men of the city said unto him on the seventh day before the sun went down, What is sweeter than honey? and what is stronger than a lion? And he said unto them, If ye had not *plowed* with my heifer, ye had not found out my riddle. And the Spirit of the LORD came upon him, and he went down to Ashkelon, and slew thirty men of them, and took their spoil, and gave change of garments unto them which expounded the riddle. And his anger was kindled, and he went up to his father's house. But Samson's wife was given to his companion, whom he had used as his friend (*Judges 14:16-20*).

And it came to pass, as he drew back his hand, that, behold, his brother came out: and she said, How hast thou *broken [break] forth*? this *breach* be upon thee: therefore his name was called *Pharez*. And afterward came out his brother, that had the scarlet thread upon his hand: and his name was called Zarah (*Genesis 38:29-30*).

Let us go up against Judah, and vex it, and let us make a *breach* therein for us, and set a king in the midst of it, even the son of Tabeal (*Isaiah 7:6*).

The sorrows of a travailing woman shall come upon him: he is an unwise son; for he should not stay long in the place of the *break[ing] forth* of children (*Hosea 13:13*).

And Israel stretched out his right hand, and laid it upon Ephraim's head, who was the younger, and his left hand upon Manasseh's head, guiding his hands wittingly; for Manasseh was the firstborn. And he blessed Joseph, and said, God, before whom my fathers Abraham and Isaac did walk, the God which fed me all my life long unto this day, The Angel which redeemed me from all evil, bless the lads; and let my name be named on them, and the name of my fathers Abraham and Isaac; and let them *grow* into a multitude in the midst of the earth. And when Joseph saw that his father laid his right hand upon the head of Ephraim, it displeased him: and he held up his father's hand, to remove it from Ephraim's head unto Manasseh's head. And Joseph said unto his father, Not so, my father: for this is the firstborn; put thy right hand upon his head (*Genesis 48:14-18*).

As thou knowest not what is the way of the spirit, nor how the bones do *grow* in the womb of her that is with child: even so thou knowest not the works of God who maketh all (*Ecclesiastes 11:5*).

And the angel of the LORD said unto her, Behold, thou art with child, and shalt *bear* a son, and shalt call his name Ishmael; because the LORD hath heard thy affliction (*Genesis 16:11*).

But the angel said unto him, Fear not, Zacharias: for thy prayer is heard; and thy wife Elisabeth shall *bear* thee a son, and thou shalt call his name John (*Luke 1:13*).

Unto the woman he said, I will greatly multiply thy sorrow and thy conception; in sorrow thou shalt *bring forth* children; and thy desire shall be to thy husband, and he shall rule over thee (*Genesis 3:16*).

And she shall *bring forth* a son, and thou shalt call his name JESUS: for he shall save his people from their sins. Now all this was done, that it might be fulfilled which was spoken of the Lord by the prophet, saying, Behold, a virgin shall be with child, and shall *bring forth* a son, and they shall call his name Emmanuel, which being interpreted is, God with us. Then Joseph being raised from sleep did as the angel of the Lord had bidden him, and took unto him his wife: And knew her not till she had brought forth her firstborn son: and he called his name JESUS (*Matthew 1:21-25*).

And Jacob begat Joseph the husband of Mary, of whom was *born* Jesus, who is called Christ (*Matthew 1:16*).

And when her days to *be delivered* were fulfilled, behold, there were twins in her womb (*Genesis 25:24*).

And his daughter in law, Phinehas' wife, was with child, near to *be delivered*: and when she heard the tidings that the ark of God was taken, and that her father in law and her husband were dead, she bowed herself and travailed; for her pains came upon her (*1 Samuel 4:19*).

A woman when she is in travail hath sorrow, because her hour is come: but as soon as she is delivered of the child, she remembereth no more the anguish, for joy that a man is born into the world (*John 16:21*).

Fear took hold upon them there, and *pain*, as of *a woman in travail* (*Psalm 48:6*).

28.   And God *saw* every thing that he had made, and, behold, it was very good. And the evening and the morning were the sixth day (*Genesis 1:31*).

And he went in unto Hagar, and she conceived: and when she *saw* that she had conceived, her mistress was despised in her eyes. And Sarai said unto Abram, My wrong be upon thee: I have given my maid into thy bosom; and when she *saw* that she had conceived, I was despised in her eyes: the LORD judge between me and thee (*Genesis 16:4-5*).

And when the LORD *saw* that Leah was hated, he opened her womb: but Rachel was barren. And Leah conceived, and bare a son, and she called his name Reuben: for she said, Surely the LORD hath looked upon my affliction; now therefore my husband will love me (*Genesis 29:31-32*).

And, *behold,* thou shalt conceive in thy womb, and bring forth a son, and shalt call his name JESUS. He shall be great, and shall be called the *Son* of the Highest: and the Lord God shall give unto him the throne of his father David (*Luke 1:31-32*).

And Leah conceived, and bare a son, and she called his name *Reuben*: for she said, Surely the Lord hath looked upon my affliction; now *therefore* my husband will love me (*Genesis 29:32*).

And when her days to be delivered were fulfilled, behold, there were twins in her womb. And the *first* came out red, all over like a hairy garment; and they called his name Esau (*Genesis 25:24-25*).

For I have heard a voice as of a woman in travail, and the anguish as of her that bringeth forth her *first* child, the voice of the daughter of Zion, that bewaileth herself, that spreadeth her hands, saying,

Woe is me now! for my soul is wearied because of murderers (*Jeremiah 4:31*).

And Adam knew his wife again; and she bare *a son*, and called his name Seth: For God, said she, hath appointed me another seed instead of Abel, whom Cain slew. And to Seth, to him also there was born *a son*; and he called his name Enos: then began men to call upon the name of the LORD (*Genesis 4:25-26*).

And I will *make* thy seed as the dust of the earth: so that if a man can number the dust of the earth, then shall thy seed also be numbered (*Genesis 13:16*).

To every thing there is a season, and a time to every purpose under the heaven: A time to be born, and a time to die; a time to plant, and a time to pluck up that which is planted; A time to kill, and a time to heal; a time to break down, and a time *to build up* (*Ecclesiastes 3:1-3*).

And I will *make* thy seed as the dust of the earth: so that if a man can number the dust of the earth, then shall thy seed also be numbered (*Genesis 13:16*).

And the angel of the LORD said unto her, Behold, thou art with child, and shalt *bear* a son, and shalt call his name Ishmael; because the LORD hath heard thy affliction (*Genesis 16:11*).

But the angel said unto him, Fear not, Zacharias: for thy prayer is heard; and thy wife Elisabeth shall *bear* thee a son, and thou shalt call his name John (*Luke 1:13*).

Unto the woman he said, I will greatly multiply thy sorrow and thy conception; in sorrow thou shalt *bring forth* children; and thy desire shall be to thy husband, and he shall rule over thee (*Genesis 3:16*).

And she shall *bring forth* a son, and thou shalt call his name JESUS: for he shall save his people from their sins. Now all this was done, that it might be fulfilled which was spoken of the Lord by the prophet, saying, Behold, a virgin shall be with child, and shall *bring forth* a son, and they shall call his name Emmanuel, which being interpreted is, God with us. Then Joseph being raised from sleep did as the angel of the Lord had bidden him, and took unto him his wife: And knew her not till she had brought forth her firstborn son: and he called his name JESUS (*Matthew 1:21-25*).

Now these are the generations of the sons of Noah, Shem, Ham, and Japheth: and unto them were sons *born* after the flood (*Genesis 10:1*).

And Abraham was an hundred years old, when his son Isaac was born unto him. And Sarah said, God hath made me to laugh, so that all that hear will laugh with me. And she said, Who would have said unto Abraham, that Sarah should have given children suck? for I have *born* him a son in his old age (*Genesis 21:5-7*).

And Jacob begat Joseph the husband of Mary, of whom was *born* Jesus, who is called Christ (*Matthew 1:16*).

And when her days to *be delivered* were fulfilled, behold, there were twins in her womb (*Genesis 25:24*).

And his daughter in law, Phinehas' wife, was with child, near to *be delivered*: and when she heard the tidings that the ark of God was taken, and that her father in law and her husband were dead, she bowed herself and travailed; for her pains came upon her (*1 Samuel 4:19*).

A woman when she is in travail hath sorrow, because her hour is come: but as soon as she is delivered of the child, she remembereth no more the anguish, for joy that a man is born into the world (*John 16:21*).

Fear took hold upon them there, and *pain*, as of *a woman in travail* (*Psalm 48:6*).

29.   When the chief baker saw that the interpretation was *good*, he said unto Joseph, I also was in my dream, and, behold, I had three white baskets on my head (*Genesis 40:16*).

And the thing was *good* in the eyes of Pharaoh, and in the eyes of all his servants (*Genesis 41:37*).

The *precious* sons of Zion, comparable to fine gold, how are they esteemed as earthen pitchers, the work of the hands of the potter! (*Lamentations 4:2*).

And for the precious fruits brought forth by the sun, and for the *precious* things put forth by the moon (*Deuteronomy 33:14*).

He that goeth forth and weepeth, bearing *precious* seed, shall doubtless come again with rejoicing, bringing his sheaves with him (*Psalm 126:6*).

And Noah begat three sons, Shem, Ham, and *Japheth* (*Genesis 6:10*).

The *son[s] of Japheth*; Gomer, and Magog, and Madai, and Javan, and Tubal, and Meshech, and Tiras (*Genesis 10:2*).

30.   And unto Eber were born two sons: the name of the one was Peleg; because in his days the earth was *divided*: and his brother's name was Joktan (*1 Chronicles 1:19*).

And when he shall stand up, his kingdom shall be broken, and shall be *divided* toward the four winds of heaven; and not to his posterity, nor according to his dominion which he ruled: for his kingdom shall be plucked up, even for others beside those. And the king of the south shall be strong, and one of his princes; and he shall be strong above him, and have dominion; his dominion shall be a great dominion. And in the end of years they shall join themselves together; for the king's daughter of the south shall come to the king of the north to make an agreement: but she shall not retain the power of the arm; neither shall he stand, nor his arm: but she shall be given up, and they that brought her, and he that begat her, and he that strengthened her in these times. But out of a branch of her roots shall one stand up in his estate, which shall come with an army, and shall enter into the fortress of the king of the north, and shall deal against them, and shall prevail (*Daniel 11:4-7*).

And Jacob lifted up his eyes, and looked, and, behold, Esau came, and with him four hundred men. And he *divided* the children unto Leah, and unto Rachel, and unto the two handmaids (*Genesis 33:1*).

And it came to pass, as he drew back his hand, that, behold, his brother came out: and she said, How hast thou *broken [break] forth?* this *breach* be upon thee: therefore his name was called *Pharez.* And afterward came out his brother, that had the scarlet thread upon his hand: and his name was called Zarah (*Genesis 38:29-30*).

Let us go up against Judah, and vex it, and let us make a *breach* therein for us, and set a king in the midst of it, even the son of Tabeal (*Isaiah 7:6*).

And Israel stretched out his right hand, and laid it upon Ephraim's head, who was the younger, and his left hand upon Manasseh's head, guiding his hands wittingly; for Manasseh was the firstborn. And he blessed Joseph, and said, God, before whom my fathers Abraham and Isaac did walk, the God which fed me all my life long unto this day, The Angel which redeemed me from all evil, bless the lads; and let my name be named on them, and the name of my fathers Abraham and Isaac; and let them *grow* into a multitude in the midst of the earth. And when Joseph saw that his father laid his right hand upon the head of Ephraim, it displeased him: and he held up his father's hand, to remove it from Ephraim's head unto Manasseh's head. And Joseph said unto his father, Not so, my father: for this is the firstborn; put thy right hand upon his head (*Genesis 48:14-18*).

As thou knowest not what is the way of the spirit, nor how the bones do *grow* in the womb of her that is with child: even so thou knowest not the works of God who maketh all (*Ecclesiastes 11:5*).

The sorrows of a travailing woman shall come upon him: he is an unwise son; for he should not stay long in the place of the *break[ing] forth* of children (*Hosea 13:13*).

And Abram said, Behold, to me thou hast given no seed: and, lo, one born in my house is mine heir. And, behold, the word of the LORD came unto him, saying, This shall not be thine heir; but he that shall come *forth* out of thine own bowels shall be thine heir. And he brought him forth abroad, and said, Look now toward heaven, and tell the stars, if thou be able to number them: and he said unto him, So shall thy seed be (*Genesis 15:3-5*).

And it came to pass, as he drew back his hand, that, behold, his brother came out: and she said, How hast thou broken forth? this breach be upon thee: therefore his name was called *Pharez* (*Genesis 38:29*).

And the angel of the LORD said unto her, Behold, thou art with child, and shalt *bear* a son, and shalt call his name Ishmael; because the LORD hath heard thy affliction (*Genesis 16:11*).

But the angel said unto him, Fear not, Zacharias: for thy prayer is heard; and thy wife Elisabeth shall *bear* thee a son, and thou shalt call his name John (*Luke 1:13*).

Unto the woman he said, I will greatly multiply thy sorrow and thy con- ception; in sorrow thou shalt *bring forth* children; and thy desire shall be to thy husband, and he shall rule over thee (*Genesis 3:16*).

And she shall *bring forth* a son, and thou shalt call his name JESUS: for he shall save his people from their sins. Now all this was done, that it might be fulfilled which was spoken of the Lord by the prophet, saying, Behold, a virgin shall be with child, and shall *bring forth* a son, and they shall call his name Emmanuel, which being interpreted is, God with us. Then Joseph being raised from sleep did as the angel of the Lord had bidden him, and took unto him his wife: And knew her not till she had brought forth her firstborn son: and he called his name JESUS (*Matthew 1:21-25*).

And Jacob begat Joseph the husband of Mary, of whom was *born* Jesus, who is called Christ (*Matthew 1:16*).

And when her days to *be delivered* were fulfilled, behold, there were twins in her womb (*Genesis 25:24*).

And his daughter in law, Phinehas' wife, was with child, near to *be delivered*: and when she heard the tidings that the ark of God was taken, and that her father in law and her husband were dead, she bowed herself and travailed; for her pains came upon her (*1 Samuel 4:19*).

A woman when she is in travail hath sorrow, because her hour is come: but as soon as she is delivered of the child, she remembereth no more the anguish, for joy that a man is born into the world (*John 16:21*).

31a. And she *called* his name Joseph; and said, The LORD shall add to me another son (*Genesis 30:24*).

And they journeyed from Bethel; and there was but a little way to come to Ephrath: and Rachel travailed, and she had hard labor. And it came to pass, when she was in hard labor, that the midwife said unto her, Fear not; thou shalt have this son also. And it came to pass, as her soul was in departing, (for she died) that she *called* his name Ben-oni: but his father called him Benjamin (*Genesis 35:16-18*).

31b. And she *called* his name Joseph; and said, The LORD shall add to me another son (*Genesis 30:24*).

And they journeyed from Bethel; and there was but a little way to come to Ephrath: and Rachel travailed, and she had hard labor. And it came to pass, when she was in hard labor, that the midwife said unto her, Fear not; thou shalt have this son also. And it came to pass, as her soul was in departing, (for she died) that she *called* his name Ben-oni: but his father called him Benjamin (*Genesis 35:16-18*).

And she shall *bring forth* a son, and thou shalt call his name JESUS: for he shall save his people from their sins. Now all this was done, that it might be fulfilled which was spoken of the Lord by the prophet, saying, Behold, a virgin shall be with child, and shall *bring forth* a son, and they shall call his name Emmanuel, which being interpreted is, God with us. Then Joseph being raised from sleep did as the angel of the Lord had bidden him, and took unto him his wife: And knew her not till she had brought forth her firstborn son: and he called his name JESUS (*Matthew 1:21-25*).

Now these are the generations of the sons of Noah, Shem, Ham, and Japheth: and unto them were sons *born* after the flood (*Genesis 10:1*).

And Abraham was an hundred years old, when his son Isaac was born unto him. And Sarah said, God hath made me to laugh, so that all that hear will laugh with me. And she said, Who would have said unto Abraham, that Sarah should have given children suck? for I have *born* him a son in his old age (*Genesis 21:5-7*).

And when her days to *be delivered* were fulfilled, behold, there were twins in her womb (*Genesis 25:24*).

And his daughter in law, Phinehas' wife, was with child, near to *be delivered*: and when she heard the tidings that the ark of God was taken, and that her father in law and her husband were dead, she bowed herself and travailed; for her pains came upon her (*1 Samuel 4:19*).

A woman when she is in travail hath sorrow, because her hour is come: but as soon as she is delivered of the child, she remembereth no more the anguish, for joy that a man is born into the world (*John 16:21*).

Fear took hold upon them there, and *pain*, as of *a woman in travail* (*Psalm 48:6*).

32.   And it came to pass the third *day*, which was Pharaoh's birthday, that he made a feast unto all his servants: and he lifted up the head of the chief butler and of the chief baker among his servants (*Genesis 40:20*).

And Isaac entreated the Lord for his wife, because she was barren: and the Lord was entreated of him, and Rebekah his wife conceived. And the children struggled together within her; and she said, If it be so, why am I thus? And she went to inquire of the Lord. And the Lord said unto her, Two nations are in thy womb, and two manner of people shall be separated from thy bowels; and the one people shall be stronger than the other people; and the elder shall serve the younger. And when her *day[s]* to be delivered were fulfilled, behold, there were twins in her womb. And the first came out red, all over like a hairy garment; and they called his name Esau (*Genesis 21-25*).

Now the *birth* of Jesus Christ was on this wise: When as his mother Mary was espoused to Joseph, before they came together, she was found with child of the Holy Ghost. Then Joseph her husband, being a just man, and not willing to make her a public example, was minded to put her away privily. But while he thought on these things, behold, the angel of the Lord appeared unto him in a dream, saying, Joseph, thou son of David, fear not to take unto thee Mary thy wife: for that which is conceived in her is of the Holy Ghost. And she shall bring forth a son, and thou shalt call his name JESUS: for he shall save his people from their sins (*Matthew 1:18-21*).

Unto the woman he said, I will greatly multiply thy sorrow and thy conception; in sorrow thou shalt *bring forth* children; and thy desire shall be to thy husband, and he shall rule over thee (*Genesis 3:16*).

And she shall *bring forth* a son, and thou shalt call his name JESUS: for he shall save his people from their sins. Now all this was done, that it might be fulfilled which was spoken of the Lord by the prophet, saying, Behold, a virgin shall be with child, and shall *bring forth* a son, and they shall call his name Emmanuel, which being interpreted is, God with us. Then Joseph being raised from sleep did as the angel of the Lord had bidden him, and took unto him his wife: And knew her not till she had brought forth her firstborn son: and he called his name JESUS (*Matthew 1:21-25*).

And when her days to *be delivered* were fulfilled, behold, there were twins in her womb (*Genesis 25:24*).

And his daughter in law, Phinehas' wife, was with child, near to *be delivered*: and when she heard the tidings that the ark of God was taken, and that her father in law and her husband were dead, she bowed herself and travailed; for her pains came upon her (*1 Samuel 4:19*).

A woman when she is in travail hath sorrow, because her hour is come: but as soon as she is delivered of the child, she remembereth no more the anguish, for joy that a man is born into the world (*John 16:21*).

Fear took hold upon them there, and *pain*, as of *a woman in travail* (*Psalm 48:6*).

33a. For I will pass through the land of Egypt this *night*, and *will smite all the firstborn in the land of Egypt, both man* and beast; and against all the gods of Egypt I will execute judgment: I am the LORD (*Exodus 12:12*).

And it came to pass, that at *[mid]night the LORD smote all the firstborn in the land of Egypt, from the firstborn of Pharaoh that sat on his throne* unto the firstborn of the captive that was in the dungeon; and all the firstborn of cattle (*Exodus 12:29*).

Then came there two women, that were harlots, unto the king, and stood before him. And the one woman said, O my lord, I and this woman dwell in one house; and I was delivered of a child with her in the house. And it came to pass the third day after that I was delivered, that this woman was delivered also: and we were together; there was no stranger with us in the house, save we two in the house. And *this woman's child died in the night*; because she overlaid it. And she arose at *[mid]night*, and took my son from beside me, while thine handmaid slept, and laid it in her bosom, *and laid her dead child in my bosom* (*1 Kings 3:16-20*).

Or as a hidden *untimely birth* I had not been; as infants which never saw light (*Job 3:16*).

And when he was come into his house, he took a knife, and laid hold on his concubine, and *divide*[d] her, together with her bones, into twelve pieces, and sent her into all the coasts of Israel (*Judges 19:29*).

33b. For I will pass through the land of Egypt this *night*, and will smite all the firstborn in the land of Egypt, both man and beast; and against all the gods of Egypt I will execute judgment: I am the LORD (*Exodus 12:12*).

For when they came into the house, he lay on his bed in his bed-chamber, and they smote him, and slew him, and beheaded him, and took his head, and gat them away through the plain all night. And they brought the head of Ish-bosheth unto David to Hebron, and said to the king, Behold the head of Ish-bosheth the son of Saul thine enemy, which sought thy life; and the LORD hath avenged my lord the king this day of Saul, and of his seed. And David answered Rechab and Baanah his brother, the sons of Rimmon the Beerothite, and said unto them, As the LORD liveth, who hath redeemed my soul out of all *adversity*, When one told me, saying, Behold, *Saul is dead*, thinking to have brought good tidings, I took hold of him, and slew him in Ziklag, who thought that I would have given him a reward for his tidings (*2 Samuel 4:7-10*).

A friend loveth at all times, and a brother is born for *adversity* (*Proverbs 17:17*).

And when the LORD saw that Leah was hated, he opened her womb: but Rachel was barren. And Leah conceived, and bare a son, and she called his name Reuben: for she said, Surely the LORD hath looked upon my *affliction*; now therefore my husband will love me. And she conceived again, and bare a son; and said, Because the LORD hath heard that I was hated, he hath therefore given me this son also: and she called his name Simeon. And she conceived again, and bare a son; and said, Now this time will my husband be joined unto me, because I have born him three sons: therefore was his name called Levi. And she conceived again, and bare a son: and she said, Now will I praise the LORD: therefore she called his name Judah; and left bearing (*Genesis 29:31-35*).

Shall I *bring to the birth*, and not cause to bring forth? saith the LORD: shall I cause to bring forth, and shut the womb? saith thy God (*Isaiah 66:9*).

34.   And he made his camels to kneel down without the city by a well of water at the time of the *evening*, even the time that women go out to draw water (*Genesis 24:11*).

And it came to pass in the *evening*, that he took Leah his daughter, and brought her to him; and he went in unto her (*Genesis 29:23*).

And Jacob came out of the field in the *evening*, and Leah went out to meet him, and said, Thou must come in unto me; for surely I have hired thee with my son's mandrakes. And he lay with her that night (*Genesis 30:16*).

And it came to pass, when he had been there a long time, that Abimelech king of the Philistines looked out at a window, and saw, and, behold, Isaac was sporting with Rebekah his wife. And Abimelech called Isaac, and said, Behold, of a *surety* she is thy wife: and how saidst thou, She is my sister? And Isaac said unto him, Because I said, Lest I die for her. And Abimelech said, What is this thou hast done unto us? one of the people might lightly have lien with thy wife, and thou shouldest have brought guiltiness upon us (*Genesis 26:8-10*).

Come, let us make our father drink wine, and we will *lie with him, that we* may preserve seed of our father (*Genesis 19:32*).

And they called unto Lot, and said unto him, Where are the men which came in to thee this night? bring them out unto us, that we may *know* them. And Lot went out at the door unto them, and shut the door after him, And said, I pray you, brethren, do not so wickedly. Behold now, I have two daughters which have not *know*[n] man; let me, I pray you, bring them out unto you, and do ye to them as is good in your eyes: only unto these men do nothing; for therefore came they under the shadow of my roof (*Genesis 19:5-8*).

Come, let us make our father drink wine, and we will *lie with him,* that we may preserve seed of our father (*Genesis 19:32*).

35. Tarry this night, and it shall be in the *morning,* that if he will perform unto thee the part of a kinsman, well; let him do the kinsman's part: but if he will not do the part of a kinsman to thee, then will I do the part of a kinsman to thee, as the LORD liveth: lie down until the morning. And she lay at his feet until the morning: and she rose up before one could know another. And he said, Let it not be known that a woman came into the floor (*Ruth 3:13-14*).

In the *morning* sow thy seed, and in the evening withhold not thine hand: for thou knowest not whether shall prosper, either this or that, or whether they both shall be alike good (*Ecclesiastes 11:6*).

In the day shalt thou make thy plant to grow, and in the *morning* shalt thou make thy seed to flourish: but the harvest shall be a heap in the day of grief and of desperate sorrow (*Isaiah 17:11*).

And Samson's wife wept before him, and said, Thou dost but hate me, and lovest me not: thou hast put forth a riddle unto the children of my people, and hast not told it me. And he said unto her, Behold, I have not told it my father nor my mother, and shall I tell it thee? And she wept before him the seven days, while their feast lasted: and it came to pass on the seventh day, that he told her, because she lay sore upon him: and she told the riddle to the children of her people. And the men of the city said unto him on the seventh day before the sun went down, What is sweeter than honey? and what is stronger than a lion? And he said unto them, If ye had not *plowed* with my heifer, ye had not found out my riddle. And the Spirit of the LORD came upon him, and he went down to Ashkelon, and slew thirty men of them, and took their spoil, and gave change of garments unto them which expounded the riddle. And his anger was kindled, and he went up to his father's house. But Samson's wife was given to his companion, whom he had used as his friend (*Judges 14:16-20*).

And it came to pass, as he drew back his hand, that, behold, his brother came out: and she said, How hast thou *broken [break] forth*? this *breach* be upon thee: therefore his name was called *Pharez*. And afterward came out his brother, that had the scarlet thread upon his hand: and his name was called Zarah (*Genesis 38:29-30*).

The sorrows of a travailing woman shall come upon him: he is an unwise son; for he should not stay long in the place of the *break*ing *forth* of children (*Hosea 13:13*).

And Israel stretched out his right hand, and laid it upon Ephraim's head, who was the younger, and his left hand upon Manasseh's head, guiding his hands wittingly; for Manasseh was the firstborn. And he blessed Joseph, and said, God, before whom my fathers Abraham and Isaac did walk, the God which fed me all my life long unto this day, The Angel which redeemed me from all evil, bless the lads; and let my name be named on them, and the name of my fathers Abraham and Isaac; and let them *grow* into a multitude in the midst of the earth. And when Joseph saw that his father laid his right hand upon the head of Ephraim, it displeased him: and he held up his father's hand, to remove it from Ephraim's head unto Manasseh's head. And Joseph said unto his father, Not so, my father: for this is the firstborn; put thy right hand upon his head (*Genesis 48:14-18*).

As thou knowest not what is the way of the spirit, nor how the bones do *grow* in the womb of her that is with child: even so thou knowest not the works of God who maketh all (*Ecclesiastes 11:5*).

And the angel of the LORD said unto her, Behold, thou art with child, and shalt *bear* a son, and shalt call his name Ishmael; because the LORD hath heard thy affliction (*Genesis 16:11*).

But the angel said unto him, Fear not, Zacharias: for thy prayer is heard; and thy wife Elisabeth shall *bear* thee a son, and thou shalt call his name John (*Luke 1:13*).

Unto the woman he said, I will greatly multiply thy sorrow and thy conception; in sorrow thou shalt *bring forth* children; and thy desire shall be to thy husband, and he shall rule over thee (*Genesis 3:16*).

And she shall *bring forth* a son, and thou shalt call his name JESUS: for he shall save his people from their sins. Now all this was done, that it might be fulfilled which was spoken of the Lord by the prophet, saying, Behold, a virgin shall be with child, and shall *bring forth* a son, and they shall call his name Emmanuel, which being interpreted is, God with us. Then Joseph being raised from sleep did as the angel of the Lord had bidden him, and took unto him his wife: And knew her not till she had brought forth her firstborn son: and he called his name JESUS (*Matthew 1:21-25*).

Now these are the generations of the sons of Noah, Shem, Ham, and Japheth: and unto them were sons *born* after the flood (*Genesis 10:1*).

And Abraham was an hundred years old, when his son Isaac was born unto him. And Sarah said, God hath made me to laugh, so that all that hear will laugh with me. And she said, Who would have said unto Abraham, that Sarah should have given children suck? for I have *born* him a son in his old age (*Genesis 21:5-7*).

And Jacob begat Joseph the husband of Mary, of whom was *born* Jesus, who is called Christ (*Matthew 1:16*).

And when her days to *be delivered* were fulfilled, behold, there were twins in her womb (*Genesis 25:24*).

And his daughter in law, Phinehas' wife, was with child, near to *be delivered*: and when she heard the tidings that the ark of God was taken, and that her father in law and her husband were dead, she bowed herself and travailed; for her pains came upon her (*1 Samuel 4:19*).

A woman when she is in travail hath sorrow, because her hour is come: but as soon as she is delivered of the child, she remembereth no more the anguish, for joy that a man is born into the world (*John 16:21*).

36. And it came to pass, when men began to multiply on the face of the earth, and daughters *were* born unto them (*Genesis 6:1*).

Now these are the generations of the sons of Noah, Shem, Ham, and Japheth: and unto them *were* sons born after the flood (*Genesis 10:1*).

And they smote all the souls that were therein with the edge of the sword, utterly destroying them: there was not any left *to breathe*: and he burnt Hazor with fire (*Joshua 11:11*).

And when her days *to be* delivered were fulfilled, behold, there were twins in her womb. And the first came out red, all over like a hairy garment; and they called his name Esau (*Genesis 25:24-25*).

And the angel of the LORD said unto her, Behold, thou art with child, and shalt *bear* a son, and shalt call his name Ishmael; because the LORD hath heard thy affliction (*Genesis 16:11*).

But the angel said unto him, Fear not, Zacharias: for thy prayer is heard; and thy wife Elisabeth shall *bear* thee a son, and thou shalt call his name John (*Luke 1:13*).

Unto the woman he said, I will greatly multiply thy sorrow and thy conception; in sorrow thou shalt *bring forth* children; and thy desire shall be to thy husband, and he shall rule over thee (*Genesis 3:16*).

Now these are the generations of the sons of Noah, Shem, Ham, and Japheth: and unto them were sons *born* after the flood (*Genesis 10:1*).

And Abraham was an hundred years old, when his son Isaac was born unto him. And Sarah said, God hath made me to laugh, so that all that hear will laugh with me. And she said, Who would have said unto Abraham, that Sarah should have given children suck? for I have *born* him a son in his old age (*Genesis 21:5-7*).

And when her days to *be delivered* were fulfilled, behold, there were twins in her womb (*Genesis 25:24*).

And his daughter in law, Phinehas' wife, was with child, near to *be delivered*: and when she heard the tidings that the ark of God was taken, and that her father in law and her husband were dead, she bowed herself and travailed; for her pains came upon her (*1 Samuel 4:19*).

A woman when she is in travail hath sorrow, because her hour is come: but as soon as she is delivered of the child, she remembereth no more the anguish, for joy that a man is born into the world (*John 16:21*).

37.   And when her days to be delivered were fulfilled, behold, there were twins in her womb. And the *first* came out red, all over like a hairy garment; and they called his name Esau (*Genesis 25:24-25*).

For I have heard a voice as of a woman in travail, and the anguish as of her that bringeth forth her *first* child, the voice of the daughter of Zion, that bewaileth herself, that spreadeth her hands, saying, Woe is me now! for my soul is wearied because of murderers (*Jeremiah 4:31*).

And Adam knew his wife again; and she bare *a son*, and called his name Seth: For God, said she, hath appointed me another seed instead of Abel, whom Cain slew. And to Seth, to him also there was born *a son*; and he called his name Enos: then began men to call upon the name of the LORD (*Genesis 4:25-26*).

To every thing there is a season, and a time to every purpose under the heaven: A time to be born, and a time to die; a time to plant, and a time to pluck up that which is planted; A time to kill, and a time to heal; a time to break down, and a time *to build* up (*Ecclesiastes 3:1-3*).

Now Sarai Abram's wife bare him no children: and she had a handmaid, an Egyptian, whose name was Hagar. And Sarai said unto Abram, Behold now, the LORD hath restrained me from bearing: I pray thee, go in unto my maid; it may be that I may *obtain children* by her. And Abram hearkened to the voice of Sarai. And Sarai Abram's wife took Hagar her maid the Egyptian, after Abram had dwelt ten years in the land of Canaan, and gave her to her husband Abram to be his wife. And he went in unto Hagar, and she con- ceived: and when she saw that she had conceived, her mistress was despised in her eyes (*Genesis 16:1-4*).

And the LORD said unto Abram, after that Lot was separated from him, Lift up now thine eyes, and look from the place where thou art northward, and southward, and eastward, and westward: For all the land which thou seest, to thee will I give it, and to thy seed for ever. And I will *make* thy seed as the dust of the earth: so that if a man can number the dust of the earth, then shall thy seed also be numbered (*Genesis 13:14-16*).

And when thy days be fulfilled, and thou shalt sleep with thy fathers, I will *set up* thy seed after thee, which shall proceed out of thy bowels, and I will establish his kingdom (*2 Samuel 7:12*).

Nevertheless for David's sake did the LORD his God give him a lamp in Jerusalem, to *set up* his son after him, and to establish Jerusalem (*1 Kings 15:4*).

And the angel of the LORD said unto her, Behold, thou art with child, and shalt *bear* a son, and shalt call his name Ishmael; because the LORD hath heard thy affliction (*Genesis 16:11*).

But the angel said unto him, Fear not, Zacharias: for thy prayer is heard; and thy wife Elisabeth shall *bear* thee a son, and thou shalt call his name John (*Luke 1:13*).

Unto the woman he said, I will greatly multiply thy sorrow and thy con-ception; in sorrow thou shalt *bring forth* children; and thy desire shall be to thy husband, and he shall rule over thee (*Genesis 3:16*).

And she shall *bring forth* a son, and thou shalt call his name JESUS: for he shall save his people from their sins. Now all this was done, that it might be fulfilled which was spoken of the Lord by the prophet, saying, Behold, a virgin shall be with child, and shall *bring forth* a son, and they shall call his name Emmanuel, which being interpreted is, God with us. Then Joseph being raised from sleep did as the angel of the Lord had bidden him, and took unto him his wife: And knew her not till she had brought forth her firstborn son: and he called his name JESUS (*Matthew 1:21-25*).

Now these are the generations of the sons of Noah, Shem, Ham, and Japheth: and unto them were sons *born* after the flood (*Genesis 10:1*).

And Abraham was an hundred years old, when his son Isaac was born unto him. And Sarah said, God hath made me to laugh, so that all that hear will laugh with me. And she said, Who would have said unto Abraham, that Sarah should have given children suck? for I have *born* him a son in his old age (*Genesis 21:5-7*).

And when her days to *be delivered* were fulfilled, behold, there were twins in her womb (*Genesis 25:24*).

And his daughter in law, Phinehas' wife, was with child, near to *be delivered*: and when she heard the tidings that the ark of God was taken, and that her father in law and her husband were dead, she bowed herself and travailed; for her pains came upon her (*1 Samuel 4:19*).

A woman when she is in travail hath sorrow, because her hour is come: but as soon as she is delivered of the child, she remembereth no more the anguish, for joy that a man is born into the world (*John 16:21*).

38. And it came to pass the third *day*, which was Pharaoh's birthday, that he made a feast unto all his servants: and he lifted up the head of the chief butler and of the chief baker among his servants (*Genesis 40:20*).

And when her *day[s]* to *be delivered* were fulfilled, behold, there were twins in her womb (*Genesis 25:24*).

Now the *birth* of Jesus Christ was on this wise: When as his mother Mary was espoused to Joseph, before they came together, she was found with child of the Holy Ghost. Then Joseph her husband, being a just man, and not willing to make her a public example, was minded to put her away privily. But while he thought on these things, behold, the angel of the Lord appeared unto him in a dream, saying, Joseph, thou son of David, fear not to take unto thee Mary thy wife: for that which is conceived in her is of the Holy Ghost. And she shall bring forth a son, and thou shalt call his name JESUS: for he shall save his people from their sins (*Matthew 1:18-21*).

Now these are the generations of the sons of Noah, Shem, Ham, and Japheth: and unto them were sons *born* after the flood (*Genesis 10:1*).

And Abraham was an hundred years old, when his son Isaac was born unto him. And Sarah said, God hath made me to laugh, so that all that hear will laugh with me. And she said, Who would have said unto Abraham, that Sarah should have given children suck? for I have *born* him a son in his old age (*Genesis 21:5-7*).

And when her days to *be delivered* were fulfilled, behold, there were twins in her womb (*Genesis 25:24*).

And his daughter in law, Phinehas' wife, was with child, near to *be delivered*: and when she heard the tidings that the ark of God was taken, and that her father in law and her husband were dead, she bowed herself and travailed; for her pains came upon her (*1 Samuel 4:19*).

A woman when she is in travail hath sorrow, because her hour is come: but as soon as she is delivered of the child, she remembereth no more the anguish, for joy that a man is born into the world (*John 16:21*).

39a. Jesus answered and said unto him, Verily, verily, I say unto thee, Except a man be *born again*, he cannot see the kingdom of God. Nicodemus saith unto him, How can a man be born when he is old? can he enter the second time into his mother's womb, and be born? Jesus answered, Verily, verily, I say unto thee, Except a man be born of water and of the Spirit, he cannot enter into the kingdom of God. That which is born of the flesh is flesh; and that which is born of the Spirit is spirit. Marvel not that I said unto thee, Ye must be *born again* (*John 3:3-7*).

As for me, behold, my covenant is with thee, and thou shalt be a *father* of many nations (*Genesis 17:4*).

And think not to say within yourselves, We have Abraham to our *father*: for I say unto you, that God is able of these stones to raise up children unto Abraham (*Matthew 3:9*).

Have we not all one *father*? hath not one God created us? why do we deal treacherously every man against his brother, by profaning the covenant of our fathers (*Malachi 2:10*)?

And Abraham was an hundred years old, when his son Isaac was born unto him. And Sarah said, God hath made me to laugh, so that all that hear will laugh with me. And she said, Who would have said unto Abraham, that Sarah should have given children suck? for I have born him *a son* in his old age (*Genesis 21:5-7*).

And Adam knew his wife again; and she bare *a son*, and called his name Seth: For God, said she, hath appointed me another seed instead of Abel, whom Cain slew (*Genesis 4:25*).

And the LORD said unto Abram, after that Lot was separated from him, Lift up now thine eyes, and look from the place where thou art northward, and southward, and eastward, and westward: For all the land which thou seest, to thee will I give it, and to thy seed for ever. And I will *make* thy seed as the dust of the earth: so that if a man can number the dust of the earth, then shall thy seed also be numbered (*Genesis 13:14-16*).

And the angel of the LORD said unto her, Behold, thou art with child, and shalt *bear* a son, and shalt call his name Ishmael; because the LORD hath heard thy affliction (*Genesis 16:11*).

But the angel said unto him, Fear not, Zacharias: for thy prayer is heard; and thy wife Elisabeth shall *bear* thee a son, and thou shalt call his name John (*Luke 1:13*).

Unto the woman he said, I will greatly multiply thy sorrow and thy conception; in sorrow thou shalt *bring forth* children; and thy desire shall be to thy husband, and he shall rule over thee (*Genesis 3:16*).

And she shall *bring forth* a son, and thou shalt call his name JESUS: for he shall save his people from their sins. Now all this was done, that it might be fulfilled which was spoken of the Lord by the prophet, saying, Behold, a virgin shall be with child, and shall *bring forth* a son, and they shall call his name Emmanuel, which being interpreted is, God with us. Then Joseph being raised from sleep did as the angel of the Lord had bidden him, and took unto him his wife: And knew her not till she had brought forth her firstborn son: and he called his name JESUS (*Matthew 1:21-25*).

Now these are the generations of the sons of Noah, Shem, Ham, and Japheth: and unto them were sons *born* after the flood (*Genesis 10:1*).

And Abraham was an hundred years old, when his son Isaac was born unto him. And Sarah said, God hath made me to laugh, so that all that hear will laugh with me. And she said, Who would have said unto Abraham, that Sarah should have given children suck? for I have *born* him a son in his old age (*Genesis 21:5-7*).

And Jacob begat Joseph the husband of Mary, of whom was *born* Jesus, who is called Christ (*Matthew 1:16*).

And when her days to *be delivered* were fulfilled, behold, there were twins in her womb (*Genesis 25:24*).

And his daughter in law, Phinehas' wife, was with child, near to *be delivered*: and when she heard the tidings that the ark of God was taken, and that her father in law and her husband were dead, she bowed herself and travailed; for her pains came upon her (*1 Samuel 4:19*).

A woman when she is in travail hath sorrow, because her hour is come: but as soon as she is delivered of the child, she remembereth no more the anguish, for joy that a man is born into the world (*John 16:21*).

39b. Jesus answered and said unto him, Verily, verily, I say unto thee, Except a man be *born again*, he cannot see the kingdom of God. Nicodemus saith unto him, How can a man be born when he is old? can he enter the second time into his mother's womb, and be born? Jesus answered, Verily, verily, I say unto thee, Except a man be born of water and of the Spirit, he cannot enter into the kingdom of God. That which is born of the flesh is flesh; and that which is born of the Spirit is spirit. Marvel not that I said unto thee, Ye must be *born again* (*John 3:7*).

And thou shalt bring it to thy *father*, that he may eat, and that he may bless thee before his death. And Jacob said to Rebekah his mother, Behold, Esau my brother is a hairy man, and I am a smooth man: My *father* peradventure will feel me, and I shall seem to him as a deceiver; and I shall bring a curse upon me, and not a blessing (*Genesis 27:10-12*).

And Adam called his wife's name Eve; because she was the *mother* of all living (*Genesis 3:20*).

And Jacob said to Rebekah his *mother*, Behold, Esau my brother is a hairy man, and I am a smooth man: My father peradventure will feel me, and I shall seem to him as a deceiver; and I shall bring a curse upon me, and not a blessing. And his *mother* said unto him, Upon me be thy curse, my son: only obey my voice, and go fetch me them. And he went, and fetched, and brought them to his *mother*: and his *mother* made savory meat, such as his father loved (*Genesis 27:11-14*).

And God said unto Abraham, As for Sarai thy wife, thou shalt not call her name Sarai, but Sarah shall her name be. And I will bless her, and give thee a son also of her: yea, I will bless her, and she shall be *a mother* of nations; kings of people shall be of her. Then Abraham fell upon his face, and laughed, and said in his heart, Shall a child be born unto him that is an hundred years old? and shall Sarah, that is ninety years old, bear (*Genesis 17:15-17*)?

And when they were come into the house, they saw the young child with Mary his *mother*, and fell down, and worshipped him: and when they had opened their treasures, they presented unto him gifts; gold, and frankincense, and myrrh (*Matthew 2:11*).

Now the LORD had said unto Abram, Get thee out of thy country, and from thy kindred, and from thy father's house, unto a land that I will show thee: And I will make of thee a great *nation*, and I will bless thee, and make thy name great; and thou shalt be a blessing (*Genesis 12:1-2*).

And Gideon had threescore and ten sons of his *body* begotten: for he had many wives (*Judges 8:30*).

Sanctify unto me all the firstborn, whatsoever openeth *the womb* among the children of Israel, both of man and of beast: it is mine (*Exodus 13:2*).

The wicked are estranged from the womb: they go astray as soon *as they be born*, speaking lies (*Psalm 58:3*).

Adam, Eve, and the S-s-s-serpent

The following footnotes relate to those found in the text of *Adam, Eve, and the S-s-s-serpent*. The author has italicized the key words for purposes of discussion. The key words are also found in *Genesis 2:9,10, 21-25 and Genesis 3:1-7* and appear in other supporting Scripture as follows:

---

40.   And out of the ground made the LORD God to grow every *tree* that is pleasant to the sight, and good for food; the *tree* of life also in the midst of the garden, and the *tree* of knowledge of good and evil (*Genesis 2:9*).

Even so every good *tree* bringeth forth good fruit; but a corrupt *tree* bringeth forth evil fruit. A good *tree* cannot bring forth evil fruit, neither can a corrupt *tree* bring forth good fruit. Every *tree* that bringeth not forth good fruit is hewn down, and cast into the fire. Wherefore by their fruits ye shall know them. Not every one that saith unto me, Lord, Lord, shall enter into the kingdom of heaven; but he that doeth the will of my Father which is in heaven (*Matthew 7:17-21*).

I am Alpha and Omega, the beginning and the end, the first and the last. Blessed are they that do his commandments, that they may have right to the *tree* of life, and may enter in through the gates into the city (*Revelation 22:13, 14*).

Weep ye not for the dead, neither bemoan him: but weep sore for him that goeth away: for he shall return no more, nor see his *native* country (*Jeremiah 22:10*).

And when a stranger shall sojourn with thee, and will keep the passover to the LORD, let all his males be circumcised, and then let him come near and keep it; and he shall be as one that is born in the land: for no uncircumcised person shall eat thereof. One law shall be to him that is *homeborn*, and unto the stranger that sojourneth among you. Thus did all the children of Israel; as the LORD commanded Moses and Aaron, so did they. And it came to pass the selfsame day, that the LORD did bring the children of Israel out of the land of Egypt by their armies (*Exodus 12:48-51*).

Now these are the generations of the sons of Noah, Shem, Ham, and Japheth: and unto them were sons *born* after the flood (*Genesis 10:1*).

And Abraham was an hundred years old, when his son Isaac was born unto him. And Sarah said, God hath made me to laugh, so that all that hear will laugh with me. And she said, Who would have said unto Abraham, that Sarah should have given children suck? for I have *born* him a son in his old age (*Genesis 21:5-7*).

And Jacob begat Joseph the husband of Mary, of whom was *born* Jesus, who is called Christ (*Matthew 1:16*).

And when her days to *be delivered* were fulfilled, behold, there were twins in her womb (*Genesis 25:24*).

And his daughter in law, Phinehas' wife, was with child, near to *be delivered*: and when she heard the tidings that the ark of God was taken, and that her father in law and her husband were dead, she bowed herself and travailed; for her pains came upon her (*1 Samuel 4:19*).

A woman when she is in travail hath sorrow, because her hour is come: but as soon as she is delivered of the child, she remembereth no more the anguish, for joy that a man is born into the world (*John 16:21*).

Fear took hold upon them there, and *pain*, as of *a woman in travail* (*Psalm 48:6*).

41a. And a *river* went out of Eden to water the garden; and from thence it was parted, and became into four heads (*Genesis 2:10*).

And unto Eber were born two sons: the name of one was *Peleg*; for in his days was the earth divided; and his brother's name was Joktan (*Genesis 10:25*).

And Adam knew his wife again; and she bare *a son*, and called his name Seth: For God, said she, hath appointed me another seed instead of Abel, whom Cain slew. And to Seth, to him also there was born *a son*; and he called his name Enos: then began men to call upon the name of the LORD (*Genesis 4:25-26*).

Then Joseph her husband, being a just man, and not willing to make her a public example, was minded to put her away privily. But while he thought on these things, behold, the angel of the Lord appeared unto him in a dream, saying, Joseph, thou son of David, fear not to take unto thee Mary thy wife: for that which is conceived in her is of the Holy Ghost. And she shall bring forth *a son*, and thou shalt call his name JESUS: for he shall save his people from their sins. Now all this was done, that it might be fulfilled which was spoken of the Lord by the prophet, saying, Behold, a virgin shall be with child, and shall bring forth *a son*, and they shall call his name Emmanuel, which being interpreted is, God with us. Then Joseph being raised from sleep did as the angel of the Lord had bidden him, and took unto him his wife: And knew her not till she had brought forth her firstborn son: and he called his name JESUS (*Matthew 1:19-25*).

And Noah begat three sons, *Shem*, Ham, and Japheth (*Genesis 6:10*).

41b.   And a *river* went out of Eden to water the garden; and from thence it was parted, and became into four heads (*Genesis 2:10*).

The priests the Levites, and all the tribe of Levi, shall have no part nor inheritance with Israel: they shall eat the offerings of the LORD made by fire, and his inheritance. Therefore shall they have no inheritance among their brethren: the LORD is their inheritance, as he hath said unto them. And this shall be the priest's due from the people, from them that offer a sacrifice, whether it be ox or sheep; and they shall give unto the priest the shoulder, and the two cheeks, and the maw. The firstfruit also of thy corn, of thy wine, and of thine oil, and the first of the fleece of thy sheep, shalt thou give him. For the LORD thy God hath chosen him out of all thy tribes, to stand to minister in the name of the LORD, him and his sons forever. And if a Levite come from any of thy gates out of all Israel, where he sojourned, and come with all the desire of his mind unto the place which the LORD shall choose; Then he shall minister in the name of the LORD his God, as all his brethren the Levites do, which stand there before the LORD. They shall have like portions to eat, beside that which cometh of the sale of his *patrimony*. When thou art come into the land which the LORD thy God giveth thee, thou shalt not learn to do after the abominations of those nations (*Deuteronomy 18:1-9*).

And David said to Abishai, and to all his servants, Behold, my son, which came *forth of* my bowels, seeketh my life: how much more now may this Benjamite do it? let him alone, and let him curse; for the LORD hath bidden him (*2 Samuel 16:11*).

As he came *forth of* his mother's womb, naked shall he return to go as he came, and shall take nothing of his labour, which he may carry away in his hand (*Ecclesiastes 5:15*).

And the days of Adam after he had *begotten* Seth were eight hundred years: and he begat sons and daughters (*Genesis 5:4*).

Now these are the generations of the sons of Noah, Shem, Ham, and Japheth: and unto them were sons *born* after the flood (*Genesis 10:1*).

And Abraham was an hundred years old, when his son Isaac was born unto him. And Sarah said, God hath made me to laugh, so that all that hear will laugh with me. And she said, Who would have said unto Abraham, that Sarah should have given children suck? for I have *born* him a son in his old age (*Genesis 21:5-7*).

And Jacob begat Joseph the husband of Mary, of whom was *born* Jesus, who is called Christ (*Matthew 1:16*).

And when her days to *be delivered* were fulfilled, behold, there were twins in her womb (*Genesis 25:24*).

And his daughter in law, Phinehas' wife, was with child, near to *be delivered*: and when she heard the tidings that the ark of God was taken, and that her father in law and her husband were dead, she bowed herself and travailed; for her pains came upon her (*1 Samuel 4:19*).

A woman when she is in travail hath sorrow, because her hour is come: but as soon as she is delivered of the child, she remembereth no more the anguish, for joy that a man is born into the world (*John 16:21*).

Fear took hold upon them there, and *pain*, as of *a woman in travail* (*Psalm 48:6*).

41c.   And a *river* went out of Eden to water the garden; and from thence it was parted, and became into four heads (*Genesis 2:10*).

And they said unto him, Thus saith Hezekiah, This day is a day of trouble, and of rebuke, and of blasphemy: for the children are come to the birth, and there is not strength to *bring* forth (*Isaiah 37:3*).

Before she travailed, she brought forth; before her pain came, she was delivered of a man child. Who hath heard such a thing? who hath seen such things? Shall the earth be made to *bring* forth in one day? or shall a nation be born at once? for as soon as Zion travailed, she brought forth her children. Shall I bring to the birth, and not cause *to bring* forth? saith the Lord: shall I cause to *bring forth*, and shut the womb? saith thy God (*Isaiah 66:7-9*).

41d.   And a *river* went out of Eden to water the garden; and from thence it was parted, and became into four heads (*Genesis 2:10*).

Shall I bring to the birth, and not cause to bring forth? saith the Lord: shall I cause to bring forth, and shut the womb? saith thy God. Rejoice ye with Jerusalem, and be glad with her, all ye that love her: rejoice for joy with her, all ye that mourn for her: That ye may suck, and be satisfied with the breasts of her consolations; that ye may milk out, and be delighted with the abundance of her glory. For thus saith the Lord, Behold, I will extend peace to her like a *river*, and the glory of the Gentiles like a flowing stream: then shall ye suck, ye shall be borne upon her sides, and be dandled upon her knees. As one whom his mother comforteth, so will I comfort you; and ye shall be comforted in Jerusalem. And when ye see this, your heart shall rejoice, and your bones shall flourish like an herb: and the hand of the Lord shall be known toward his servants, and his indignation toward his enemies (*Isaiah 66:9-14*).

The word of the Lord that came to Jeremiah the prophet against the Philistines, before that Pharaoh smote Gaza. Thus saith the Lord; Behold, *water[s] rise up out of the north*, and shall be an overflowing flood, and shall overflow the land, and all that is therein; the city, and them that dwell therein: then the men shall cry, and all the inhabitants of the land shall howl. At the noise of the stamping of the hoofs of his strong horses, at the rushing of his chariots, and at the rumbling of his wheels, the fathers shall not look back to their children for feebleness of hands; Because of the day that cometh to spoil all the Philistines, and to cut off from Tyrus and Zidon every helper that remaineth: for the Lord will spoil the Philistines, the remnant of the country of Caphtor (*Jeremiah 47:1-4*).

42.   And Cain *went* out from the presence of the Lord, and dwelt in the land of Nod, on the east of Eden. And Cain knew his wife; and she conceived, and bare Enoch: and he builded a city, and called the name of the city, after the name of his son, Enoch (*Genesis 4:16-17*).

And Noah *went* in, and his sons, and his wife, and his sons' wives with him, into the ark, because of the waters of the flood (*Genesis 7:7*).

And he said, I am God, the God of thy father: fear not *to go* down into Egypt; for I will there make of thee a great nation (*Genesis 46:3*).

And the man that stood among the myrtle trees answered and said, These are they whom the Lord hath sent *to walk* to and fro through the earth (*Zechariah 1:10*).

43.   Now the Lord had said unto Abram, Get thee *out* of thy country, and from thy kindred, and from thy father's house, unto a land that I will show thee (*Genesis 12:1*).

And the beginning of his kingdom was Babel, and Erech, and Accad, and Calneh, in the land of Shinar. *Out of* that land went forth Asshur, and builded Nineveh, and the city Rehoboth, and Calah (*Genesis 10:10-11*).

44a.   And the LORD God took the man, and put him into the Garden of *Eden* to dress it and to keep it (*Genesis 2:15*).

Now Abraham and Sarah were old and well stricken in age; and it ceased to be with Sarah after the manner of women. Therefore Sarah laughed within herself, saying, After I am waxed old shall I have *pleasure*, my lord being old also? And the Lord said unto Abraham, Wherefore did Sarah laugh, saying, Shall I of a surety bear a child, which am old (*Genesis 18:11-13*)?

And the drinking was according to the law; none did compel: for so the king had appointed to all the officers of his house, that they should do according to every man's *pleasure*. Also Vashti the queen made a feast for the women in the royal house which belonged to king Ahasuerus (*Esther 1:8-9*).

44b.   And the LORD God took the man, and put him into the Garden of *Eden* to dress it and to keep it (*Genesis 2:15*).

And when a stranger shall sojourn with thee, and will keep the passover to the LORD, let all his males be circumcised, and then let him come near and keep it; and he shall be as one that is born in the land: for no uncircumcised person shall eat thereof. One law shall be to him that is *homeborn*, and unto the stranger that sojourneth among you. Thus did all the children of Israel; as the LORD commanded Moses and Aaron, so did they. And it came to pass the selfsame day, that the LORD did bring the children of Israel out of the land of Egypt by their armies (*Exodus 12:48-51*).

And the angel of the LORD said unto her, Behold, thou art with child, and shalt *bear* a son, and shalt call his name Ishmael; because the LORD hath heard thy affliction (*Genesis 16:11*).

But the angel said unto him, Fear not, Zacharias: for thy prayer is heard; and thy wife Elisabeth shall *bear* thee a son, and thou shalt call his name John (*Luke 1:13*).

Unto the woman he said, I will greatly multiply thy sorrow and thy conception; in sorrow thou shalt *bring forth* children; and thy desire shall be to thy husband, and he shall rule over thee (*Genesis 3:16*).

And she shall *bring forth* a son, and thou shalt call his name JESUS: for he shall save his people from their sins. Now all this was done, that it might be fulfilled which was spoken of the Lord by the prophet, saying, Behold, a virgin shall be with child, and shall *bring forth* a son, and they shall call his name Emmanuel, which being interpreted is, God with us. Then Joseph being raised from sleep did as the angel of the Lord had bidden him, and took unto him his wife: And knew her not till she had brought forth her firstborn son: and he called his name JESUS (*Matthew 1:21-25*).

Now these are the generations of the sons of Noah, Shem, Ham, and Japheth: and unto them were sons *born* after the flood (*Genesis 10:1*).

And Abraham was an hundred years old, when his son Isaac was born unto him. And Sarah said, God hath made me to laugh, so that all that hear will laugh with me. And she said, Who would have said unto Abraham, that Sarah should have given children suck? for I have *born* him a son in his old age (*Genesis 21:5-7*).

And Jacob begat Joseph the husband of Mary, of whom was *born* Jesus, who is called Christ (*Matthew 1:16*).

And when her days to *be delivered* were fulfilled, behold, there were twins in her womb (*Genesis 25:24*).

And his daughter in law, Phinehas' wife, was with child, near to *be delivered*: and when she heard the tidings that the ark of God was taken, and that her father in law and her husband were dead, she bowed herself and travailed; for her pains came upon her (*1 Samuel 4:19*).

A woman when she is in travail hath sorrow, because her hour is come: but as soon as she is delivered of the child, she remembereth no more the anguish, for joy that a man is born into the world (*John 16:21*).

Fear took hold upon them there, and *pain*, as of *a woman in travail* (*Psalm 48:6*).

45a. He shall pour the water out of his buckets, and *his seed shall be in many water[s]*, and his king shall be higher than Agag, and his kingdom shall be exalted (*Numbers 24:7*).

And he made his camels to kneel down without the city by a well of water at the time of the evening, even the time that women go out to draw *water* (*Genesis 24:11*).

Behold, I stand by the well of water; and it shall come to pass, that when the virgin cometh forth to draw *water*, and I say to her, Give me, I pray thee, a little water of thy pitcher to drink (*Genesis 24:41*).

And the angel of the LORD said unto her, Behold, thou art with child, and shalt *bear* a son, and shalt call his name Ishmael; because the LORD hath heard thy affliction (*Genesis 16:11*).

And Jacob begat Joseph the husband of Mary, of whom was *born* Jesus, who is called Christ (*Matthew 1:16*).

And when her days to *be delivered* were fulfilled, behold, there were twins in her womb (*Genesis 25:24*).

And his daughter in law, Phinehas' wife, was with child, near to *be delivered*: and when she heard the tidings that the ark of God was taken, and that her father in law and her husband were dead, she bowed herself and travailed; for her pains came upon her (*1 Samuel 4:19*).

A woman when she is in travail hath sorrow, because her hour is come: but as soon as she is delivered of the child, she remembereth no more the anguish, for joy that a man is born into the world (*John 16:21*).

Fear took hold upon them there, and *pain*, as of *a woman in travail* (*Psalm 48:6*).

45b. He shall pour the *water* out of his buckets, and *his seed shall be in many water[s]*, and his king shall be higher than Agag, and his kingdom shall be exalted (*Numbers 24:7*).

And he made his camels to kneel down without the city by a well of water at the time of the evening, even the time that women go out to draw *water* (*Genesis 24:11*).

Behold, I stand by the well of water; and it shall come to pass, that when the virgin cometh forth to draw *water*, and I say to her, Give me, I pray thee, a little water of thy pitcher to drink (*Genesis 24:41*).

When Moses heard this, he fell facedown. Then he said to Korah and all his followers: "In the morning the LORD will show who belongs to him and who is holy, and he will have that person come near him. The man he chooses he will *cause to* come near him. You, Korah, and all your followers are to do this: Take censers and tomorrow put fire and incense in them before the LORD. The man the LORD chooses will be the one who is holy. You Levites have gone too far!" (*Numbers 16:4-7*).

But God came to Abimelech in a dream by night, and said to him, Behold, thou art but a dead man, for the woman which thou hast taken; for she is a man's wife. But Abimelech had not *come near* her: and he said, LORD, wilt thou slay also a righteous nation (*Genesis 20:3-4*)?

And she shall *bring forth* a son, and thou shalt call his name JESUS: for he shall save his people from their sins. Now all this was done, that it might be fulfilled which was spoken of the Lord by the prophet, saying, Behold, a virgin shall be with child, and shall *bring forth* a son, and they shall call his name Emmanuel, which being interpreted is, God with us. Then Joseph being raised from sleep did as the angel of the Lord had bidden him, and took unto him his wife: And knew her not till she had brought forth her firstborn son: and he called his name JESUS (*Matthew 1:21-25*).

Now these are the generations of the sons of Noah, Shem, Ham, and Japheth: and unto them were sons *born* after the flood (*Genesis 10:1*).

And Abraham was an hundred years old, when his son Isaac was born unto him. And Sarah said, God hath made me to laugh, so that all that hear will laugh with me. And she said, Who would have said unto Abraham, that Sarah should have given children suck? for I have *born* him a son in his old age (*Genesis 21:5-7*).

And Jacob begat Joseph the husband of Mary, of whom was *born* Jesus, who is called Christ (*Matthew 1:16*).

And when her days to *be delivered* were fulfilled, behold, there were twins in her womb (*Genesis 25:24*).

And his daughter in law, Phinehas' wife, was with child, near to *be delivered*: and when she heard the tidings that the ark of God was taken, and that her father in law and her husband were dead, she bowed herself and travailed; for her pains came upon her (*1 Samuel 4:19*).

A woman when she is in travail hath sorrow, because her hour is come: but as soon as she is delivered of the child, she remembereth no more the anguish, for joy that a man is born into the world (*John 16:21*).

Fear took hold upon them there, and *pain*, as of *a woman in travail* (*Psalm 48:6*).

46.   For the land, whither thou goest in to possess it, is not as the land of Egypt, from whence ye came out, where thou sowedst thy seed, and wateredst it with thy foot, as a *garden* of herbs (Deuteronomy 11:10):

And Ahab spake unto Naboth, saying, Give me thy vineyard, that I may have it for a *garden* of herbs, because it is near unto my house: and I will give thee for it a better vineyard than it; or, if it seem good to thee, I will give thee the worth of it in money (*1 Kings 21:2*).

A *garden* enclosed is my sister, my spouse; a spring shut up, a fountain sealed (*Song 4:12*).

Awake, O north wind; and come, thou south; blow upon my *garden*, that the spices thereof may flow out. Let my beloved come into his garden, and eat his pleasant fruits (*Song 4:16*).

I am come into *my garden, my sister, my spouse*: I have gathered my myrrh with my spice; I have eaten my honeycomb with my honey; I have drunk my wine with my milk: eat, O friends; drink, yea, drink abundantly, O beloved (*Song 5:1*).

Whither is thy beloved gone, O thou fairest among women? whither is thy beloved turned aside? that we may seek him with thee. My beloved is gone down into his *garden*, to the beds of spices, to feed in the gardens, and to gather lilies. I am my beloved's, and my beloved is mine: he feedeth among the lilies (*Song 6:1-3*).

Gather the people, sanctify the congregation, assemble the elders, gather the children, and those that suck the breasts: let the bridegroom go forth of his chamber, and the *bride* out of her closet (*Joel 2:16*).

And Judah took a wife for Er his firstborn, whose name was Tamar. And Er, Judah's firstborn, was wicked in the sight of the LORD; and the LORD slew him. And Judah said unto Onan, Go in unto thy brother's wife, and marry her, and raise up seed to thy brother. And Onan knew that the seed should not be his; and it came to pass, when he went in unto his brother's wife, that he spilled it on the ground, lest that he should give seed to his brother. And the thing which he did displeased the LORD: wherefore he slew him also. Then said Judah to Tamar his *daughter in law*, Remain a widow at thy father's house, till Shelah my son be grown: for he said, Lest peradventure he die also, as his brethren did. And Tamar went and dwelt in her father's house (*Genesis 38:6-11*).

Come with me from Lebanon, my *spouse*, with me from Lebanon: look from the top of Amana, from the top of Shenir and Hermon, from the lions' dens, from the mountains of the leopards. Thou hast ravished my heart, my sister, my *spouse*; thou hast ravished my heart with one of thine eyes, with one chain of thy neck. How fair is thy love, my sister, my *spouse*! how much better is thy love than wine! and the smell of thine ointments than all spices! Thy lips, O my *spouse*, drop as the honeycomb: honey and milk are under thy tongue; and the smell of thy garments is like the smell of Lebanon. A garden enclosed is my sister, my *spouse*; a spring shut up, a fountain sealed (*Song 4:8-12*).

47. So the L ORD scattered them abroad from *thence* upon the face of all the earth: and they left off to build the city. Therefore is the name of it called Babel; because the L ORD did there confound the language of all the earth: and from *thence* did the L ORD scatter them abroad upon the face of all the earth (*Genesis 11:8-9*).

And to Seth, to him also *there* was born a son; and he called his name Enos: then began men to call upon the name of the L ORD (*Genesis 4:26*).

And I will make thy seed as the dust of the earth: so that if a man can number the dust of the earth, *then* shall thy seed also be numbered (*Genesis 13:16*).

48. For, behold, in those days, and in that time, when I shall bring again the captivity of Judah and Jerusalem, I will also gather all nations, and will bring them down into the valley of Jehoshaphat, and will plead with them there for my people and for my heritage Israel, whom they have scattered among the nations, and *parted* my land. And they have cast lots for my people; and have given a boy for a harlot, and sold a girl for wine, that they might drink (*Joel 3:1-3*).

And the Lord said unto her, Two nations are in thy womb, and two manner of people shall be *separated from thy bowels*; and the one people shall be stronger than the other people; and the elder shall serve the younger. And when her days to be delivered were fulfilled, behold, there were twins in her womb (*Genesis 25:23-24*).

And when he shall stand up, his kingdom shall be broken, and shall be *divide[d]* toward the four winds of heaven; and not to his posterity, nor according to his dominion which he ruled: for his kingdom shall be plucked up, even for others beside those. And the king of the south shall be strong, and one of his princes; and he shall be strong above him, and have dominion; his dominion shall be a great dominion. And in the end of years they shall join themselves together; for the king's daughter of the south shall come to the king of the north to make an agreement: but she shall not retain the power of the arm; neither shall he stand, nor his arm: but she shall be given up, and they that brought her, and he that begat her, and he that strengthened her in these times. But out of a branch of her roots shall one stand up in his estate, which shall come with an army, and shall enter into the fortress of the king of the north, and shall deal against them, and shall prevail (*Daniel 11:4 7*).

And unto Eber were born two sons: the name of the one was Peleg; because in his days the earth was *divide[d]*: and his brother's name was Joktan (*1 Chronicles 1:19*).

And Jacob lifted up his eyes, and looked, and, behold, Esau came, and with him four hundred men. And he *divide[d]* the children unto Leah, and unto Rachel, and unto the two handmaids (*Genesis 33:1*).

The sorrows of a travailing woman shall come upon him: he is an unwise son; for he should not stay long in the place of the *break[ing] forth* of children (*Hosea 13:13*).

And it came to pass, as he drew back his hand, that, behold, his brother came out: and she said, How hast thou *broken [break] forth*? this *breach* be upon thee: therefore his name was called *Pharez*. And afterward came out his brother, that had the scarlet thread upon his hand: and his name was called Zarah (*Genesis 38:29-30*).

And Abram said, Behold, to me thou hast given no seed: and, lo, one born in my house is mine heir. And, behold, the word of the LORD came unto him, saying, This shall not be thine heir; but he that shall come *forth* out of thine own bowels shall be thine heir. And he brought him forth abroad, and said, Look now toward heaven, and tell the stars, if thou be able to number them: and he said unto him, So shall thy seed be (*Genesis 15:3-5*).

And it came to pass, as he drew back his hand, that, behold, his brother came out: and she said, How hast thou broken forth? this breach be upon thee: therefore his name was called *Pharez* (*Genesis 38:29*).

And Abram said, Behold, to me thou hast given no seed: and, lo, one born in my house is mine heir. And, behold, the word of the LORD came unto him, saying, This shall not be thine heir; but he that shall come *forth* out of thine own bowels shall be thine heir.

And he brought him forth abroad, and said, Look now toward heaven, and tell the stars, if thou be able to number them: and he said unto him, So shall thy seed be (*Genesis 15:3-5*).

And the angel of the LORD said unto her, Behold, thou art with child, and shalt *bear* a son, and shalt call his name Ishmael; because the LORD hath heard thy affliction (*Genesis 16:11*).

But the angel said unto him, Fear not, Zacharias: for thy prayer is heard; and thy wife Elisabeth shall *bear* thee a son, and thou shalt call his name John (*Luke 1:13*).

And she shall *bring forth* a son, and thou shalt call his name JESUS: for he shall save his people from their sins. Now all this was done, that it might be fulfilled which was spoken of the Lord by the prophet, saying, Behold, a virgin shall be with child, and shall *bring forth* a son, and they shall call his name Emmanuel, which being interpreted is, God with us. Then Joseph being raised from sleep did as the angel of the Lord had bidden him, and took unto him his wife: And knew her not till she had brought forth her firstborn son: and he called his name JESUS (*Matthew 1:21-25*).

Unto the woman he said, I will greatly multiply thy sorrow and thy conception; in sorrow thou shalt *bring forth* children; and thy desire shall be to thy husband, and he shall rule over thee (*Genesis 3:16*).

And Jacob begat Joseph the husband of Mary, of whom was *born* Jesus, who is called Christ (*Matthew 1:16*).

And when her days to *be delivered* were fulfilled, behold, there were twins in her womb (*Genesis 25:24*).

And his daughter in law, Phinehas' wife, was with child, near to *be delivered*: and when she heard the tidings that the ark of God was taken, and that her father in law and her husband were dead, she bowed herself and travailed; for her pains came upon her (*1 Samuel 4:19*).

A woman when she is in travail hath sorrow, because her hour is come: but as soon as she is delivered of the child, she remembereth no more the anguish, for joy that a man is born into the world (*John 16:21*).

Fear took hold upon them there, and *pain*, as of *a woman in travail* (*Psalm 48:6*).

49.   There were giants in the earth in those days; and also after that, when the sons of God came in unto the daughters of men, and they bare children to them, the same *became* mighty men which were of old, men of renown (*Genesis 6:4*).

And they smote all the souls that were therein with the edge of the sword, utterly destroying them: there was not any left *to breathe*: and he burnt Hazor with fire (*Joshua 11:11*).

And when her days *to be* delivered were fulfilled, behold, there were twins in her womb. And the first came out red, all over like a hairy garment; and they called his name Esau (*Genesis 25:24-25*).

And the angel of the Lord said unto her, Behold, thou art with child, and shalt *bear* a son, and shalt call his name Ishmael; because the Lord hath heard thy affliction (*Genesis 16:11*).

But the angel said unto him, Fear not, Zacharias: for thy prayer is heard; and thy wife Elisabeth shall *bear* thee a son, and thou shalt call his name John (*Luke 1:13*).

Unto the woman he said, I will greatly multiply thy sorrow and thy conception; in sorrow thou shalt *bring forth* children; and thy desire shall be to thy husband, and he shall rule over thee (*Genesis 3:16*).

Now these are the generations of the sons of Noah, Shem, Ham, and Japheth: and unto them were sons *born* after the flood (*Genesis 10:1*).

And Abraham was an hundred years old, when his son Isaac was born unto him. And Sarah said, God hath made me to laugh, so that all that hear will laugh with me. And she said, Who would have said unto Abraham, that Sarah should have given children suck? for I have *born* him a son in his old age (*Genesis 21:5-7*).

And when her days to *be delivered* were fulfilled, behold, there were twins in her womb (*Genesis 25:24*).

And his daughter in law, Phinehas' wife, was with child, near to *be delivered*: and when she heard the tidings that the ark of God was taken, and that her father in law and her husband were dead, she bowed herself and travailed; for her pains came upon her (*1 Samuel 4:19*).

A woman when she is in travail hath sorrow, because her hour is come: but as soon as she is delivered of the child, she remembereth no more the anguish, for joy that a man is born into the world (*John 16:21*).

Fear took hold upon them there, and pain, as of *a woman in travail* (*Psalm 48:6*).

50. These *four* were born to the giant in Gath, and fell by the hand of David, and by the hand of his servants (*2 Samuel 21:22*).

And these were born unto him in Jerusalem; Shimea, and Shobab, and Nathan, and Solomon, *four*, of Bath-shua the daughter of Ammiel (*1 Chronicles 3:5*).

Now the sons of Issachar were, Tola, and Puah, Jashub, and Shimrom, *four* (*1 Chronicles 7:1*).

And Ornan turned back, and saw the angel; and his *four* sons with him hid themselves. Now Ornan was threshing wheat (*1 Chronicles 21:20*).

Thou shalt not lie with mankind, as with womankind: it is abomination. Neither shalt thou lie with any beast to defile thyself therewith: neither shall any woman stand before a beast *to lie down* thereto: it is confusion (*Leviticus 18:22-23*).

And when Boaz had eaten and drunk, and his heart was merry, he went *to lie down* at the end of the heap of corn: and she came softly, and uncovered his feet, and laid her down. And it came to pass at midnight, that the man was afraid, and turned himself: and, behold, a woman lay at his feet. And he said, Who art thou? And she answered, I am Ruth thine handmaid: spread therefore thy skirt over thine handmaid; for thou art a near kinsman (*Ruth 3:7-9*).

And Adam knew his wife again; and she bare a son, and called his name Seth: For God, said she, hath appointed me another *seed* instead of Abel, whom Cain slew (*Genesis 4:25*).

And Jacob's anger was kindled against Rachel: and he said, Am I in God's stead, who hath withheld from thee the *fruit* of the womb (*Genesis 30:2*)?

51.   And the LORD spake unto Moses and unto Aaron, and gave them a charge unto the children of Israel, and unto Pharaoh king of Egypt, to bring the children of Israel out of the land of Egypt. These be the *heads* of their fathers' houses: The sons of Reuben the firstborn of Israel; Hanoch, and Pallu, Hezron, and Carmi: these be the families of Reuben (*Exodus 6:13-14*).

And Canaan begat Sidon his *first*born, and Heth (*Genesis 10:15*).

And the LORD said unto her, Two nations are in thy womb, and two manner of people shall be separated from thy bowels; and the one people shall be stronger than the other people; and the elder shall serve the younger. And when her days to be delivered were fulfilled, behold, there were twins in her womb. And the *first* came out red, all over like a hairy garment; and they called his name Esau. And after that came his brother out, and his hand took hold on Esau's heel; and his name was called Jacob: and Isaac was threescore years old when she bare them (*Genesis 25:23-26*).

And it came to pass in the time of her travail, that, behold, twins were in her womb. And it came to pass, when she travailed, that the one put out his hand: and the midwife took and bound upon his hand a scarlet thread, saying, This came out *first*, And it came to pass, as he drew back his hand, that, behold, his brother came out: and she said, How hast thou broken forth? this breach be upon thee: therefore his name was called Pharez. And afterward came out his brother, that had the scarlet thread upon his hand: and his name was called Zarah (*Genesis 38:27-30*).

And Adam knew his wife again; and she bare *a son*, and called his name Seth: For God, said she, hath appointed me another seed instead of Abel, whom Cain slew (*Genesis 4:25*).

And the LORD said unto Abram, after that Lot was separated from him, Lift up now thine eyes, and look from the place where thou art northward, and southward, and eastward, and westward: For all the land which thou seest, to thee will I give it, and to thy seed for ever. And I will *make* thy seed as the dust of the earth: so that if a man can number the dust of the earth, then shall thy seed also be numbered (*Genesis 13:14-16*).

And the angel of the LORD said unto her, Behold, thou art with child, and shalt *bear* a son, and shalt call his name Ishmael; because the LORD hath heard thy affliction (*Genesis 16:11*).

But the angel said unto him, Fear not, Zacharias: for thy prayer is heard; and thy wife Elisabeth shall *bear* thee a son, and thou shalt call his name John (*Luke 1:13*).

Unto the woman he said, I will greatly multiply thy sorrow and thy conception; in sorrow thou shalt *bring forth* children; and thy desire shall be to thy husband, and he shall rule over thee (*Genesis 3:16*).

And she shall *bring forth* a son, and thou shalt call his name JESUS: for he shall save his people from their sins. Now all this was done, that it might be fulfilled which was spoken of the Lord by the prophet, saying, Behold, a virgin shall be with child, and shall *bring forth* a son, and they shall call his name Emmanuel, which being interpreted is, God with us. Then Joseph being raised from sleep did as the angel of the Lord had bidden him, and took unto him his wife: And knew her not till she had brought forth her firstborn son: and he called his name JESUS (*Matthew 1:21-25*).

Now these are the generations of the sons of Noah, Shem, Ham, and Japheth: and unto them were sons *born* after the flood (*Genesis 10:1*).

And Abraham was an hundred years old, when his son Isaac was born unto him. And Sarah said, God hath made me to laugh, so that all that hear will laugh with me. And she said, Who would have said unto Abraham, that Sarah should have given children suck? for I have *born* him a son in his old age (*Genesis 21:5-7*).

And Jacob begat Joseph the husband of Mary, of whom was *born* Jesus, who is called Christ (*Matthew 1:16*).

And when her days to *be delivered* were fulfilled, behold, there were twins in her womb (*Genesis 25:24*).

And his daughter in law, Phinehas' wife, was with child, near to *be delivered*: and when she heard the tidings that the ark of God was taken, and that her father in law and her husband were dead, she bowed herself and travailed; for her pains came upon her (*1 Samuel 4:19*).

A woman when she is in travail hath sorrow, because her hour is come: but as soon as she is delivered of the child, she remembereth no more the anguish, for joy that a man is born into the world (*John 16:21*).

Fear took hold upon them there, and pain, as of *a woman in travail* (*Psalm 48:6*).

52a. Even by the God of thy father, who shall help thee; and by the Almighty, who shall bless thee with blessings of heaven above, blessings of the *deep* that lieth under, blessings of the breasts, and of the womb (*Genesis 49:25*).

Hath the rain a father? or who hath begotten the drops of dew? Out of whose womb came the ice? and the hoary frost of heaven, who hath gendered it? The waters are hid as with a stone, and the face of the *deep* is frozen (*Job 38:28-30*).

And the angel of the LORD said unto her, I will *multiply* thy seed exceedingly, that it shall not be numbered for multitude (*Genesis 16:10*).

If the clouds *be full of* rain, they empty themselves upon the earth: and if the tree fall toward the south, or toward the north, in the place where the tree falleth, there it shall be. He that observeth the wind shall not sow; and he that regardeth the clouds shall not reap. As thou knowest not what is the way of the spirit, nor how the bones do grow in the womb of her that is with child: even so thou knowest not the works of God who maketh all. In the morning sow thy seed, and in the evening withhold not thine hand: for thou knowest not whether shall prosper, either this or that, or whether they both shall be alike good (*Ecclesiastes 11:3-6*).

And the sucking child shall play on the hole of the asp, and the weaned child shall put his hand on the cockatrice' den. They shall not hurt nor destroy in all my holy mountain: for the earth shall *be full of* the knowledge of the LORD, as the waters cover the sea. And in that day there shall be a root of Jesse, which shall stand for an ensign of the people; to it shall the Gentiles seek: and his rest shall be glorious (*Isaiah 11:8-10*).

From men which are thy hand, O LORD, from men of the world, which have their portion in this life, and whose belly thou fillest with thy hid treasure: they are *full* of children, and leave the rest of their substance to their babes (*Psalm 17:14*).

As thou knowest not what is the way of the spirit, nor how the bones do grow in the womb of *her that is with child*: even so thou knowest not the works of God who maketh all (*Ecclesiastes 11:5*).

Now the birth of Jesus Christ was on this wise: When as his mother Mary was espoused to Joseph, before they came together, *she was found with child* of the Holy Ghost (*Matthew 1:18*).

52b. Even by the God of thy father, who shall help thee; and by the Almighty, who shall bless thee with blessings of heaven above, blessings of the *deep* that lieth under, blessings of the breasts, and of the womb (*Genesis 49:25*).

Hath the rain a father? or who hath begotten the drops of dew? Out of whose womb came the ice? and the hoary frost of heaven, who hath gendered it? The waters are hid as with a stone, and the face of the *deep* is frozen (*Job 38:28-30*).

And when a stranger shall sojourn with thee, and will keep the passover to the LORD, let all his males be circumcised, and then let him come near and keep it; and he shall be as one that is born in the land: for no uncircumcised person shall eat thereof. One law shall be to him that is *homeborn*, and unto the stranger that sojourneth among you. Thus did all the children of Israel; as the

L ORD commanded Moses and Aaron, so did they. And it came to pass the selfsame day, that the L ORD did bring the children of Israel out of the land of Egypt by their armies (*Exodus 12:48-51*).

And the angel of the L ORD said unto her, Behold, thou art with child, and shalt *bear* a son, and shalt call his name Ishmael; because the L ORD hath heard thy affliction (*Genesis 16:11*).

Unto the woman he said, I will greatly multiply thy sorrow and thy conception; in sorrow thou shalt *bring forth* children; and thy desire shall be to thy husband, and he shall rule over thee (*Genesis 3:16*).

And she shall *bring forth* a son, and thou shalt call his name JESUS: for he shall save his people from their sins. Now all this was done, that it might be fulfilled which was spoken of the Lord by the prophet, saying, Behold, a virgin shall be with child, and shall *bring forth* a son, and they shall call his name Emmanuel, which being interpreted is, God with us. Then Joseph being raised from sleep did as the angel of the Lord had bidden him, and took unto him his wife: And knew her not till she had brought forth her firstborn son: and he called his name JESUS (*Matthew 1:21-25*).

Now these are the generations of the sons of Noah, Shem, Ham, and Japheth: and unto them were sons *born* after the flood (*Genesis 10:1*).

And Abraham was an hundred years old, when his son Isaac was born unto him. And Sarah said, God hath made me to laugh, so that all that hear will laugh with me. And she said, Who would have said unto Abraham, that Sarah should have given children suck? for I have *born* him a son in his old age (*Genesis 21:5-7*).

And Jacob begat Joseph the husband of Mary, of whom was *born* Jesus, who is called Christ (*Matthew 1:16*).

And when her days to *be delivered* were fulfilled, behold, there were twins in her womb (*Genesis 25:24*).

And his daughter in law, Phinehas' wife, was with child, near to *be delivered*: and when she heard the tidings that the ark of God was taken, and that her father in law and her husband were dead,

she bowed herself and travailed; for her pains came upon her (*1 Samuel 4:19*).

A woman when she is in travail hath sorrow, because her hour is come: but as soon as she is delivered of the child, she remembereth no more the anguish, for joy that a man is born into the world (*John 16:21*).

Fear took hold upon them there, and pain, as of *a woman in travail* (*Psalm 48:6*).

53. When thou liest down, thou shalt not be afraid: yea, thou shalt lie down, and thy *sleep* shall be sweet (*Proverbs 3:24*).

And *she made him sleep upon her knees*; and she called for a man, and she caused him to shave off the seven locks of his head; and she began to afflict him, and his strength went from him (*Judges 16:19*).

Thou shalt not lie with mankind, as with womankind: it is abomination. Neither shalt thou lie with any beast to defile thyself therewith: neither shall any woman stand before a beast *to lie down* thereto: it is confusion (*Leviticus 18:22-23*).

And when Boaz had eaten and drunk, and his heart was merry, he went *to lie down* at the end of the heap of corn: and she came softly, and uncovered his feet, and laid her down. And it came to pass at midnight, that the man was afraid, and turned himself: and, behold, a woman lay at his feet. And he said, Who art thou? And she answered, I am Ruth thine handmaid: spread therefore thy skirt over thine handmaid; for thou art a near kinsman (*Ruth 3:7-9*).

54a. And Lamech *took* unto him two wives: the name of the one was Adah, and the name of the other Zillah (*Genesis 4:19*).

And Abram and Nahor *took* them wives: the name of Abram's wife was Sarai; and the name of Nahor's wife, Milcah, the daughter of Haran, the father of Milcah, and the father of Iscah. But Sarai was barren; she had no child (*Genesis 11:29-30*).

When Esau saw that Isaac had blessed Jacob, and sent him away to Padan-aram, *to take* him a wife from thence; and that as he blessed him he gave him a charge, saying, Thou shalt not take a wife of the daughters of Canaan (*Genesis 28:6*).

But thou shalt go unto my country, and to my kindred, and *take* a wife unto my son Isaac. And the servant said unto him, Peradventure the woman will not be willing to follow me unto this land: must I needs bring thy son again unto the land from whence thou camest? And Abraham said unto him, Beware thou that thou bring not my son thither again. The Lord God of heaven, which took me from my father's house, and from the land of my kindred, and which spake unto me, and that sware unto me, saying, Unto thy seed will I give this land; he shall send his angel before thee, and thou shalt *take* a wife unto my son from thence (*Genesis 24:4-7*).

And he went down, and talked with the woman; and she pleased Samson well. And after a time he returned *to take* her, and he turned aside to see the carcass of the lion: and, behold, there was a swarm of bees and honey in the carcass of the lion *(Judges 14:7-8)*.

And whereas thou sawest iron mixed with miry clay, they shall *mingle* themselves with the seed of men: but they shall not cleave one to another, even as iron is not mixed with clay (*Daniel 2:43*).

And it came to pass, when he had been there a long time, that Abimelech king of the Philistines looked out at a window, and saw, and, behold, Isaac was sporting with Rebekah his wife. And Abimelech called Isaac, and said, Behold, of a *surety* she is thy wife: and how saidst thou, She is my sister? And Isaac said unto him, Because I said, Lest I die for her. And Abimelech said, What is this thou hast done unto us? one of the people might lightly have lien with thy wife, and thou shouldest have brought guiltiness upon us (*Genesis 26:8-10*).

Come, let us make our father drink wine, and we will *lie with him*, that we may preserve seed of our father (*Genesis 19:32*).

And it came to pass after these things, that his master's wife cast her eyes upon Joseph; and she said, *Lie* with me (*Genesis 39:7*).

And she said unto her, Is it a small matter that thou hast taken my husband? and wouldest thou take away my son's mandrakes also?

And Rachel said, Therefore he shall *lie* with thee to night for thy son's mandrakes. And Jacob came out of the field in the evening, and Leah went out to meet him, and said, Thou must come in unto me; for surely I have hired thee with my son's mandrakes. And he lay with her that night. And God hearkened unto Leah, and she conceived, and bare Jacob the fifth son (*Genesis 30:15-17*).

And they called unto Lot, and said unto him, Where are the men which came in to thee this night? bring them out unto us, that we may *know* them. Lot went out at the door unto them, and shut the door after him, And said, I pray you, brethren, do not so wickedly. Behold now, I have two daughters which have not *know*n man; let me, I pray you, bring them out unto you, and do ye to them as is good in your eyes: only unto these men do nothing; for therefore came they under the shadow of my roof (*Genesis 19:5-8*).

55.   And the *rib*, which the LORD God had taken from man, made he a woman, and brought her unto the man (*Genesis 2:22*).

Do not prostitute thy daughter, to cause her to be a whore; lest the and *fall* to whoredom, and the land become full of wickedness (*Leviticus 19:29*).

Thou shalt not lie with mankind, as with womankind: it is abomination. Neither shalt thou lie with any beast to defile thyself therewith: neither shall any woman stand before a beast to *lie down* thereto: it is confusion. Defile not ye yourselves in any of these things: for in all these the nations are defiled which I cast out before you (*Leviticus 18:22-24*).

Tarry this night, and it shall be in the morning, that if he will perform unto thee the part of a kinsman, well; let him do the kinsman's part: but if he will not do the part of a kinsman to thee, then will I do the part of a kinsman to thee, as the Lord liveth: *lie down* until the morning (*Ruth 3:13*).

56.   And the LORD God caused a deep sleep to fall upon Adam and he slept: and he took one of his ribs, and *closed* up the flesh instead thereof (*Genesis 2:21*).

For the LORD had fast *closed* up all the wombs of the house of Abimelech, because of Sarah Abraham's wife (*Genesis 20:18*).

57.　What? know ye not that he which is joined to an harlot is one body? for two, saith he, shall be one *flesh* (*1 Corinthians 6:16*).

And the LORD God caused a deep sleep to fall upon Adam and he slept: and he took one of his ribs, and closed up the *flesh* instead thereof; And the rib, which the LORD God had taken from man, made he a woman, and brought her unto the man. And Adam said, This is now bone of my bones, and *flesh* of my *flesh*: she shall be called Woman, because she was taken out of Man. Therefore shall a man leave his father and his mother, and shall cleave unto his wife: and they shall be one *flesh* (*Genesis 2:21-24*).

And he said, Who art thou? And she answered, I am Ruth thine handmaid: spread therefore thy skirt over thine handmaid; for thou art a near *kin*sman (*Ruth 3:9*).

And Judah said unto Onan, *Go in unto thy brother's wife, and marry her*, and raise up seed to thy brother (*Genesis 38:8*).

None of you shall approach to any that is near of kin to him, to uncover their *nakedness*: I am the Lord. The *nakedness* of thy father, or the *nakedness* of thy mother, shalt thou not uncover: she is thy mother; thou shalt not uncover her *nakedness*. The *nakedness* of thy father's wife shalt thou not uncover: it is thy father's *nakedness*. The *nakedness* of thy sister, the daughter of thy father, or daughter of thy mother, whether she be born at home, or born abroad, even their *nakedness* thou shalt not uncover. (*Leviticus 18:6-9*)

And the man that lieth with his father's wife hath uncovered his father's *nakedness*: both of them shall surely be put to death; their blood shall be upon them (*Leviticus 20:11*).

Thus will I make thy lewdness to cease from thee, and thy whoredom brought from the land of Egypt: so that thou shalt not lift up thine eyes unto them, nor remember Egypt any more. For thus saith the Lord God; Behold, I will deliver thee into the hand of them whom thou hatest, into the hand of them from whom thy mind is alienated: And they shall deal with thee hatefully, and shall take away all thy labour, and shall leave thee naked and bare: and the *nakedness* of thy whoredoms shall be discovered, both thy lewdness and thy whoredoms (*Ezekiel 23:27-29*).

58a. And she *made* him sleep upon her knees; and she called for a man, and she caused him to shave off the seven locks of his head; and she began to afflict him, and his strength went from him (*Judges 16:19*).

And the king loved Esther above all the women, and she obtained grace and favour in his sight more than all the virgins; so that he set the royal crown upon her head, and *made* her queen instead of Vashti (*Esther 2:17*).

And it came to pass after this, that Absalom the son of David had a fair sister, whose name was Tamar; and Amnon the son of David loved her. And Amnon was so vexed, that he fell sick for his sister Tamar; for she was a virgin; and Amnon thought it hard for him *to do* anything to her (*2 Samuel 13:1-2*).

Son of man, there were two women, the daughters of one mother: *And they committed whoredoms in Egypt; they committed whoredoms in their youth: there were their breasts pressed, and there they bruised the teats of their virginity.* And the names of them were Aholah the elder, and Aholibah her sister: and they were mine, and they bare sons and daughters. Thus were their names; Samaria is Aholah, and Jerusalem Aholibah. And Aholah played the harlot when she was mine; and she doted on her lovers, on the Assyrians her neighbours, Which were clothed with blue, captains and rulers, all of them desirable young men, horsemen riding upon horses. Thus she committed her whoredoms with them, with all them that were the chosen men of Assyria, and with all on whom she doted: with all their idols she defiled herself. *Neither left she her whoredoms brought from Egypt: for in her youth they lay with her, and they bruised the breasts of her virginity, and poured their whoredom upon her.* Wherefore I have delivered her into the hand of her lovers, into the hand of the Assyrians, upon whom she doted. These discovered her nakedness: they took her sons and her daughters, and slew her with the sword: and she became famous among women; for they had executed judgment upon her. And when her sister Aholibah saw this, she was more corrupt in her inordinate love than she, and in her whoredoms more than her sister in her whoredoms. She doted upon the Assyrians her neighbours, captains and rulers clothed most gorgeously, horsemen riding upon horses, all of them desirable young men. Then I saw that she was defiled, that they took both one way, And that she increased her whoredoms: for when she saw men pourtrayed upon the wall, the images of the Chaldeans pourtrayed with vermilion, Girded with girdles upon their loins, exceeding in dyed attire upon their heads, all of them princes to look to, after the manner of the Babylonians of Chaldea, the land of their nativity: And as soon as she saw them with her eyes, she doted upon them, and sent messengers unto them into Chaldea. And the Babylonians came to her into the bed of love, and they defiled her with their whoredom, and she was polluted with them, and her mind was alienated from them. So she discovered her whoredoms, and discovered her nakedness: then my mind was alienated from her, like as my mind was alienated from her sister. Yet she multiplied her whoredoms, in calling to remembrance the days of her youth, wherein she had played the harlot in the land of Egypt. For she doted upon their paramours, whose flesh is as the flesh of asses, and whose issue is like the issue of horses. Thus thou calledst to remembrance the lewdness of thy youth, in bruising thy teats by the Egyptians for the paps of thy youth. There, O Aholibah, thus saith the Lord God; Behold, I will raise up thy lovers against thee, from whom thy mind is alienated, and I will bring them against thee on every side; The Babylonians, and all the Chaldeans, Pekod, and Shoa, and Koa, and all the Assyrians with them: all of them desirable young men, captains and rulers, great lords and renowned, all of them riding upon horses (*Ezekiel 23:2-23*).

58b.   And she *made* him sleep upon her knees; and she called for a man, and she caused him to shave off the seven locks of his head; and she began to afflict him, and his strength went from him (*Judges 16:19*).

And the king loved Esther above all the women, and she obtained grace and favour in his sight more than all the virgins; so that he set the royal crown upon her head, and *made* her queen instead of Vashti (*Esther 2:17*).

Behind the doors also and the posts hast thou set up thy remembrance: for thou hast discovered thyself to another than me, and art gone up; thou hast enlarged thy bed, and made thee a *covenant* with them; thou lovedst their bed where thou sawest it (*Isaiah 57:8*).

Then may also my *covenant* be broken with David my servant, that he should not have a son to reign upon his throne; and with the Levites the priests, my ministers (*Jeremiah 33:21*).

When a man hath taken a wife, and married her, and it come to pass that she find no favor in his eyes, because he hath found some uncleanness in her: then let him write her a bill of *divorce[ment]*, and give it in her hand, and send her out of his house. And when she is departed out of his house, she may go and be another man's wife. And if the latter husband hate her, and write her a bill of *divorce[ment]*, and giveth it in her hand, and sendeth her out of his house; or if the latter husband die, which took her to be his wife; Her former husband, which sent her away, may not take her again to be his wife, after that she is defiled; for that is abomination before the Lord: and thou shalt not cause the land to sin, which the Lord thy God giveth thee for an inheritance. When a man hath taken a new wife, he shall not go out to war, neither shall he be charged with any business: but he shall be free at home one year, and shall cheer up his wife which he hath taken (*Deuteronomy 24:1-5*).

The Lord said also unto me in the days of Josiah the king, Hast thou seen that which backsliding Israel hath done? she is gone up upon every high mountain and under every green tree, and there hath played the harlot. And I said after she had done all these things, Turn thou unto me. But she returned not. And her treacherous sister Judah saw it. And I saw, when for all the causes whereby backsliding Israel committed adultery I had put her away, and given her a bill of *divorce*; yet her treacherous sister Judah feared not, but went and played the harlot also. And it came to pass through the lightness of her whoredom, that she defiled the land, and committed adultery with stones and with stocks (*Jeremiah 3:6-9*).

59.   And Adam said, This is now *bone* of my bones, and flesh of my flesh: she shall be called Woman, because she was taken out of Man (*Genesis 2:23*).

And a man lie with her carnally, and it be hid from the eyes of her husband, and be kept *close*, and she be defiled, and there be no witness against her, neither she be taken with the manner (*Numbers 5:13*).

When Esau saw that Isaac had blessed Jacob, and sent him away to Padan-aram, to *take* him a wife from thence; and that as he blessed him he gave him a charge, saying, Thou shalt not take a wife of the daughters of Canaan (*Genesis 28:6*).

The princes also of Pharaoh saw her, and commended her before Pharaoh: and the woman was *taken* into Pharaoh's house. And he entreated Abram well for her sake: and he had sheep, and oxen, and he asses, and menservants, and maidservants, and she asses, and camels. And the LORD plagued Pharaoh and his house with great plagues because of Sarai Abram's wife. And Pharaoh called Abram, and said, What is this that thou hast done unto me? why didst thou not tell me that she was thy wife? Why saidst thou, She is my sister? so I might have *taken* her to me to wife: now therefore behold thy wife, take her, and go thy way (*Genesis 12:15-18*).

And he went down, and talked with the woman; and she pleased Samson well. And after a time he returned *to take* her, and he turned aside to see the carcass of the lion: and, behold, there was a swarm of bees and honey in the carcass of the lion *(Judges 14:7-8)*.

When Esau saw that Isaac had blessed Jacob, and sent him away to Padan-aram, *to take* him a wife from thence; and that as he blessed him he gave him a charge, saying, Thou shalt not take a wife of the daughters of Canaan (*Genesis 28:6*).

And he went down, and talked with the woman; and she pleased Samson well. And after a time he returned *to take* her, and he turned aside to see the carcass of the lion: and, behold, there was a swarm of bees and honey in the carcass of the lion *(Judges 14:7-8)*.

60a. Therefore shall a man leave his father and his mother, and shall *cleave* unto his wife: and they shall be one flesh (*Genesis 2:24*).

And she conceived again, and bare a son; and said, Now this time will my husband *be joined* unto me, because I have born him three sons: therefore was his name called Levi (*Genesis 29:34*).

And Sarai Abram's wife took Hagar her maid the Egyptian, after Abram had dwelt ten years in the land of Canaan, and gave her to her husband Abram *to be* his wife. And he went in unto Hagar, and she conceived: and when she saw that she had conceived, her mistress was despised in her eyes (*Genesis 16:3-4*).

And seest among the captives a beautiful woman, and hast a *desire* unto her, that thou wouldest have her to thy wife (*Deuteronomy 21:11*).

60b. Therefore shall a man leave his father and his mother, and shall *cleave* unto his wife: and they shall be one flesh (*Genesis 2:24*).

And she conceived again, and bare a son; and said, Now this time will my husband *be joined* unto me, because I have born him three sons: therefore was his name called Levi (*Genesis 29:34*).

And Sarai Abram's wife took Hagar her maid the Egyptian, after Abram had dwelt ten years in the land of Canaan, and gave her to her husband Abram *to be* his wife. And he went in unto Hagar, and she conceived: and when she saw that she had conceived, her mistress was despised in her eyes (*Genesis 16:3-4*).

Thou shalt not covet thy neighbor's house, thou shalt not *covet* thy neighbor's wife, nor his manservant, nor his maidservant, nor his ox, nor his ass, nor any thing that is thy neighbor's (*Exodus 20:17*).

To keep thee from the evil woman, from the flattery of the tongue of a strange woman. *Lust* not *after* her beauty in thine heart; neither let her take thee with her eyelids. For by means of a whorish woman a man is brought to a piece of bread: and the adulteress will hunt for the precious life. Can a man take fire in his bosom, and his clothes not be burned (*Proverbs 6:24-27*)?

61. Now the *serpent* was more subtil than any beast of the field which the Lord God had made. And he said unto the woman, Yea, hath God said, Ye shall not eat of every tree of the garden? And the woman said unto the *serpent*, We may eat of the fruit of the trees of the garden (*Genesis 3:1-2*):

And Jacob called unto his sons, and said, Gather yourselves together, that I may tell you that which shall befall you in the last days. Gather yourselves together, and hear, ye sons of Jacob; and hearken unto Israel your father... Dan shall be a *serpent* by the way, an adder in the path, that biteth the horse heels, so that his rider shall fall backward (*Genesis 49:1-2, 17*).

But I fear, lest by any means, as the *serpent* beguiled Eve *through his subtlety*, so your minds should be corrupted from the simplicity that is in Christ (*2 Corinthians 11:3*).

62. That they may keep thee from the strange woman, from the stranger which flattereth with her words. For at the window of my house I looked through my casement, And beheld among the simple ones, I discerned among the youths, a young man void of understanding, Passing through the street near her corner; and he went the way to her house, In the twilight, in the evening, in the black and dark night: And, behold, there met him a woman with the attire of an harlot, and *subtle* of heart. (She is loud and stubborn; her feet abide not in her house: Now is she without, now in the streets, and lieth in wait at every corner.) So she caught him, and kissed him, and with an impudent face said unto him (*Proverbs 7:5-13*).

But the boys grew: and Esau was a *cunning* hunter, a man of the field; and Jacob was a plain man, dwelling in tents (*Genesis 25:27*).

63. So foolish was I, and ignorant: I was as a *beast* before thee (*Psalm 73:22*).

Issachar is a *strong* ass couching down between two burdens (*Genesis 49:14*).

And that bringeth me forth from mine enemies: thou also hast lifted me up on high above them that rose up against me: thou hast delivered me from the *violent* man (*2 Samuel 22:49*).

O my soul, come not thou into their secret; unto their assembly, mine honor, be not thou united: for in their anger they slew a man, and in their selfwill they digged down a wall. Cursed be their anger, for it was fierce; and their wrath, for it was *cruel*: I will divide them in Jacob, and scatter them in Israel (*Genesis 49:6-7*).

64. And it came to pass in the evening, that he took Leah his daughter, and brought her to him; and he went in unto her. And Laban gave unto his daughter Leah Zilpah his maid for a handmaid. And it came to pass, that in the morning, behold, it was Leah: and he said to Laban, What is this thou hast done unto me? did not I serve with thee for Rachel? wherefore then hast thou *beguiled* me (*Genesis 29:23-25*)?

But I fear, lest by any means, as the serpent *beguiled* Eve through his subtlety, so your minds should be corrupted from the simplicity that is in Christ (*2 Corinthians 11:3*).

Notwithstanding I have a few things against thee, because thou sufferest that woman Jezebel, which calleth herself a prophetess, to teach and *to seduce* my servants to commit fornication, and to eat things sacrificed unto idols. And I gave her space to repent of her fornication; and she repented not Behold, I will cast her into a bed, and them that commit adultery with her into great tribulation, except they repent of their deeds (*Revelation 2:20-22*).

65a. When thou sittest to *eat* with a ruler, consider diligently what is before thee: And put a knife to thy throat, if thou be a man given to appetite. Be not desirous of his dainties: for they are deceitful meat (*Proverbs 23:1-3*).

And Amnon said unto Tamar, Bring the meat into the chamber, *that I may eat of thine hand.* And Tamar took the cakes which she had made, and brought them into the chamber to Amnon her brother. And when she had brought them unto him to eat, he took hold of her, and said unto her, Come lie with me, my sister (*2 Samuel 13:10-11*).

Do not *prostitute* thy daughter, to cause her to be a whore; lest the land fall to whoredom, and the land become full of wickedness (*Leviticus 19:29*).

65b. When thou sittest to *eat* with a ruler, consider diligently what is before thee: And put a knife to thy throat, if thou be a man given to appetite. Be not desirous of his dainties: for they are deceitful meat (*Proverbs 23:1-3*).

And Amnon said unto Tamar, Bring the meat into the chamber, *that I may eat of thine hand.* And Tamar took the cakes which she had made, and brought them into the chamber to Amnon her brother. And when she had brought them unto him to eat, he took hold of her, and said unto her, Come lie with me, my sister (*2 Samuel 13:10-11*).

Behold, thou art fair, my love; behold, thou art fair; thou hast doves' eyes within thy locks: thy hair is as a flock of goats, that appear from mount Gilead. Thy teeth are like a flock of sheep that are even shorn, which came up from the washing; whereof every one bear twins, and none is barren among them. Thy lips are like a thread of scarlet, and thy speech is comely: thy temples are like a piece of a pomegranate within thy locks. Thy neck is like the tower of David builded for an armoury, whereon there hang a thousand bucklers, all shields of mighty men. Thy two breasts are like two young roes that are twins, which feed among the lilies. Until the day break, and the shadows flee away, I will get me to the mountain of myrrh, and to the hill of frankincense. Thou art all fair, my love; there is no spot in thee. Come with me from Lebanon, my spouse, with me from Lebanon: look from the top of Amana, from the top of Shenir and Hermon, from the lions' dens, from the mountains of the leopards. Thou hast ravished my heart, my sister, my spouse; thou hast ravished my heart with one of thine eyes, with one chain of thy neck. How fair is thy love, my sister, my spouse! how much better is thy love than wine! and the smell of thine ointments than all spices! Thy lips, O my spouse, drop as the honeycomb: honey and milk are under thy tongue; and the smell of thy garments is like the smell of Lebanon. A garden inclosed is my sister, my spouse; a spring shut up, a fountain sealed. Thy plants are an orchard of pomegranates, with pleasant fruits; camphire, with spikenard, Spikenard and saffron; calamus and cinnamon, with all trees of frankincense; myrrh and aloes, with all the chief spices: A fountain of gardens, a well of living waters, and streams from Lebanon. Awake, O north wind; and come, thou south; blow upon my garden, that the spices thereof may flow out. Let my beloved come into his garden, and *eat* his pleasant fruits (*Song of Solomon 4:1-16*).

Have they not sped? have they not divided the *prey*; to every man a damsel or two; to Sisera a prey of divers colors, a prey of divers colors of needlework, of divers colors of needlework on both sides, meet for the necks of them that take the spoil (*Judges 5:30*)?

But thou shalt go unto my country, and to my kindred, and *take* a wife unto my son Isaac (*Genesis 24:4*).

And whereas thou sawest iron mixed with miry clay, they shall *mingle* themselves with the seed of men: but they shall not cleave one to another, even as iron is not mixed with clay (*Daniel 2:43*).

And it came to pass, when he had been there a long time, that Abimelech king of the Philistines looked out at a window, and saw, and, behold, Isaac was sporting with Rebekah his wife. And Abimelech called Isaac, and said, Behold, of a *surety* she is thy wife: and how saidst thou, She is my sister? And Isaac said unto him, Because I said, Lest I die for her. And Abimelech said, What is this thou hast done unto us? one of the people might lightly have lien with thy wife, and thou shouldest have brought guiltiness upon us (*Genesis 26:8-10*).

Come, let us make our father drink wine, and we will *lie with him*, that we may preserve seed of our father (*Genesis 19:32*).

And it came to pass after these things, that his master's wife cast her eyes upon Joseph; and she said, *Lie with me* (*Genesis 39:7*).

And she said unto her, Is it a small matter that thou hast taken my husband? and wouldest thou take away my son's mandrakes also? And Rachel said, Therefore he shall *lie* with thee to night for thy son's mandrakes. And Jacob came out of the field in the evening, and Leah went out to meet him, and said, Thou must come in unto me; for surely I have hired thee with my son's mandrakes. And he lay with her that night. And God hearkened unto Leah, and she conceived, and bare Jacob the fifth son (*Genesis 30:15-17*).

And they called unto Lot, and said unto him, Where are the men which came in to thee this night? bring them out unto us, that we may *know* them. Lot went out at the door unto them, and shut the door after him, And said, I pray you, brethren, do not so wickedly. Behold now, I have two daughters which have not *know[n]* man; let me, I pray you, bring them out unto you, and do ye to them as is good in your eyes: only unto these men do nothing; for therefore came they under the shadow of my roof (*Genesis 19:5-8*).

66.   But God came to Abimelech in a dream by night, and said to him, Behold, thou art but a dead man, for the woman which thou hast taken; for she is a man's wife. But Abimelech had not come near her: and he said, Lord, wilt thou slay also a righteous nation? Said he not unto me, She is my sister? and she, even she herself said, He is my brother: in the integrity of my heart and innocency of my hands have I done this. And God said unto him in a dream, Yea, I know that thou didst this in the integrity of thy heart; for I also withheld thee from sinning against me: therefore suffered I thee not to *touch* her. Now therefore restore the man his wife; for he is a prophet, and he shall pray for thee, and thou shalt live: and if thou restore her not, know thou that thou shalt surely die, thou, and all that are thine (*Genesis 20:3-7*).

Now concerning the things whereof ye wrote unto me: It is good for a man not to *touch* a woman. Nevertheless, to avoid fornication, let every man have his own wife, and let every woman have her own husband. Let the husband render unto the wife due benevolence: and likewise also the wife unto the husband. The wife hath not power of her own body, but the husband: and likewise also the husband hath not power of his own body, but the wife (*1 Corinthians 7:1-4*).

Come, let us make our father drink wine, and we will *lie with him*, that we may preserve seed of our father (*Genesis 19:32*).

And it came to pass after these things, that his master's wife cast her eyes upon Joseph; and she said, *Lie* with me (*Genesis 39:7*).

And she said unto her, Is it a small matter that thou hast taken my husband? and wouldest thou take away my son's mandrakes also? And Rachel said, Therefore he shall *lie* with thee to night for thy son's mandrakes. And Jacob came out of the field in the evening, and Leah went out to meet him, and said, Thou must come in unto me; for surely I have hired thee with my son's mandrakes. And he lay with her that night. And God hearkened unto Leah, and she conceived, and bare Jacob the fifth son (*Genesis 30:15-17*).

67a.   And when the woman saw that the tree was good for food, and that it was pleasant to the eyes, and a tree to be desired to make one wise, she took of the *fruit* thereof, and did eat, and gave also unto her husband with her; and he did eat (*Genesis 3:6*).

Behold, thou art fair, my love; behold, thou art fair; thou hast doves' eyes within thy locks: thy hair is as a flock of goats, that appear from mount Gilead. Thy teeth are like a flock of sheep that are even shorn, which came up from the washing; whereof every one bear twins, and none is barren among them. Thy lips are like a thread of scarlet, and thy speech is comely: thy temples are like a piece of a pomegranate within thy locks. Thy neck is like the tower of David builded for an armoury, whereon there hang a thousand bucklers, all shields of mighty men. Thy two breasts are like two young roes that are twins, which feed among the lilies. Until the day break, and the shadows flee away, I will get me to the mountain of myrrh, and to the hill of frankincense. Thou art all fair, my love; there is no spot in thee. Come with me from Lebanon, my spouse, with me from Lebanon: look from the top of Amana, from the top of Shenir and Hermon, from the lions' dens, from the mountains of the leopards. Thou hast ravished my heart, my sister, my spouse; thou hast ravished my heart with one of thine eyes, with one chain of thy neck. How fair is thy love, my sister, my spouse! how much better is thy love than wine! and the smell of thine ointments than all spices! Thy lips, O my spouse, drop as the honeycomb: honey and milk are under thy tongue; and the smell of thy garments is like the smell of Lebanon. A garden inclosed is my sister, my spouse; a spring shut up, a fountain sealed. Thy plants are an orchard of pomegranates, with pleasant fruits; camphire, with spikenard, Spikenard and saffron; calamus and cinnamon, with all trees of frankincense; myrrh and aloes, with all the chief spices: A fountain of gardens, a well of living waters, and streams from Lebanon. Awake, O north wind; and come, thou south; blow upon my garden, that the spices thereof may flow out. Let my beloved come into his garden, and eat his pleasant *fruit[s]* (*Song of Solomon 4:1-16*).

And God blessed Noah and his sons, and said unto them, *Be fruitful*, and multiply, and replenish the earth (*Genesis 9:1*).

And God said, Sarah thy wife shall bear thee a son indeed; and thou shalt call his name Isaac: and I will establish my covenant with him for an everlasting covenant, and with his seed after him. And as for Ishmael, I have heard thee: Behold, I have blessed him, and will *make* him *fruitful,* and will multiply him exceedingly; twelve princes shall he beget, and I will make him a great nation. But my covenant will I establish with Isaac, which Sarah shall bear unto thee at this set time in the next year (*Genesis 17:19-21*).

67b.   And when the woman saw that the tree was good for food, and that it was pleasant to the eyes, and a tree to be desired to make one wise, she took of the *fruit* thereof, and did eat, and gave also unto her husband with her; and he did eat (*Genesis 3:6*).

Awake, O north wind; and come, thou south; blow upon my garden, that the spices thereof may flow out. Let my beloved come into his garden, and eat his pleasant *fruit[s]* (*Song of Solomon 4:16*).

The way of man is froward and strange: but as for the pure, his work is right. It is better to dwell in a corner of the housetop, than with a brawling woman in a wide house. The soul of the wicked desireth evil: his neighbor findeth no favor in his eyes. When the scorner is punished, the simple is made wise: and when the wise is instructed, he receiveth knowledge. The righteous man wisely considereth the house of the wicked: but God overthroweth the wicked for their wickedness. Whoso stoppeth his ears at the cry of the poor, he also shall cry himself, but shall not be heard. A gift in secret pacifieth anger: and a *reward* in the bosom strong wrath (*Proverbs 21:8-14*).

And Hamor communed with them, saying, The soul of my son Shechem longeth for your daughter: I pray you give her him to wife. And make ye marriages with us, and give your daughters unto us, and take our daughters unto you. And ye shall dwell with us: and the land shall be before you; dwell and trade ye therein, and get you possessions therein. And Shechem said unto her father and unto her brethren, Let me find grace in your eyes, and what ye shall say unto me I will give. Ask me never so much dowry and *gift,* and I will give according as ye shall say unto me: but give me the damsel to wife. And the sons of Jacob answered Shechem and Hamor his father deceitfully, and said, because he had defiled Dinah their sister (*Genesis 34:8-13*).

And it came to pass, that in the morning, behold, it was Leah: and he said to Laban, What is this thou hast done unto me? did not I serve with thee for Rachel? wherefore then hast thou beguiled me? And Laban said, It must not be so done in our country, *to give* the younger before the firstborn. Fulfill her week, and we will give thee this also for the service which thou shalt serve with me yet seven other years. And Jacob did so, and fulfilled her week: and he gave him Rachel his daughter to wife also (*Genesis 29:25-28*).

And it came to pass after this, that Absalom the son of David had a fair sister, whose name was Tamar; and Amnon the son of David loved her. And Amnon was so vexed, that he fell sick for his sister Tamar; for she was a virgin; and Amnon thought it hard for him to *do* anything to her (*2 Samuel 13:1-2*).

67c. And when the woman saw that the tree was good for food, and that it was pleasant to the eyes, and a tree to be desired to make one wise, she took of the *fruit* thereof, and did eat, and gave also unto her husband with her; and he did eat (*Genesis 3:6*).

Awake, O north wind; and come, thou south; blow upon my garden, that the spices thereof may flow out. Let my beloved come into his garden, and eat his pleasant *fruit[s]* (*Song of Solomon 4:16*).

The way of man is froward and strange: but as for the pure, his work is right. It is better to dwell in a corner of the housetop, than with a brawling woman in a wide house. The soul of the wicked desireth evil: his neighbor findeth no favor in his eyes. When the scorner is punished, the simple is made wise: and when the wise is instructed, he receiveth knowledge. The righteous man wisely considereth the house of the wicked: but God overthroweth the wicked for their wickedness. Whoso stoppeth his ears at the cry of the poor, he also shall cry himself, but shall not be heard. A gift in secret pacifieth anger: and a *reward* in the bosom strong wrath (*Proverbs 21:8-14*).

And Hamor communed with them, saying, The soul of my son Shechem longeth for your daughter: I pray you give her him to wife. And make ye marriages with us, and give your daughters unto us, and take our daughters unto you. And ye shall dwell with us: and the land shall be before you; dwell and trade ye therein, and get you possessions therein. And Shechem said unto her father and unto her brethren, Let me find grace in your eyes, and what ye shall say unto me I will give. Ask me never so much dowry and *gift*, and I will give according as ye shall say unto me: but give me the damsel to wife. And the sons of Jacob answered Shechem and Hamor his father deceitfully, and said, because he had defiled Dinah their sister (*Genesis 34:8-13*).

And it came to pass, that in the morning, behold, it was Leah: and he said to Laban, What is this thou hast done unto me? did not I serve with thee for Rachel? wherefore then hast thou beguiled me? And Laban said, It must not be so done in our country, *to give* the younger before the firstborn. Fulfill her week, and we will give thee this also for the service which thou shalt serve with me yet seven other years. And Jacob did so, and fulfilled her week: and he gave him Rachel his daughter to wife also (*Genesis 29:25-28*).

And Dinah the daughter of Leah, which she bare unto Jacob, went out to see the daughters of the land. And when Shechem the son of Hamor the Hivite, prince of the country, saw her, he took her, and *lay* with her, and defiled her (*Genesis 34:1-2*).

67d. And when the woman saw that the tree was good for food, and that it was pleasant to the eyes, and a tree to be desired to make one wise, she took of the *fruit* thereof, and did eat, and gave also unto her husband with her; and he did eat (*Genesis 3:6*).

Awake, O north wind; and come, thou south; blow upon my garden, that the spices thereof may flow out. Let my beloved come into his garden, and eat his pleasant *fruit[s]* (*Song of Solomon 4:16*).

The way of man is froward and strange: but as for the pure, his work is right. It is better to dwell in a corner of the housetop, than with a brawling woman in a wide house. The soul of the wicked desireth evil: his neighbour findeth no favour in his eyes. When the scorner is punished, the simple is made wise: and when the wise is instructed, he receiveth knowledge. The righteous man wisely considereth the house of the wicked: but God overthroweth the wicked for their wickedness. Whoso stoppeth his ears at the cry of the poor, he also shall cry himself, but shall not be heard. A gift in secret pacifieth anger: and a *reward* in the bosom strong wrath (*Proverbs 21:8-14*).

And Hamor communed with them, saying, The soul of my son Shechem longeth for your daughter: I pray you give her him to wife. And make ye marriages with us, and give your daughters unto us, and take our daughters unto you. And ye shall dwell with us: and the land shall be before you; dwell and trade ye therein, and get you possessions therein. And Shechem said unto her father and unto her brethren, Let me find grace in your eyes, and what ye shall say unto me I will give. Ask me never so much dowry and *gift*, and I will give according as ye shall say unto me: but give me the damsel to wife. And the sons of Jacob answered Shechem and Hamor his father deceitfully, and said, because he had defiled Dinah their sister (*Genesis 34:8-13*).

And it came to pass, that in the morning, behold, it was Leah: and he said to Laban, What is this thou hast done unto me? did not I serve with thee for Rachel? wherefore then hast thou beguiled me? And Laban said, It must not be so done in our country, *to give* the younger before the firstborn. Fulfill her week, and we will give thee this also for the service which thou shalt serve with me yet seven other years. And Jacob did so, and fulfilled her week: and he gave him Rachel his daughter to wife also (*Genesis 29:25-28*).

And it came to pass after these things, that his master's wife cast her eyes upon Joseph; and she said, *Lie* with me. But he refused, and said unto his master's wife, Behold, my master wotteth not what is with me in the house, and he hath committed all that he hath to my hand; There is none greater in this house than I; neither hath he kept back any thing from me but thee, because thou art his wife: how then can I do this great wickedness, and sin against God? And it came to pass, as she spake to Joseph day by day, that he hearkened not unto her, to *lie* by her, or to be with her (*Genesis 39:7-10*).

67e. And when the woman saw that the tree was good for food, and that it was pleasant to the eyes, and a tree to be desired to make one wise, she took of the *fruit* thereof, and did eat, and gave also unto her husband with her; and he did eat (*Genesis 3:6*).

Awake, O north wind; and come, thou south; blow upon my garden, that the spices thereof may flow out. Let my beloved come into his garden, and eat his pleasant *fruit[s]* (*Song of Solomon 4:16*).

The way of man is froward and strange: but as for the pure, his work is right. It is better to dwell in a corner of the housetop, than with a brawling woman in a wide house. The soul of the wicked desireth evil: his neighbor findeth no favor in his eyes. When the scorner is punished, the simple is made wise: and when the wise is instructed, he receiveth knowledge. The righteous man wisely considereth the house of the wicked: but God overthroweth the wicked for their wickedness. Whoso stoppeth his ears at the cry of the poor, he also shall cry himself, but shall not be heard. A gift in secret pacifieth anger: and a *reward* in the bosom strong wrath (*Proverbs 21:8-14*).

And Hamor communed with them, saying, The soul of my son Shechem longeth for your daughter: I pray you give her him to wife. And make ye marriages with us, and give your daughters unto us, and take our daughters unto you. And ye shall dwell with us: and the land shall be before you; dwell and trade ye therein, and get you possessions therein. And Shechem said unto her father and unto her brethren, Let me find grace in your eyes, and what ye shall say unto me I will give. Ask me never so much dowry and *gift*, and I will give according as ye shall say unto me: but give me the damsel to wife. And the sons of Jacob answered Shechem and Hamor his father deceitfully, and said, because he had defiled Dinah their sister (*Genesis 34:8-13*).

And it came to pass, that in the morning, behold, it was Leah: and he said to Laban, What is this thou hast done unto me? did not I serve with thee for Rachel? wherefore then hast thou beguiled me? And Laban said, It must not be so done in our country, *to give* the younger before the firstborn. Fulfill her week, and we will give thee this also for the service which thou shalt serve with me yet seven other years. And Jacob did so, and fulfilled her week: and he gave him Rachel his daughter to wife also (*Genesis 29:25-28*).

When Esau saw that Isaac had blessed Jacob, and sent him away to Padan-aram, to *take* him a wife from thence; and that as he blessed him he gave him a charge, saying, Thou shalt not take a wife of the daughters of Canaan (*Genesis 28:6*).

And he went down, and talked with the woman; and she pleased Samson well. And after a time he returned to *take* her, and he turned aside to see the carcass of the lion: and, behold, there was a swarm of bees and honey in the carcass of the lion *(Judges 14:7-8)*.

67f.   And when the woman saw that the tree was good for food, and that it was pleasant to the eyes, and a tree to be desired to make one wise, she took of the *fruit* thereof, and did eat, and gave also unto her husband with her; and he did eat *(Genesis 3:6)*.

Awake, O north wind; and come, thou south; blow upon my garden, that the spices thereof may flow out. Let my beloved come into his garden, and eat his pleasant *fruit[s] (Song of Solomon 4:16)*.

When Esau saw that Isaac had blessed Jacob, and sent him away to Padan-aram, to *take* him a wife from thence; and that as he blessed him he gave him a charge, saying, Thou shalt not take a wife of the daughters of Canaan *(Genesis 28:6)*.

And if the man like not *to take* his brother's wife, then let his brother's wife go up to the gate unto the elders, and say, My husband's brother refuseth to raise up unto his brother a name in Israel, he will not perform the duty of my husband's brother *(Deuteronomy 25:7)*.

And he went down, and talked with the woman; and she pleased Samson well. And after a time he returned *to take* her, and he turned aside to see the carcass of the lion: and, behold, there was a swarm of bees and honey in the carcass of the lion *(Judges 14:7-8)*.

And when David heard that Nabal was dead, he said, Blessed be the LORD, that hath pleaded the cause of my reproach from the hand of Nabal, and hath kept his servant from evil: for the LORD hath returned the wickedness of Nabal upon his own head, And David sent and communed with Abigail, *to take* her to him to wife *(1 Samuel 25:39)*.

68.   And Sarai said unto Abram, Behold now, the LORD hath restrained me from bearing: I pray thee, go in unto my maid; it may be that I may obtain children by her. And Abram hearkened to the voice of Sarai. And Sarai Abram's wife took Hagar her maid the Egyptian, after Abram had dwelt ten years in the land of Canaan, and *gave* her to her husband Abram to be his wife. And he went in unto Hagar, and she conceived: and when she saw that she had conceived, her mistress was despised in her eyes *(Genesis 16:2-4)*.

And it came to pass, that in the morning, behold, it was Leah: and he said to Laban, What is this thou hast done unto me? did not I serve with thee for Rachel? wherefore then hast thou beguiled me? And Laban said, It must not be so done in our country, *to give* the younger before the firstborn. Fulfill her week, and we will give thee this also for the service which thou shalt serve with me yet seven other years. And Jacob did so, and fulfilled her week: and he gave him Rachel his daughter to wife also. And Laban gave to Rachel his daughter Bilhah his handmaid to be her maid. And he went in also unto Rachel, and he loved also Rachel more than Leah, and served with him yet seven other years. And when the LORD saw that Leah was hated, he opened her womb: but Rachel was barren. And Leah conceived, and bare a son, and she called his name Reuben: for she said, Surely the LORD hath looked upon my affliction; now therefore my husband will love me. And she conceived again, and bare a son; and said, Because the LORD hath heard that I was hated, he hath therefore given me this son also: and she called his name Simeon. And she conceived again, and bare a son; and said, Now this time will my husband be joined unto me, because I have born him three sons: therefore was his name called Levi. And she conceived again, and bare a son: and she said, Now will I praise the LORD: therefore she called his name Judah; and left bearing (*Genesis 29:25-35*).

Therefore shall a man leave his father and his mother, and shall *cleave* unto his wife: and they shall be one flesh (*Genesis 2:24*).

And she conceived again, and bare a son; and said, Now this time will my husband *be joined* unto me, because I have born him three sons: therefore was his name called Levi (*Genesis 29:34*).

And Sarai Abram's wife took Hagar her maid the Egyptian, after Abram had dwelt ten years in the land of Canaan, and gave her to her husband Abram *to be* his wife. And he went in unto Hagar, and she conceived: and when she saw that she had conceived, her mistress was despised in her eyes (*Genesis 16:3-4*).

And seest among the captives a beautiful woman, and hast a *desire* unto her, that thou wouldest have her to thy wife (*Deuteronomy 21:11*).

69.   So he *drove out* the man; and he placed at the east of the garden of Eden Cherubims, and a flaming sword which turned every way, to keep the way of the tree of life (*Genesis 3:24*).

And I saw, when for all the causes whereby backsliding Israel committed adultery I had put her away, and given her a bill of *divorce*; yet her treacherous sister Judah feared not, but went and played the harlot also (*Jeremiah 3:8*).

The Lord's Prayer

The following footnotes relate to those found in the text of *The Lord's Prayer*. The author has italicized the key words for purposes of discussion. The key words are also found in *Matthew 6:9-10* and appear in other supporting Scripture as follows:

70.　And he said, The God of *our* fathers hath chosen thee, that thou shouldest know his will, and see that Just One, and shouldest hear the voice of his mouth (*Acts 22:14*).

Therefore it is of faith, that it might be by grace; to the end the promise might be sure to all the seed; not to that only which is of the law, but to that also which is of the faith of Abraham; who is the father *of us* all, (As it is written, I have made thee a father of many nations,) before him whom he believed, even God, who quickeneth the dead, and calleth those things which be not as though they were (*Romans 4:16-17*).

71.　And he arose, and took the young child and his mother, and came into the land of Israel. But when he heard that Archelaus did reign in Judaea in the room of his *father* Herod, he was afraid to go thither: notwithstanding, being warned of God in a dream, he turned aside into the parts of Galilee: And he came and dwelt in a city called Nazareth: that it might be fulfilled which was spoken by the prophets, He shall be called a Nazarene (*Matthew 2:21-23*).

And think not to say within yourselves, We have Abraham to our *father*: for I say unto you, that God is able of these stones to raise up children unto Abraham. And now also the axe is laid unto the root of the trees: therefore every tree which bringeth not forth good fruit is hewn down, and cast into the fire (*Matthew 3:9-10*).

And it came to pass in those days, that there went out a decree from Caesar Augustus, that all the world should be taxed. (And this taxing was first made when Cyrenius was governor of Syria.) And all went to be taxed, every one into his own city. And Joseph also went up from Galilee, out of the city of Nazareth, into Judaea, unto the city of David, which is called Bethlehem; (because he was of the house and *lineage* of David:) To be taxed with Mary his espoused wife, being great with child. And so it was, that, while they were there, the days were accomplished that she should be delivered. And she brought forth her firstborn son, and wrapped him in swaddling clothes, and laid him in a manger; because there was no room for them in the inn (*Luke 2:1-7*).

Now these are the generations of the sons of Noah, Shem, Ham, and Japheth: and unto them were sons *born* after the flood (*Genesis 10:1*).

And Abraham was an hundred years old, when his son Isaac was born unto him. And Sarah said, God hath made me to laugh, so that all that hear will laugh with me. And she said, Who would have said unto Abraham, that Sarah should have given children suck? for I have *born* him a son in his old age (*Genesis 21:5-7*).

And Jacob begat Joseph the husband of Mary, of whom was *born* Jesus, who is called Christ (*Matthew 1:16*).

And when her days to *be delivered* were fulfilled, behold, there were twins in her womb (*Genesis 25:24*).

And his daughter in law, Phinehas' wife, was with child, near to *be delivered*: and when she heard the tidings that the ark of God was taken, and that her father in law and her husband were dead, she bowed herself and travailed; for her pains came upon her (*1 Samuel 4:19*).

A woman when she is in travail hath sorrow, because her hour is come: but as soon as she is delivered of the child, she remembereth no more the anguish, for joy that a man is born into the world (*John 16:21*).

72. But while he thought on these things, behold, the angel of the Lord appeared unto him in a dream, saying, Joseph, thou son of

David, fear not to take unto thee Mary thy wife: for that *which* is conceived in her is of the Holy Ghost (*Matthew 1:20*).

What and if ye shall see the Son of man ascend up *where* he was before? (*John 6:62*).

73.   He shall cry unto me, Thou *art* my father, my God, and the rock of my salvation. Also I will make him my firstborn, higher than the kings of the earth (*Psalm 89:26-27*).

74.   Jesus saith unto him, I am the way, the truth, and the life: no man cometh unto the Father, but by me. If ye had known me, ye should have known my Father also: and from henceforth ye know him, and have seen him. Philip saith unto him, Lord, show us the Father, and it sufficeth us. Jesus saith unto him, Have I been so long time with you, and yet hast thou not known me, Philip? he that hath seen me hath seen the Father; and how sayest thou then, Show us the Father? Believest thou not that I am *in* the Father, and the Father *in* me? the words that I speak unto you I speak not of myself: but the Father that dwelleth *in* me, he doeth the works. Believe me that I am *in* the Father, and the Father *in* me: or else believe me for the very works' sake (*John 14:6-11*).

75a.   And it came to pass, that, as he was praying in a certain place, when he ceased, one of his disciples said unto him, Lord, teach us to pray, as John also taught his disciples. And he said unto them, When ye pray, say, Our Father which art in *heaven*, Hallowed be thy name. Thy kingdom come. Thy will be done, as in heaven, so in earth (*Luke 11:1-2*).

And lo a voice from *heaven*, saying, This is my beloved Son, in whom I am well pleased (*Matthew 3:17*).

Then said the Jews, Forty and six years was this temple in building, and wilt thou *rear* it up in three days? (*John 2:20*).

But the angel said unto him, Fear not, Zacharias: for thy prayer is heard; and thy wife Elisabeth shall *bear* thee a son, and thou shalt call his name John (*Luke 1:13*).

And she shall *bring forth* a son, and thou shalt call his name JESUS: for he shall save his people from their sins (*Matthew 1:21*).

Now these are the generations of the sons of Noah, Shem, Ham, and Japheth: and unto them were sons *born* after the flood (*Genesis 10:1*).

And Abraham was an hundred years old, when his son Isaac was born unto him. And Sarah said, God hath made me to laugh, so that all that hear will laugh with me. And she said, Who would have said unto Abraham, that Sarah should have given children suck? for I have *born* him a son in his old age (*Genesis 21:5-7*).

And Jacob begat Joseph the husband of Mary, of whom was *born* Jesus, who is called Christ (*Matthew 1:16*).

And when her days to *be delivered* were fulfilled, behold, there were twins in her womb (*Genesis 25:24*).

And his daughter in law, Phinehas' wife, was with child, near to *be delivered*: and when she heard the tidings that the ark of God was taken, and that her father in law and her husband were dead, she bowed herself and travailed; for her pains came upon her (*1 Samuel 4:19*).

A woman when she is in travail hath sorrow, because her hour is come: but as soon as she is delivered of the child, she remembereth no more the anguish, for joy that a man is born into the world (*John 16:21*).

75b.   And it came to pass, that, as he was praying in a certain place, when he ceased, one of his disciples said unto him, Lord, teach us to pray, as John also taught his disciples. And he said unto them, When ye pray, say, Our Father which art in *heaven*, Hallowed be thy name. Thy kingdom come. Thy will be done, as in heaven, so in earth (*Luke 11:1-2*).

And lo a voice from *heaven*, saying, This is my beloved Son, in whom I am well pleased (*Matthew 3:17*).

Male and female created he them; and blessed them, and called their *name* Adam, in the day when they were created (*Genesis 5:2*).

Again I say unto you, That if two of you shall agree on earth as touching any thing that they shall ask, it shall be done for them of my Father which is in heaven. For where two or three are gathered together in my *name*, there am I in the midst of them (*Matthew 18:19-20*).

And when thy days be fulfilled, and thou shalt sleep with thy fathers, I will *set up* thy seed after thee, which shall proceed out of thy bowels, and I will establish his kingdom (*2 Samuel 7:12*).

Nevertheless for David's sake did the Lord his God give him a lamp in Jerusalem, to *set up* his son after him, and to establish Jerusalem (*1 Kings 15:4*).

And the Lord said unto Abram, after that Lot was separated from him, Lift up now thine eyes, and look from the place where thou art northward, and southward, and eastward, and westward: For all the land which thou seest, to thee will I give it, and to thy seed for ever. And I will *make* thy seed as the dust of the earth: so that if a man can number the dust of the earth, then shall thy seed also be numbered (*Genesis 13:14-16*).

And the angel of the Lord said unto her, Behold, thou art with child, and shalt *bear* a son, and shalt call his name Ishmael; because the Lord hath heard thy affliction (*Genesis 16:11*).

But the angel said unto him, Fear not, Zacharias: for thy prayer is heard; and thy wife Elisabeth shall *bear* thee a son, and thou shalt call his name John (*Luke 1:13*).

Unto the woman he said, I will greatly multiply thy sorrow and thy conception; in sorrow thou shalt *bring forth* children; and thy desire shall be to thy husband, and he shall rule over thee (*Genesis 3:16*).

And she shall *bring forth* a son, and thou shalt call his name JESUS: for he shall save his people from their sins. Now all this was done, that it might be fulfilled which was spoken of the Lord by the prophet, saying, Behold, a virgin shall be with child, and shall *bring forth* a son, and they shall call his name Emmanuel, which being interpreted is, God with us. Then Joseph being raised from sleep did as the angel of the Lord had bidden him, and took unto him his wife: And knew her not till she had brought forth her firstborn son: and he called his name JESUS (*Matthew 1:21-25*).

Now these are the generations of the sons of Noah, Shem, Ham, and Japheth: and unto them were sons *born* after the flood (*Genesis 10:1*).

And Abraham was an hundred years old, when his son Isaac was born unto him. And Sarah said, God hath made me to laugh, so that all that hear will laugh with me. And she said, Who would have said unto Abraham, that Sarah should have given children suck? for I have *born* him a son in his old age (*Genesis 21:5-7*).

And Jacob begat Joseph the husband of Mary, of whom was *born* Jesus, who is called Christ (*Matthew 1:16*).

And when her days to *be delivered* were fulfilled, behold, there were twins in her womb (*Genesis 25:24*).

And his daughter in law, Phinehas' wife, was with child, near to *be delivered*: and when she heard the tidings that the ark of God was taken, and that her father in law and her husband were dead, she bowed herself and travailed; for her pains came upon her (*1 Samuel 4:19*).

A woman when she is in travail hath sorrow, because her hour is come: but as soon as she is delivered of the child, she remembereth no more the anguish, for joy that a man is born into the world (*John 16:21*).

75c. And it came to pass, that, as he was praying in a certain place, when he ceased, one of his disciples said unto him, Lord, teach us to pray, as John also taught his disciples. And he said unto them, When ye pray, say, Our Father which art in *heaven*, Hallowed be thy name. Thy kingdom come. Thy will be done, as in heaven, so in earth (*Luke 11:1-2*).

And lo a voice from *heaven*, saying, This is my beloved Son, in whom I am well pleased (*Matthew 3:17*).

Male and female created he them; and blessed them, and called their *name* Adam, in the day when they were created (*Genesis 5:2*).

Again I say unto you, That if two of you shall agree on earth as touching any thing that they shall ask, it shall be done for them of my Father which is in heaven. For where two or three are gathered together in my *name*, there am I in the midst of them (*Matthew 18:19-20*).

And Noah begat three sons, *Shem*, Ham, and Japheth (*Genesis 6:10*).

And Adam knew his wife again; and she bare *a son*, and called his name Seth: For God, said she, hath appointed me another seed instead of Abel, whom Cain slew (*Genesis 4:25*).

And the LORD said unto Abram, after that Lot was separated from him, Lift up now thine eyes, and look from the place where thou art northward, and southward, and eastward, and westward: For all the land which thou seest, to thee will I give it, and to thy seed for ever. And I will *make* thy seed as the dust of the earth: so that if a man can number the dust of the earth, then shall thy seed also be numbered (*Genesis 13:14-16*).

And the angel of the LORD said unto her, Behold, thou art with child, and shalt *bear* a son, and shalt call his name Ishmael; because the LORD hath heard thy affliction (*Genesis 16:11*).

But the angel said unto him, Fear not, Zacharias: for thy prayer is heard; and thy wife Elisabeth shall *bear* thee a son, and thou shalt call his name John (*Luke 1:13*).

Unto the woman he said, I will greatly multiply thy sorrow and thy conception; in sorrow thou shalt *bring forth* children; and thy desire shall be to thy husband, and he shall rule over thee (*Genesis 3:16*).

And she shall *bring forth* a son, and thou shalt call his name JESUS: for he shall save his people from their sins. Now all this was done,

that it might be fulfilled which was spoken of the Lord by the prophet, saying, Behold, a virgin shall be with child, and shall *bring forth* a son, and they shall call his name Emmanuel, which being interpreted is, God with us. Then Joseph being raised from sleep did as the angel of the Lord had bidden him, and took unto him his wife: And knew her not till she had brought forth her firstborn son: and he called his name JESUS (*Matthew 1:21-25*).

Now these are the generations of the sons of Noah, Shem, Ham, and Japheth: and unto them were sons *born* after the flood (*Genesis 10:1*).

And Abraham was an hundred years old, when his son Isaac was born unto him. And Sarah said, God hath made me to laugh, so that all that hear will laugh with me. And she said, Who would have said unto Abraham, that Sarah should have given children suck? for I have *born* him a son in his old age (*Genesis 21:5-7*).

And Jacob begat Joseph the husband of Mary, of whom was *born* Jesus, who is called Christ (*Matthew 1:16*).

And when her days to *be delivered* were fulfilled, behold, there were twins in her womb (*Genesis 25:24*).

And his daughter in law, Phinehas' wife, was with child, near to *be delivered*: and when she heard the tidings that the ark of God was taken, and that her father in law and her husband were dead, she bowed herself and travailed; for her pains came upon her (*1 Samuel 4:19*).

A woman when she is in travail hath sorrow, because her hour is come: but as soon as she is delivered of the child, she remembereth no more the anguish, for joy that a man is born into the world (*John 16:21*).

76.   And he said unto them, When ye pray, say, Our Father which art in heaven, *Hallowed* be thy name. Thy kingdom come. Thy will be done, as in heaven, so in earth (*Luke 11:2*).

Draw nigh to God, and he will draw nigh to you. Cleanse your hands, ye sinners; and *purify* your hearts, ye double minded (*James 4:8*).

The gold for things of gold, and the silver for things of silver, and for all manner of work to be made by the hands of artificers. And who then is willing to *consecrate* his service this day unto the LORD (*1 Chronicles 29:5*)?

And the LORD spake unto Moses, saying, Speak unto Aaron and to his sons, that they separate themselves from the holy things of the children of Israel, and that they profane not my holy name in those things which they hallow unto me: I am the LORD. Say unto them, Whosoever he be of all your seed among your generations, that goeth unto the holy things, which the children of Israel *hallow* unto the LORD, having his uncleanness upon him, that soul shall be cut off from my presence: I am the LORD (*Leviticus 22:1-3*).

77. Now all this was done, that it might *be* fulfilled which was spoken of the Lord by the prophet, saying, Behold, a virgin shall *be* with child, and shall bring forth a son, and they shall call his name Emmanuel, which being interpreted is, God with us (*Matthew 1:22-23*).

78. Now the LORD had said unto Abram, Get thee out of thy country, and from thy kindred, and from *thy* father's house, unto a land that I will show thee: And I will make of thee a great nation, and I will bless thee, and make thy name great; and thou shalt be a blessing (*Genesis 12:1-2*).

And, behold, the word of the LORD came unto him, saying, This shall not be thine heir; but he that shall come forth out of *thine own* bowels shall be thine heir (*Genesis 15:4*).

79. And she shall bring forth a son, and thou shalt call his *name* JESUS: for he shall save his people from their sins. Now all this was done, that it might be fulfilled which was spoken of the Lord by the prophet, saying, Behold, a virgin shall be with child, and shall bring forth a son, and they shall call his *name* Emmanuel, which being interpreted is, God with us. Then Joseph being raised from sleep did as the angel of the Lord had bidden him, and took

unto him his wife: And knew her not till she had brought forth her firstborn son: and he called his *name* JESUS (*Matthew 1:21-25*).

Again I say unto you, That if two of you shall agree on earth as touching any thing that they shall ask, it shall be done for them of my Father which is in heaven. For where two or three are gathered together in my *name*, there am I in the midst of them (*Matthew 18:19-20*).

Beware of false prophets, which come to you in sheep's clothing, but inwardly they are ravening wolves. Ye shall *know* them by their fruits. Do men gather grapes of thorns, or figs of thistles? Even so every good tree bringeth forth good fruit; but a corrupt tree bringeth forth evil fruit. A good tree cannot bring forth evil fruit, neither can a corrupt tree bring forth good fruit. Every tree that bringeth not forth good fruit is hewn down, and cast into the fire. Wherefore by their fruits ye shall *know* them (*Matthew 7:15-20*).

And she shall bring forth a son, and thou shalt call his name JESUS: for he shall save his people from their sins. Now all this was done, that it might be fulfilled which was spoken of the Lord by the prophet, saying, *Behold*, a virgin shall be with child, and shall bring forth a son, and they shall call his name Emmanuel, which being interpreted is, God with us. Then Joseph being raised from sleep did as the angel of the Lord had bidden him, and took unto him his wife: And knew her not till she had brought forth her firstborn son: and he called his name JESUS (*Matthew 1:21-25*).

80. And it shall come to pass, when thy days be expired that thou must go to be with thy fathers, that I will raise up thy seed after thee, which shall be of thy sons; and I will establish his *kingdom* (*1 Chronicles 17:11*).

In his days did Hiel the Bethelite build Jericho: he laid the *foundation* thereof in Abiram his firstborn, and set up the gates thereof in his youngest son Segub, according to the word of the LORD, which he spake by Joshua the son of Nun (*1 Kings 16:34*).

And the angel said unto her, Fear not, Mary: for thou hast found favor with God. And, behold, thou shalt *conceive* in thy womb, and bring forth a son, and shalt call his name JESUS (*Luke 1:30-31*).

81.   Neither shall thy name any more be called Abram, but thy name shall be Abraham; for a father of many nations have I made thee. And I will make thee exceeding fruitful, and I will make nations of thee, and kings shall *come* out of thee. And I will establish my covenant between me and thee and thy seed after thee in their generations for an everlasting covenant, to be a God unto thee, and to thy seed after thee. And I will give unto thee, and to thy seed after thee, the land wherein thou art a stranger, all the land of Canaan, for an everlasting possession; and I will be their God (*Genesis 17:5-8*).

And Abram said, Behold, to me thou hast given no seed: and, lo, one born in my house is mine heir. And, behold, the word of the LORD came unto him, saying, This shall not be thine heir; but he that shall *come forth* out of thine own bowels shall be thine heir. And he brought him forth abroad, and said, Look now toward heaven, and tell the stars, if thou be able to number them: and he said unto him, So shall thy seed be (*Genesis 15:3-5*).

And now thy two sons, Ephraim and Manasseh, which were born unto thee in the land of Egypt before I came unto thee into Egypt, are mine; as Reuben and Simeon, they shall be mine. And thy *issue*, which thou begettest after them, shall be thine, and shall be called after the name of their brethren in their inheritance (*Genesis 48:5-6*).

Now the LORD had said unto Abram, Get thee out of thy country, and from thy *kindred*, and from thy father's house, unto a land that I will show thee: And I will make of thee a great nation, and I will bless thee, and make thy name great; and thou shalt be a blessing (*Genesis 12:1-2*).

Verily I say unto you, Among them that are *born* of women there hath not risen a greater than John the Baptist: notwithstanding he that is least in the kingdom of heaven is greater than he (*Matthew 11:11*).

But the angel said unto him, Fear not, Zacharias: for thy prayer is heard; and thy wife Elisabeth shall *bear* thee a son, and thou shalt call his name John (*Luke 1:13*).

And as for Ishmael, I have heard thee: Behold, I have blessed him, and will make him fruitful, and will multiply him exceedingly; twelve princes shall he *beget*, and I will make him a great nation (*Genesis 17:20*).

Then Abraham fell upon his face, and laughed, and said in his heart, Shall a child *be born* unto him that is an hundred years old? and shall Sarah, that is ninety years old, bear (*Genesis 17:17*)?

And she shall *bring forth* a son, and thou shalt call his name JESUS: for he shall save his people from their sins (*Matthew 1:21*).

And the angel said unto her, Fear not, Mary: for thou hast found favor with God. And, behold, thou shalt *conceive* in thy womb, and bring forth a son, and shalt call his name JESUS (*Luke 1:30-31*).

82a.   Unto the woman he said, I *will* greatly multiply thy sorrow and thy conception; in sorrow thou shalt bring forth children; and thy desire shall be to thy husband, and he shall rule over thee (*Genesis 3:16*).

Then said the lord of the vineyard, What shall I do? I *will* send my beloved son: it may be they will reverence him when they see him (*Luke 20:13*).

And, behold, the word of the LORD came unto him, saying, This *shall* not be thine heir; but he that *shall* come forth out of thine own bowels *shall* be thine heir. And he brought him forth abroad, and said, Look now toward heaven, and tell the stars, if thou be able to number them: and he said unto him, So *shall* thy seed be (*Genesis 15:4-5*).

For, lo, thou shalt conceive, and bear a son; and no razor shall come on his head: for the child shall be a Nazarite unto God from the womb: and he *shall* begin to deliver Israel out of the hand of the Philistines (*Judges 13:5*).

But the angel said unto him, Fear not, Zacharias: for thy prayer is heard; and thy wife Elisabeth shall *bear* thee a son, and thou shalt call his name John (*Luke 1:13*).

Then Abraham fell upon his face, and laughed, and said in his heart, Shall a child *be born* unto him that is an hundred years old? and shall Sarah, that is ninety years old, bear (*Genesis 17:17*)?

And she shall *bring forth* a son, and thou shalt call his name JESUS: for he shall save his people from their sins (*Matthew 1:21*).

And when her days to *be delivered* were fulfilled, behold, there were twins in her womb (*Genesis 25:24*).

And his daughter in law, Phinehas' wife, was with child, near to *be delivered*: and when she heard the tidings that the ark of God was taken, and that her father in law and her husband were dead, she bowed herself and travailed; for her pains came upon her (*1 Samuel 4:19*).

82b. Unto the woman he said, I *will* greatly multiply thy sorrow and thy conception; in sorrow thou shalt bring forth children; and thy desire shall be to thy husband, and he shall rule over thee (*Genesis 3:16*).

Then said the lord of the vineyard, What shall I do? I *will* send my beloved son: it may be they will reverence him when they see him (*Luke 20:13*).

For, lo, thou shalt conceive, and bear a son; and no razor shall come on his head: for the child shall be a Nazarite unto God from the womb: and he *shall begin* to deliver Israel out of the hand of the Philistines (*Judges 13:5*).

For I have heard a voice as of a *woman in travail*, and the anguish as of her that bringeth forth her first child, the voice of the daughter of Zion, that bewaileth herself, that spreadeth her hands, saying, Woe is me now! for my soul is wearied because of murderers (*Jeremiah 4:31*).

Then Abraham fell upon his face, and laughed, and said in his heart, Shall a child be *born* unto him that is an hundred years old? and shall Sarah, that is ninety years old, bear (*Genesis 17:17*)?

And when her days to *be delivered* were fulfilled, behold, there were twins in her womb (*Genesis 25:24*).

And his daughter in law, Phinehas' wife, was with child, near to *be delivered*: and when she heard the tidings that the ark of God was taken, and that her father in law and her husband were dead, she bowed herself and travailed; for her pains came upon her (*1 Samuel 4:19*).

A woman when she is in travail hath sorrow, because her hour is come: but as soon as she is delivered of the child, she remembereth no more the anguish, for joy that a man is born into the world (*John 16:21*).

77.   Now all this was done, that it might *be* fulfilled which was spoken of the Lord by the prophet, saying, Behold, a virgin shall *be* with child, and shall bring forth a son, and they shall call his name Emmanuel, which being interpreted is, God with us (*Matthew 1:22-23*).

83.   If ye abide in me, and my words abide in you, ye shall ask what ye will, and it shall be *done* unto you. Herein is my Father glorified, that ye bear much fruit; so shall ye be my disciples (*John 15:7-8*).

He was in the world, and the world was made by him, and the world knew him not. He came unto his own, and his own received him not. But as many as received him, to them gave he power *to become* the sons of God, even to them that believe on his name: Which were born, not of blood, nor of the will of the flesh, nor of the will of man, but of God. And the Word was made flesh, and dwelt among us, (and we beheld his glory, the glory as of the only begotten of the Father,) full of grace and truth (*John 1:10-14*).

And she shall bring forth a son, and thou shalt call his name JESUS: for he shall save his people from their sins. Now all this was done, that it might *be* fulfilled which was spoken of the Lord by the prophet, saying, Behold, a virgin shall *be* with child, and shall bring forth a son, and they shall call his name Emmanuel, which be being interpreted is, God with us (*Matthew 1:21-23*).

And the angel said unto her, Fear not, Mary: for thou hast found favor with God. And, behold, thou shalt *conceive* in thy womb, and bring forth a son, and shalt call his name JESUS (*Luke 1:30-31*).

74.   And the LORD said unto her, Two nations are *in* thy womb, and two manner of people shall be separated from thy bowels; and the one people shall be stronger than the other people; and the elder shall serve the younger. And when her days to be delivered were fulfilled, behold, there were twins *in* her womb (*Genesis 25:23-24*).

Now the birth of Jesus Christ was on this wise: When as his mother Mary was espoused to Joseph, before they came together, she was found with child of the Holy Ghost. Then Joseph her husband, being a just man, and not willing to make her a public example, was minded to put her away privily. But while he thought on these things, behold, the angel of the Lord appeared unto him in a dream, saying, Joseph, thou son of David, fear not to take unto thee Mary thy wife: for that which is conceived *in* her is of the Holy Ghost. And she shall bring forth a son, and thou shalt call his name JESUS: for he shall save his people from their sins (*Matthew 1:18-21*).

84a.   There were giants *in the earth* in those days; and also after that, when the sons of God came in unto the daughters of men, and they bare children to them, the same became mighty men which were of old, men of renown (*Genesis 6:4*).

And Cush begat Nimrod: he began to be a mighty one *in the earth* (*Genesis 10:8*).

And God sent me before you to preserve you posterity *in the earth*, and to save your lives by a great deliverance (*Genesis 45:7*).

Now therefore thus shalt thou say unto my servant David, Thus saith the LORD of hosts, I took thee from the sheepcote, even from following the sheep, that thou shouldest be ruler over my people Israel: And I have been with thee whithersoever thou hast walked, and have cut off all thine enemies from before thee, and have made thee a name like the name of the great men that are *in the earth*... And it shall come to pass, when thy days be expired that thou must go to be with thy fathers, that I will raise up thy seed after thee, which shall be of thy sons; and I will establish his kingdom... But I will settle him in mine house and in my kingdom for ever: and his throne shall be established for evermore (*1 Chronicles 17:7-8, 11, 14*).

Behold, this is the joy of his way, and *out of the earth shall others grow*. Behold, God will not cast away a perfect man, neither will he help the evil doers (*Job 8:19-20*).

And when a stranger shall sojourn with thee, and will keep the passover to the LORD, let all his males be circumcised, and then let him come near and keep it; and he shall be as one that is born in the land: for no uncircumcised person shall eat thereof. One law shall be to him that is *homeborn*, and unto the stranger that sojourneth among you. Thus did all the children of Israel; as the LORD commanded Moses and Aaron, so did they. And it came to pass the selfsame day, that the LORD did bring the children of Israel out of the land of Egypt by their armies (*Exodus 12:48-51*).

And the angel of the LORD said unto her, Behold, thou art with child, and shalt *bear* a son, and shalt call his name Ishmael; because the LORD hath heard thy affliction (*Genesis 16:11*).

But the angel said unto him, Fear not, Zacharias: for thy prayer is heard; and thy wife Elisabeth shall *bear* thee a son, and thou shalt call his name John (*Luke 1:13*).

Unto the woman he said, I will greatly multiply thy sorrow and thy con- ception; in sorrow thou shalt *bring forth* children; and thy desire shall be to thy husband, and he shall rule over thee (*Genesis 3:16*).

And she shall *bring forth* a son, and thou shalt call his name JESUS: for he shall save his people from their sins. Now all this was done, that it might be fulfilled which was spoken of the Lord by the prophet, saying, Behold, a virgin shall be with child, and shall *bring forth* a son, and they shall call his name Emmanuel, which being interpreted is, God with us. Then Joseph being raised from sleep did as the angel of the Lord had bidden him, and took unto him his wife: And knew her not till she had brought forth her firstborn son: and he called his name JESUS (*Matthew 1:21-25*).

Now these are the generations of the sons of Noah, Shem, Ham, and Japheth: and unto them were sons *born* after the flood (*Genesis 10:1*).

And Abraham was an hundred years old, when his son Isaac was born unto him. And Sarah said, God hath made me to laugh, so that all that hear will laugh with me. And she said, Who would have said unto Abraham, that Sarah should have given children suck? for I have *born* him a son in his old age (*Genesis 21:5-7*).

And Jacob begat Joseph the husband of Mary, of whom was *born* Jesus, who is called Christ (*Matthew 1:16*).

And when her days to *be delivered* were fulfilled, behold, there were twins in her womb (*Genesis 25:24*).

And his daughter in law, Phinehas' wife, was with child, near to *be delivered*: and when she heard the tidings that the ark of God was taken, and that her father in law and her husband were dead, she bowed herself and travailed; for her pains came upon her (*1 Samuel 4:19*).

A woman when she is in travail hath sorrow, because her hour is come: but as soon as she is delivered of the child, she remembereth no more the anguish, for joy that a man is born into the world (*John 16:21*).

84b. There were giants *in the earth* in those days; and also after that, when the sons of God came in unto the daughters of men, and they bare children to them, the same became mighty men which were of old, men of renown (*Genesis 6:4*).

And Cush begat Nimrod: he began to be a mighty one *in the earth* (*Genesis 10:8*).

And God sent me before you to preserve you a posterity *in the earth*, and to save your lives by a great deliverance (*Genesis 45:7*).

Now therefore thus shalt thou say unto my servant David, Thus saith the LORD of hosts, I took thee from the sheepcote, even from following the sheep, that thou shouldest be ruler over my people Israel: And I have been with thee whithersoever thou hast walked, and have cut off all thine enemies from before thee, and have made thee a name like the name of the great men that are *in the earth...* And it shall come to pass, when thy days be expired that thou must go to be with thy fathers, that I will raise up thy seed after thee, which shall be of thy sons; and I will establish his kingdom ... But I will settle him in mine house and in my kingdom for ever: and his throne shall be established for evermore (*1 Chronicles 17:7-8, 11, 14*).

Behold, this is the joy of his way, and *out of the earth shall others grow.* Behold, God will not cast away a perfect man, neither will he help the evil doers (*Job 8:19-20*).

Say ye unto your brethren, Ammi; and to your sisters, Ruhamah. Plead with your mother, plead: for she is not my wife, neither am I her husband: let her therefore put away her whoredoms out of her sight, and her adulteries from between her breasts; Lest I strip her naked, and set her as in the day that she was born, and make her as a wilderness, and set her like a dry *land*, and slay her with thirst. And I will not have mercy upon her children; for they be the children of whoredoms. For their mother hath played the harlot: she that conceived them hath done shamefully: for she said, I will go after my lovers, that give me my bread and my water, my wool and my flax, mine oil and my drink (*Hosea 2:1-5*).

And I will make thee exceeding fruitful, and I will make *nations* of thee, and kings shall come out of thee (*Genesis 17:6*).

And in thy seed shall all the *nations* of the earth be blessed; because thou hast obeyed my voice (*Genesis 22:18*).

And Isaac entreated the LORD for his wife, because she was barren: and the LORD was entreated of him, and Rebekah his wife conceived. And the children struggled together within her; and she said, If it be so, why am I thus? And she went to inquire of the LORD. And the LORD said unto her, Two *nations* are in thy womb, and two manner of people shall be separated from thy bowels; and the one people shall be stronger than the other people; and the elder shall serve the younger. And when her days to be delivered were fulfilled, behold, there were twins in her womb (*Genesis 25:21-24*).

And I will bless her, and give thee a son also of her: yea, I will bless her, and she shall be *a mother* of nations; kings of people shall be of her (*Genesis 17:16*).

As for me, behold, my covenant is with thee, and thou shalt be a *father* of many nations (*Genesis 17:4*).

And think not to say within yourselves, We have Abraham to our *father*: for I say unto you, that God is able of these stones to raise up children unto Abraham (*Matthew 3:9*).

Have we not all one *father*? hath not one God created us? why do we deal treacherously every man against his brother, by profaning the covenant of our fathers (*Malachi 2:10*)?

And Adam knew his wife again; and she bare *a son*, and called his name Seth: For God, said she, hath appointed me another seed instead of Abel, whom Cain slew (*Genesis 4:25*).

And the LORD said unto Abram, after that Lot was separated from him, Lift up now thine eyes, and look from the place where thou art northward, and southward, and eastward, and westward: For all the land which thou seest, to thee will I give it, and to thy seed for ever. And I will *make* thy seed as the dust of the earth: so that if a man can number the dust of the earth, then shall thy seed also be numbered (*Genesis 13:14-16*).

And the angel of the LORD said unto her, Behold, thou art with child, and shalt *bear* a son, and shalt call his name Ishmael; because the LORD hath heard thy affliction (*Genesis 16:11*).

But the angel said unto him, Fear not, Zacharias: for thy prayer is heard; and thy wife Elisabeth shall *bear* thee a son, and thou shalt call his name John (*Luke 1:13*).

Unto the woman he said, I will greatly multiply thy sorrow and thy conception; in sorrow thou shalt *bring forth* children; and thy desire shall be to thy husband, and he shall rule over thee (*Genesis 3:16*).

And she shall *bring forth* a son, and thou shalt call his name JESUS: for he shall save his people from their sins. Now all this was done,

that it might be fulfilled which was spoken of the Lord by the prophet, saying, Behold, a virgin shall be with child, and shall *bring forth* a son, and they shall call his name Emmanuel, which being interpreted is, God with us. Then Joseph being raised from sleep did as the angel of the Lord had bidden him, and took unto him his wife: And knew her not till she had brought forth her firstborn son: and he called his name JESUS (*Matthew 1:21-25*).

Now these are the generations of the sons of Noah, Shem, Ham, and Japheth: and unto them were sons *born* after the flood (*Genesis 10:1*).

And Abraham was an hundred years old, when his son Isaac was born unto him. And Sarah said, God hath made me to laugh, so that all that hear will laugh with me. And she said, Who would have said unto Abraham, that Sarah should have given children suck? for I have *born* him a son in his old age (*Genesis 21:5-7*).

And Jacob begat Joseph the husband of Mary, of whom was *born* Jesus, who is called Christ (*Matthew 1:16*).

And when her days to *be delivered* were fulfilled, behold, there were twins in her womb (*Genesis 25:24*).

And his daughter in law, Phinehas' wife, was with child, near to *be delivered*: and when she heard the tidings that the ark of God was taken, and that her father in law and her husband were dead, she bowed herself and travailed; for her pains came upon her (*1 Samuel 4:19*).

A woman when she is in travail hath sorrow, because her hour is come: but as soon as she is delivered of the child, she remembereth no more the anguish, for joy that a man is born into the world (*John 16:21*).

85. And he entered into a ship, and passed over, and came into his own city. And, behold, they brought to him a man sick of the palsy, lying *on* a bed: and Jesus seeing their faith said unto the sick of the palsy; Son, be of good cheer; thy sins be forgiven thee. And, behold, certain of the scribes said within themselves, This man blasphemeth. And Jesus knowing their thoughts said, Wherefore think ye evil in your hearts? For whether is easier, to say, Thy sins be forgiven thee; or to say, Arise, and walk? But that ye may know that the Son of man hath power *on* earth to forgive sins, (then saith he to the sick of the palsy,) Arise, take up thy bed, and go unto thine house (*Matthew 9:1-6*).

Addendum

Defined Word Approach Applied to "Networking"

Every word contains a story .... Willie J. Alexander

First Step—Define "Networking"
A supportive system of sharing information and services among individuals and groups having a common interest. *Random House Webster's Unabridged Dictionary*

Second Step—Define the words that define networking. *Random House Webster's Unabridged Dictionary*

I.   *A*—one; one sort of

II.   *supportive*—providing support

III.   *system*—an assemblage or combination of things or parts forming a complex or unitary whole.

IV.   *of*—from; specifically, derived or coming from.

V.   *sharing*—a portion allotted or assigned a member of a group.

VI.   *information*—knowledge communicated or received concerning a particular fact or circumstance.

VII.   *and*—in addition; also; as well as: used to join elements of similar syntactic structure.

VIII.   *services*—an act of assistance; help; aid.

IX.   *among*—in or into the midst of.

X.   *individuals*—people

XI.   *groups*—any collection or assemblage of persons.

XII.   *having*—possessing or owning; holding for some use.

XIII.   *common*—belonging equally to or shared alike by two or more of all in question.

XIV.   *interest*—one's feelings or attitudes of concern, involvement, or curiosity as aroused by something or someone.

Glossary

1. affliction – mental or physical pain
2. beast – a cruel and sometimes violent person
3. beginning – the birth of a male and married male and female's first baby
4. became – to exist
5. beguile – to lead astray
6. bone – the male's reproductive organ
7. bone of my bone – a male and female engaged in coitus
8. called – a person's name
9. cleaved – a male and female joined in matrimony
10. closed – a male's penetration during coitus
11. created – marriage of an adult female and male
12. covenant - a male and female consummate marriage
13. darkness – a miscarriage; the newborn baby's eyes are closed
14. day – a baby is born; birthday
15. deep – the female's womb
16. divided – separation between the birth of children
17. drove out – a man divorces his wife
18. earth – an adult female
19. east – the front of an adult male or female
20. eat – male and female engage in coitus with someone other than their spouse; adultery
21. Eden – a place of pleasure
22. evening – the start of male and female foreplay
23. face – a newborn baby; an individual's physical presence
24. father – God in heaven and earthly male parent
25. first – baby number one
26. first day – birth of first child

27. flesh – the puenda of a man
28. flesh of my flesh – a male and female engaged in coitus
29. form – a fetus in the womb;
30. four – literally, the number four
31. fruit – male or female genitalia
32. garden – a bride
33. gave – to give permission to marry or engage in coitus
34. God – The Holy Spirit
35. ground - the female's genitalia
36. hallowed – to revere or worship
37. heads – patriarch's of different families
38. heaven – an adult male
39. in the beginning – the birth of a married male and female's first baby
40. kingdom – children
41. let there be light – a newborn baby opens its eyes
42. light – a newborn baby open its eyes
43. made – a female engages in coitus
44. man – a newborn baby; an adult male
45. mist – after effect of aminiotic fluid spilling on hot desert sand
46. morning – a male impregnates a female
47. moved – a baby shows signs of life after taking first breath; body movement
48. name – literally a person's name; an individuals identification
49. night – death of a newborn shortly after delivery
50. out – to leave a place
51. parted – give birth to more than one baby
52. rib – the male pudenda
53. river – an adult male who leaves a geographical area
54. said – commanded
55. saw – looked upon
56. serpent – a crafty and deceitful adult male
57. sleep – male and female engaged in coitus
58. spirit – a baby takes first breath of air
59. subtil – cunning

60. there was light – a newborn eyes have opened
61. took – a female becomes a wife
62. touch – to initiate the sexual act
63. tree of knowledge of good and evil – a native born adult female who has lost virginity
64. tree of life – a native born adult female who maintains virginity; Jesus Christ
65. upon – covers entire body
66. void – an adult female's womb is empty or has given birth to a stillborn baby
67. was – to breathe; to exist
68. water – to impregnate a female; semen
69. waters – new life; the amniotic fluids that surrounds the fetus in the womb and precedes the baby's birth
70. went – to leave a place
71. were – continue breathing
72. west – the rear of an adult male or female
73. without – an adult female showing no physical signs of pregnancy
74. without – outside appearance
75. without form – an adult female showing no physical signs of pregnancy after delivering baby
76. woman – a female who has engaged in coitus; an adult female

References

Preface

Willie J. Alexander, *Entering The Promised Land,* (Houston, TX: Entering The Promised Land Houston, TX, 2007).

Robert Draper, "The Black Pharaohs: Conquerors of Ancient Egypt," *National Geographic,* February, 2008.

Spencer Wells, *The Journey of Man: A Genetic Odyssey,* (Princeton, NJ: Princeton University Press, 2002).

Donald Johnson, Maitland Edey, *Lucy: The Beginnings of Humankind,* (New York: Simon & Schuster, 1981).

Chapter 1

Susan Hertog, *Dangerous Ambition: Rebecca West and Dorothy Thompson: New Women In Search of Love and Power,* (New York: Ballantine Books, 2011).

Fr. Jonathan Morris, "Fox & Friends," *Fox News Network, L.L.C.,* October 30, 2011.

"'Nones' on the Rise: One in Five Adults Have No Religious Affiliation," *The Pew Forum on Religion and Public Life,* October 9, 2012.

Gary Whitta, Screenplay, "The Book of Eli," *Columbia Pictures and Warner Brothers,* 2010.

Chapter 3

Willie J. Alexander, *Entering The Promised Land,* (Houston, TX: Entering The Promised Land Houston, TX, 2007).

Random House Webster's Unabridged Dictionary, 2nd ed.

Webster's New World College Dictionary, 4th ed.

Chapter 4

Spiros Zodhiates, *King James Version Hebrew-Greek Key Word Study Bible,* (Chattanooga, TN: AMG Publishing, 2008).

James Strong, S.T.D., L.L.D., *A Concise Dictionary of The Words in The Hebrew Bible with Their Renderings in the Authorized Version,* (Madison, NJ: 1890).

Chapter 5

Thomas Nelson, *The Holy Bible: New King James Version,* (Nashville, TN: Thomas Nelson Publishers, 1997).

Holy Bible, The Life Application Study Bible, (Carol Stream, IL: Tyndale House Publishers, Inc., 1996).

Holy Bible, New International Version Study Bible, (Grand Rapids, MI: Zondervan, 2002).

Holy Bible, English Standard Version Study Bible, (Wheaton, IL: Crossway Bibles, 2008).

Spiros Zodhiates, *King James Version Hebrew-Greek Key Word Study Bible,* (Chattanooga, TN: AMG Publishing, 2008).

Chapter 6

Matti Friedman, "Scholars Trace Hebrew Bible's Evolution," *Houston Chronicle,* August 13, 2011.

Chapter 7

Joseph Blenkinsopp, *The Pentateuch: An Introduction to the First Five Books of the Bible,* (New Haven, CT: Yale University Press, 2000).

R.K. Harrison, *Old Testament Times: A Social, Political, and Cultural Context,* (Grand Rapids, MI, Baker Books, 2005).

Chapter 8

Spiros Zodhiates, *King James Version Hebrew-Greek Key Word Study Bible,* (Chattanooga, TN: AMG Publishing, 2008).

Biblesoft Complete Reference Library (CD Rom, version 5.0)

Holy Bible, New International Version Study Bible, (Grand Rapids, MI: Zondervan, 2002).

Holy Bible, The Life Application Study Bible, (Carol Stream, IL: Tyndale House Publishers, Inc., 1996).

Holy Bible, English Standard Version Study Bible, (Wheaton, IL: Crossway Bibles, 2008).

Holy Bible, The Interpreter's Bible, (Nashville, TN: Abingdon Press, 1953).

Willie J. Alexander, *Entering The Promised Land,* (Houston, TX: Entering The Promised Land Houston, TX, 2007).

James Strong, S.T.D., L.L.D., *A Concise Dictionary of The Words in The Hebrew Bible with Their Renderings in the Authorized Version,* (Madison, NJ: 1890).

James Strong, S.T.D., L.L.D., *A Concise Dictionary of The Words in The Greek Testament with Their Renderings in the Authorized Version,* (Madison, NJ: 1890).

Chapter 9

Random House Webster's Unabridged Dictionary, 2nd ed.

Spiros Zodhiates, *King James Version Hebrew-Greek Key Word Study Bible,* (Chattanooga, TN: AMG Publishing, 2008).

James Strong, S.T.D., L.L.D., *A Concise Dictionary of The Words in The Hebrew Bible with Their Renderings in the Authorized Version,* (Madison, NJ: 1890).

James Strong, S.T.D., L.L.D., *A Concise Dictionary of The Words in The Greek Testament with Their Renderings in the Authorized Version,* (Madison, NJ: 1890).

Jeff A. Brenner, "The Origin of the Hebrew Language," *Ancient Hebrew Research Center*

Chapter 10

Spencer Wells, "The Greatest Journey Ever Told: The Trail of Our DNA," *National Geographic Magazine,* March 2006.

Donald Johnson, Maitland Edey, *Lucy: The Beginnings of Humankind,* (New York: Simon & Schuster, 1981).

Willie J. Alexander, *Entering The Promised Land,* (Houston, TX: Entering The Promised Land Houston, TX, 2007).

James Strong, S.T.D., L.L.D., *A Concise Dictionary of The Words in The Hebrew Bible with Their Renderings in the Authorized Version*, (Madison, NJ: 1890).

James Strong, S.T.D., L.L.D., *A Concise Dictionary of The Words in The Greek Testament with Their Renderings in the Authorized Version*, (Madison, NJ: 1890).

Random House Webster's Unabridged Dictionary, 2nd ed.

Spiros Zodhiates, *King James Version Hebrew-Greek Key Word Study Bible*, (Chattanooga, TN: AMG Publishing, 2008).

Biblesoft Complete Reference Library (CD Rom, version 5.0)

Chapter 11

Spiros Zodhiates, *King James Version Hebrew-Greek Key Word Study Bible*, (Chattanooga, TN: AMG Publishing, 2008).

Addendum

Random House Webster's Unabridged Dictionary, 2nd ed.

Made in the USA
Coppell, TX
06 March 2021

51348303R00193